SPEECH
for Christian Schools®

Donna L. Hess and Dawn L. Watkins

Authors
  Donna Hess, B.S., M.A.
  Dawn Watkins, B.A., M.Ed., M.A.

Consultants
  Elizabeth Edwards, B.A., M.A.
  DeWitt Jones, B.A., M.A.
  William Moose, B.A., M.A.
  Dale Savidge, B.S., M.A.

Contributors
  Miriam Bonner
  Joseph Brazeal
  Karen Duncan
  Chuck Nicholas
  Daniel Olinger
  Lonnie Polson
  Laura Pratt
  JoAnn Shields
  Ronald Shields
  Margaret Yearick

NOTE:
The fact that materials produced by other publishers are referred to in this volume does not constitute an endorsement by Bob Jones University Press of the content or theological position of these materials or any other materials produced by such publishers. The position of Bob Jones University Press, and the University itself, is well known. Any references and ancillary materials are listed as an aid to the student or the teacher in an attempt to maintain accepted academic standards of the publishing industry.

SPEECH for Christian Schools®

©1985 by Bob Jones University Press
Greenville, South Carolina 29614

All rights reserved

**Produced in cooperation with Bob Jones University
Division of Speech and Bob Jones Academy**

Printed in the United States of America
ISBN 0-89084-302-3 (hardbound)
ISBN 0-89084-315-5 (softbound)

20   19   18   17   16   15   14   13   12   11   10   9   8   7

Table of Contents

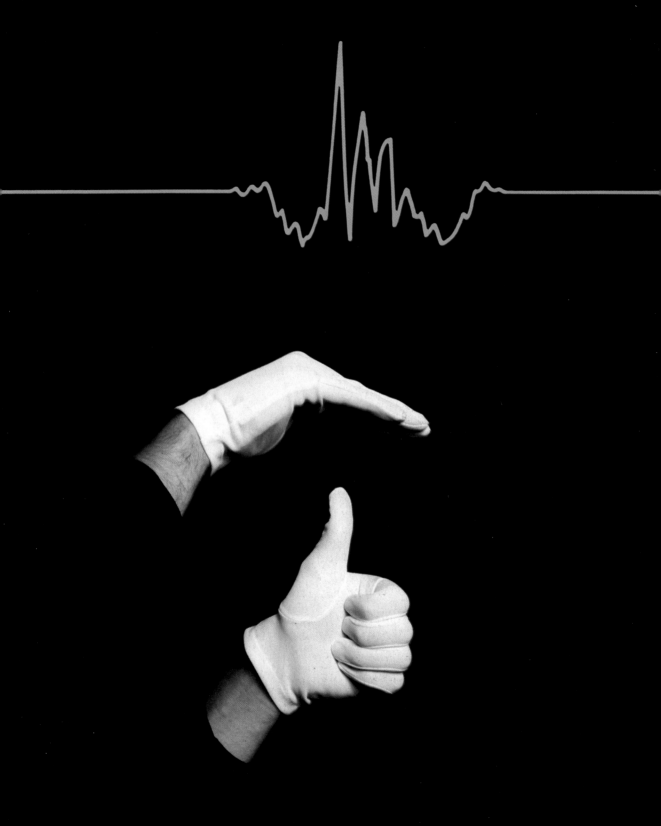

BENETH JONES

Profession: Housewife/speaker/writer

Professional Experience: Teaching speech, speaking at conferences, performing, directing plays

Hobbies: Reading, tennis, horseback riding

Interviewer: Why did you choose speech as a major?

Beneth Jones: My choosing the field of speech was clearly the Lord's leading. I took speech when I started to a Christian school just to fill a class hour. Once into the course, I was encouraged and counseled to continue in the field. My parents also encouraged me; too, I soon felt the attraction and the challenge of speech work.

Interviewer: You have been a director, performer, and public speaker. How would you say each of these areas has helped you glorify God and edify others?

Beneth Jones: I often think of the scriptural phrase "Do all to the glory of God," and in all my speech activities I have tried to do that. As for directing, I feel strongly that the doors of human hearts swing on different hinges. Since drama is such a strong communication tool, it can be a means of opening people's hearts and minds to scriptural truth. This applies not only in religious drama but in nonreligious drama. For example, Shakespearean plays underline the scriptural principle of right triumphing and of wrong being punished. This truth which we read in the Word of God and hear preached from our pulpits is powerfully reinforced when we see it well acted in a creditable production.

In performing, I feel it is valuable to present a characterization "for the glory of God" and for the edification of others. A personal experience that comes to mind is the film *SHEFFEY*. By performing in this film, I had one of my richest opportunities for ministry because of the clear spiritual impact of that film.

Even in nonreligious roles there is an opportunity for helping others. We all need times of relaxation and refreshment. By performing good drama we can provide an audience with such times.

Over the years, my public speaking has become my number two ministry, after my home. As the devil tries harder than ever to destroy homes, he uses heavy artillery against Christian women. Speaking at retreats and conferences gives me the privilege of using God's Word to strengthen these women against satanic assault.

Interviewer: If you had chosen another career, do you think your speech training would still have been beneficial?

Beneth Jones: Oh, definitely. In fact, as a teenager there were several other careers I considered. For awhile, I thought about medicine, and I had a biology teacher who encouraged that interest. If I had gone into medicine, my speech training would have been vital. It would have helped me in communicating both to my patients and to my fellow medical personnel.

Another field which beckoned me was clothing design. Again, the art of communication would have been very valuable. How else could I have expressed what I wanted in a design for those who were to construct the garment? And how else would I have sold my designs to retailers?

I also considered banking. Summer work in a bank demonstrated the importance of effective communication both to the public and to fellow employees. Actually, I think *any* career benefits by some speech training. That includes homemaking.

Even if a woman's communication would be only to her husband and children—which is very unlikely—the ability to express herself clearly would be an important asset.

Interviewer: Does the speaker's character really influence the credibility of his message?

Beneth Jones: Very definitely. A person's character is strongly communicated from the platform. I can immediately think of a couple of examples. For instance, I remember listening to one tiny, frail preacher's wife who was so short she could hardly reach the microphone and whose voice was so weak she could hardly make herself heard. Nevertheless, a large audience of women sat absolutely still, listening to her. Her godly character was so evident and so powerfully communicated that everyone was eager to hear what she had to say.

Another time, I had the sad experience of going to a seminar workshop and listening to a woman who was trying to communicate to us the importance of laboring for the Lord. Unfortunately, all through her presentation it was painfully evident that she had not invested *any* labor of preparation! The restless, inattentive audience responded to the speaker's character, negating her words. Those examples could be expanded by similar instances with male speakers. Character does tell.

Interviewer: You have given us two specific examples to show that character is communicated to an audience. Can you also give us some general ways that could help convey the proper message?

Beneth Jones: I think the most important thing in communication is willingness to be honest with the audience, willingness to be vulnerable. In other words, if a speaker tries to give an impression of perfection, he sets up psychological blocks to communication. People in an audience recognize imperfections in the world and in themselves; they respond to someone who speaks to them as a fellow flawed human—not as an oracle. An up-to-date spiritual life and a view of self as God sees him is the speaker's necessary foundation for having and communicating good character.

Interviewer: When you speak or perform, are you ever nervous?

Beneth Jones: I am always terrified when I speak. As a matter of fact, on the way to the platform I invariably wonder, "Why didn't I major in home economics?"

Interviewer: What do you do to overcome your fear?

Beneth Jones: Physically, the only thing I can do is some deep breathing. The real help comes through a great deal of prayer for every speaking occasion. Specifically, I pray that my own heart will be right, that I might be like clear glass through which Jesus Christ is seen, and that God will give me a positive attitude toward the speaking situation. Seeing the platform time as an *opportunity* helps take the teeth out of the monster terror.

Further, there is a wonderful verse in Proverbs 16:3 which says, "Commit thy works unto the Lord, and thy thoughts shall be established." I hold on to that verse when I speak—otherwise my timidity and terror would destroy my mental processes no matter how diligently I had prepared. When I give the speaking situation to the Lord, as a service, He proves Himself true and establishes my thoughts. Throughout every speaking assignment I find His strength in my weakness.

Interviewer: So in essence, your speaking builds your faith?

Beneth Jones: Very definitely. As you see God do the impossible in each speaking situation, your faith grows and you trust Him more. Speech offers an excellent opportunity for a Christian young person to build his confidence in God.

Interviewer: In giving advice to a beginning speech student, what one pitfall would you warn him to guard against?

Beneth Jones: Avoid copying anybody else. It is easy as a beginning student to look at a classmate who speaks well, or at an admired teacher or pastor and think, "That is the speaker I want to be." But copying anyone else in speech is deadly; the only things you pick up are the externals—the physical and vocal mannerisms. Those will hinder rather than help you. Be yourself. Learn good speech techniques, and learn them well. Then add to the "skeleton" of technique the flesh and blood of the interesting, uniquely-created person that is *you.*

Chapter 1

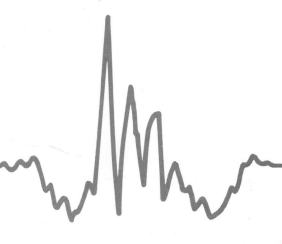

A Matter of Life and Death

Death and life are in the power of the tongue:
and they that love it shall eat the fruit thereof.
—Proverbs 18:21

World War II, the greatest conflict the world has ever seen, was fought with submarines, battleships, tanks, howitzers, rifles, grenades, airplanes, atomic bombs, and—no less important—words. The Third Reich was led by a man who understood that words could be weapons. The leaders of the Allied forces had an arsenal of words as well. When Adolph Hitler fired his threats, Winston Churchill thundered back: "Whatever the cost may

5

be, we shall fight on the beaches, we shall fight on the landing grounds, we shall fight in the fields and in the streets, we shall fight in the hills, we shall never surrender." As Lance Morrow has observed: "Hitler's ranting persuasions worked enough black magic to send his audiences pouring out of the stadium to conquer the world. Churchill's answering eloquence quite literally, physically pushed back the Reich."

It is easy to examine the lives of famous men and see the effect of their speech on others. But how often do we examine our own words? It is important for us to realize that even in daily conversation our speech has the potential to influence others for good or evil.

Speech, however, is not limited to what we *say*. Studies have shown that only 7 percent of the total effect of our speaking actually comes from the words we use. The remaining 93 percent of our message is conveyed by our facial expressions, posture, tone of voice, voice inflection, and gestures. Communication, then, is the combination of both our words and our actions.

Communication is a gift from God. Its purpose it to praise Him and to edify, to encourage, and to exhort others. If we Christians are to use this gift as God intended, then our communication must reflect God's character and works. This is not to say that unregenerate men can never fulfill the true purpose of communication. Shakespeare, though we do not know that he was a Christian, often presented biblical truth through his drama. The primary difference between a Christian communicator and a non-Christian communicator is responsibility. A non-Christian may *at times* reflect God's character and works; you, the Christian, must strive to do so *at all times*.

The Process of Communication

There are five elements in the process of communication: the source, the speaker, the message, the channel, and the audience. These elements are, of course, closely related and may at times overlap, but to simplify our discussion we will cover them separately.

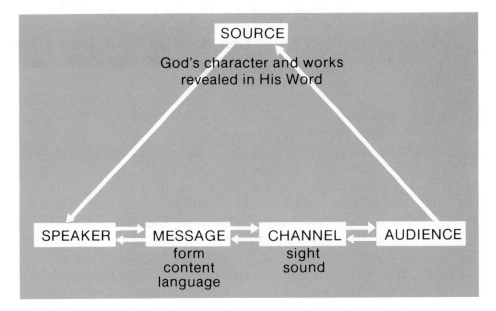

As you can see in the diagram, both the speaker and the audience have an active role in communication. Essentially these are your responsibilities in communication:

■ The speaker is responsible to reflect the character and the works of God through the message and the channel.

■ The audience is then responsible to evaluate the message. As an audience member, a Christian would evaluate the message by comparing it to the source.

■ The audience then sends back to the speaker their response to his message, enabling him to know if the message was perceived as he intended it to be.

Source

The source is the originator of the message. For the Christian speaker the source of his message is God. This does not, of course, imply that your speech is in any way "inspired." Nor does this mean that every speech will be a devotional or that every utterance will be a sermon. It does mean that as a Christian you should look to the Holy Spirit for guidance in your communication to insure that what you say never conflicts with God's Word.

You may initially feel that recognizing God as the source of your message is restrictive. But think of this: God is eternal, all-powerful, ever-present, unchanging, infinite, all-knowing, holy, and just. Your source is comprehensive, unlimited, and infallible. However, the speaker who anchors his message in self is bound by his own understanding and experience.

Speaker

Christ said to his disciples on the eve of His Crucifixion, "The words that I speak unto you I speak not of myself: but the Father that dwelleth in me, he doeth the works." (John 14:10) Throughout His ministry here on earth Christ reflected His Father through His words. So you should reflect Christ. An example may help you understand your role as a "mirrored image." On the walls of the Alamo in Texas are pictures of the heroes who gave their lives in the great battle to free Texas. One of these heroes was named James Butler Bonam. Above his name is a picture, but the picture is not of him. It is of his nephew, James Bonam. Under the picture is the following inscription: "James Butler Bonam. No picture of him exists. This portrait is of his nephew, James Bonam, deceased, who greatly resembled his uncle. It is placed here by the family that people might see the appearance of the man who died for freedom." You are placed here on earth to show forth Christ who died for all. When you speak, people should see not you, but your Lord.

Message

Your message is made up of both content and form. Content is the idea you want to express. The form of your message may be either written (as in letters, essays, poems, short stories, novels, or plays) or oral (as in conversation, public speeches, debates, interviews, or dramatic and interpretative performances). Scripture contains examples of all types of communication: impassioned oratory (Jeremiah, Ezekiel), close reasoning (Romans, Galatians, and Hebrews), tactful persuasion (Philemon), sublime lyricism (the Psalms and Isaiah), artfully shaped narratives (Ruth and Jonah), and abundant instances of ordinary discourse perfectly suited to subject, audience, and situation (e.g., John 4:1-26). Of course, you can also learn from studying nonbiblical writers and speakers. For example, studying the writings of men like Francis Bacon and John Bunyan or analyzing the speeches of orators like Daniel Webster and Winston Churchill can teach you much about content and form.

Channel

The message is conveyed by the means—or channel—of sight and sound. The speaking situation determines which of these senses will be most important in delivering your message. For example, when you are speaking to an audience face to face, how you look and how you sound are equally important. On the other hand, if you are speaking to a radio audience, obviously sound is more important.

Audience

Whether your audience is one or many, you should have one of the three following intentions for communicating: to edify, to encourage, or to exhort. To edify means to *instruct or enlighten* so as to encourage intellectual, moral, or spiritual improvement; to encourage means to *inspire* with hope, courage, or confidence; and to *exhort* means to *incite by strong argument, advice, or appeal.* These definitions correspond to the three types of formal speeches: informative, inspirational, and persuasive. They also emphasize your responsibilities to your audience.

My brethren, be not many masters, knowing that we shall receive the greater condemnation.

For in many things we offend all. If any man offend not in word, the same is a perfect man, and able also to bridle the whole body.

Behold, we put bits in the horses' mouths, that they may obey us; and we turn about their whole body.

Behold also the ships, which though they be so great, and are driven of fierce winds, yet are they turned about with a very small helm, whithersoever the governor listeth.

Even so the tongue is a little member, and boasteth great things. Behold, how great a matter a little fire kindleth!

And the tongue is a fire, a world of iniquity: so is the tongue among our members, that it defileth the whole body, and setteth on fire the course of nature; and it is set on fire of hell.

For every kind of beasts, and of birds, and of serpents, and of things in the sea, is tamed, and hath been tamed of mankind:

But the tongue can no man tame; it is an unruly evil, full of deadly poison.

Therewith bless we God, even the Father; and therewith curse we men, which are made after the similitude of God.

Out of the same mouth proceedeth blessing and cursing. My brethren, these things ought not so to be.

Doth a fountain send forth at the same place sweet water and bitter?

Can the fig tree, my brethren, bear olive berries? either a vine, figs? so can no fountain both yield salt water and fresh.

Who is a wise man and endued with knowledge among you? let him show out of a good conversation his works with meekness of wisdom.

(James 3:1-13)

The Christian Communicator

Christ said in Matthew 12:37: "For by thy words thou shalt be justified, and by thy words thou shalt be condemned." *By thy words* literally means "out of thy words." John Broadus, a nineteenth-century theologian and scholar, wrote that "the repetition of the phrase 'by thy words' makes the statement more weighty and impressive. Words are important because they reveal character and because they powerfully affect others. The only sin declared unpardonable is a sin of speech; on the other hand, 'if any man offend not in speech, the same is a perfect man.' Speech is indeed one of the grand distinctions of human beings, and a mighty power for good or evil. But this passage must not be understood as condemning all light pleasantries of conversation; it simply declares that *the idlest nothings we ever utter are included within the range of accountability to God.*"

If we are responsible for the "idlest nothings" how much more responsible are we for our formal speech? Scripture says, "Out of the abundance of the heart the mouth speaketh." A good speaker, then, must first have a good heart. Do you want to be a good speaker? Then take an honest look at yourself.

- Are you pure? (Luke 6:45; I Tim. 4:12)

- Are you humble? (I Cor. 1:26-31)

- Are you unselfish? (Heb. 10:24)

- Are you trustworthy? (Eph. 4:24-25)

- Are you competent? (Isa. 50:4a)

- Are you teachable? (James 3:17-18)

- Are you discerning? (Col. 4:6; Phil. 1:9-10)

We cannot ask God to bless us if we are impure, proud, selfish, deceitful, incompetent, unteachable, or willfully naive. The success of our speaking rests more on what we *are* than on how we can perform. Even if it were possible to hone our speaking skills to perfection, without Christ-like attitudes we would fall short of our true goal—to mirror our Lord.

On Your Mark! Get Set! Go!

Now you are ready to learn *how* to become a good speaker. Or are you? Haven't you always found that it is far easier to talk of doing something than it is actually to *do* it? For example, it is simple to discuss the value of a runner's disciplined training and the joy of a victorious race. However, such discussion is not half as demanding as the actual training. Likewise, it is one thing to discuss the value of communication, but quite another matter to begin training and to make your way to the platform. If you feel a bit apprehensive—take heart—you're not alone.

According to a study published in *The Sunday Times* (London), 41 percent of the three thousand Americans surveyed named fear of public speaking as their greatest fear. Most people ranked stage fright ahead of their fear of heights, insects, financial disaster, deep water, sickness, and even death. It is not surprising, then, that even experienced public speakers like preachers, teachers, and politicians confess to experiencing "butterflies." All this is not to confirm the adage that "misery loves company" but rather to assure you that you can succeed and even enjoy this experience. How? Let's return to our analogy of the runner. Imagine yourself approaching the track to begin training. Your first job is to *concentrate* on the following four areas:

■ developing your physical skills

■ focusing your mental energies

■ keeping your eye on the goal

■ practicing! practicing! practicing!

Chapters 2 and 3 should help you develop your physical skills. Chapter 4 directs you to focus your mental energies, and Chapter 5 teaches you to keep your eye on the goal. The rest of the book introduces specific types of communication, such as public speaking, debating, and performing. Every chapter has *Work Out* sections that provide ample opportunity for practicing! practicing! practicing! So, on your mark! Get set! Go!

- Read the following two famous speeches that are found in Appendix A:

  1. Adolf Hitler's speech entitled *Germany's Claims* February 20, 1938.

  2. Winston Churchill's speech titled *Dunkirk* delivered June 4, 1940.

- After reading the speeches, answer the following questions:

  1. What can you tell about the character of each speaker from his speech?

  2. How did each speech affect the audience?

  3. What techniques did each speaker use to move his audience?

  4. Were there differences between Churchill's techniques and Hitler's techniques? If so, what were the differences?

  5. How did each of these men use his ability to communicate to influence men?

Chapter 2

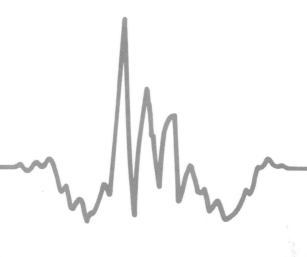

The Speaker We Hear

Let thy speech be better than silence; or be silent.
                                        —*Dionysius*

Most of your friends can probably identify you by a simple "hello" on the telephone. This recognition shows that your voice is as distinctive as your handwriting. It is your verbal "signature."

As a graphologist forms an impression of your personality by examining your handwriting, so others form impressions of you by listening to your voice. Think for a moment. What is your impression of someone who mumbles? How would you describe someone with an extremely high-pitched voice? How do you feel about someone who speaks gruffly? We tend to believe that high-pitched voices indicate nervousness or irritability and that gruffness means impatience and unfriendliness. Whether these initial assumptions are valid or not, we must realize that people *do* make certain assumptions based on how we sound to them. As Christians, then, we should learn to speak well.

A good way to begin improving your voice is to learn to identify good and bad speech habits. The following are characteristics of a good voice:

Vocal variety Your voice should be flexible and clearly expressive.

Vocal quality You should be able to use your voice for long periods of time without hoarseness, cracking, or stridency.

Adequate volume Your speaking should appear effortless and free from strain. You should also be capable of adjusting your volume to any speaking occasion.

- To begin learning the difference between good and bad speech, listen to the following tape. While listening, write down your impressions of each speaker you hear. For example, do any of the speakers sound haughty, antagonistic, indecisive, or childish? Which voices sound authoritative, agreeable, or sincere?

- Now that you've had an opportunity to test your evaluative skills, you can analyze your own voice. Begin by filling in the following checklist.

☐ Y ☐ N Are you forced to swallow frequently while speaking?

☐ Y ☐ N Does your voice "give out" toward the end of each sentence, creating repetitive, falling inflections?

☐ Y ☐ N Do your friends complain that you mumble?

□ Y □ N Do people enjoy listening to you read aloud?
□ Y □ N Does your throat hurt after speaking to a group for
short periods?

■ As you read the following selection, record your reading on
a tape recorder:

A Young Man's First Speech

When he got
up to speak
some stared too hard
and let on, and
some started to
twitch and
shuffle awkward feet,
and some squirmed
with smiles and
flagrant signs; and
he sputtered and
slurred over sounds that
came out
without sense,
until he broke out
in a warm laugh, and
we all knew that
he would force himself
to a finish; and
it would be and
was and still is all right.

Ronald Groba

■ Play the tape back, and then answer the following questions:

□ Y □ N Is your voice pleasant?
□ Y □ N Is your voice expressive of the varying ideas and
emotions in the piece?
□ Y □ N Do you sound sincere?
□ Y □ N Do you hear particular sounds you don't like?
□ Y □ N Do you feel that your voice accurately conveys "who
you are"?

Vocal Production

Now that you have identified some problems, what should you do? You first need to understand how the voice works. Three basic elements work together to produce your voice. These elements are the source of power, the source of vibration, and the chief resonators.

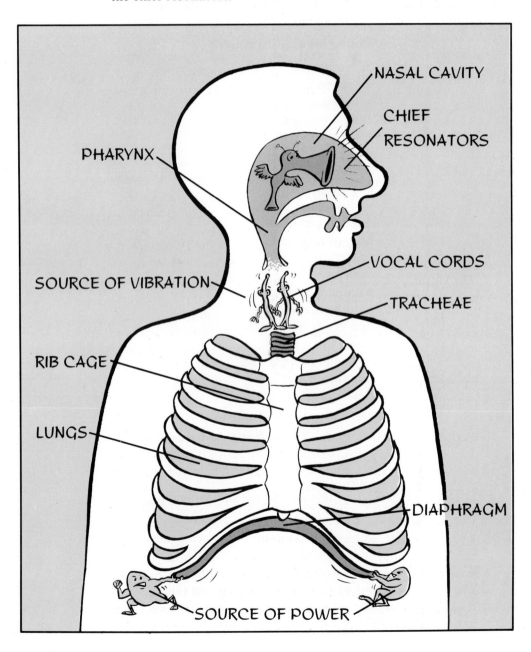

NASAL CAVITY

CHIEF RESONATORS

PHARYNX

VOCAL CORDS

SOURCE OF VIBRATION

TRACHEAE

RIB CAGE

LUNGS

DIAPHRAGM

SOURCE OF POWER

Source of power The lungs, diaphragm, and other muscles of breathing are the source of power. Your lungs operate constantly like a pair of bellows.

As shown in the diagram, when you inhale, the dome-shaped muscle called the *diaphragm* contracts and pulls down while the ribs move upward and outward. These movements increase the size and the volume of the chest cavity, reducing the air pressure in the lungs. Consequently, the air rushes into the lungs to equalize the air pressure. When you exhale, the diaphragm moves back up into its relaxed position in the chest cavity, forcing air out of the lungs. For an effective, pleasing voice, you must inhale and exhale correctly. (See the breathing and relaxation exercises in Appendix B.)

Source of vibration The larynx houses the vocal folds and is the source of vibration. The voice is produced when air passes over the vocal folds, or vocal cords. (Strictly speaking, they are neither cords nor folds.) When the diaphragm pushes air from the lungs through the trachea (windpipe), the air passes between the vocal folds. When the vocal folds are lightly closed, ready for voicing, the air passing through makes them vibrate.

The vibration of the vocal folds produces high and low tones. A man's longer and thicker vocal folds naturally produce lower tones than a woman's vocal folds. Both men and women can vary the tone, or pitch, of their vocal folds. Greater tension allows faster vibration, which produces higher tones. Greater loudness, though, is mainly caused by the amount of air pressure coming from the lungs.

Chief resonators The mouth, the pharynx, and the nasal cavity are the main resonators. When the vocal folds vibrate, they produce only a weak sound. To be heard, this sound must be enriched and amplified by your resonators. These resonators, depending on their size, shape, texture, and structure, reinforce the vibrated sound. Working together, they amplify and modify your sounds into a recognizable voice.

The pharynx and the oral cavity are both adjustable resonators. You cannot alter the shape of your larynx or nasal cavities, but you can adjust the size and shape of the pharynx and oral cavity. Sound must travel through the pharynx and the mouth without interference or restriction. If the muscular action within the larynx is disturbed or constricted by the pull and strain of the muscles in the neck and shoulders, the vocal tone will suffer. Consequently, you must remember to keep the throat, jaw, and shoulders as relaxed as possible.

Articulation and Pronunciation

Marzedotes endozedotes en lidellambzedivey, a kidel edivey too. Wouldn't you? Can you guess what this song says? It says, *Mares eat oats and does eat oats, and little lambs eat ivy. A kid will eat ivy too. Wouldn't you?* Of course, the songwriter slurred the words for fun. When you speak, you do not try to slur your words. Unless you want your listeners to have to guess what you are saying, you must speak clearly and pronounce your words correctly. Correct pronunciation is putting the proper sounds together and stressing the appropriate syllables.

Vowel and Consonant Sounds

Words are combinations of vowel and consonant sounds. Observe the following vowel sounds.

ē - eat, meat, sleep	ah - father, hot, object
ĭ - it, pig, sit	aw - paw, bought, lost
ā - may, date, trade	ō - gold, notice, alone
ĕ - ever, bed, said	ŏo - put, book, hook
ă - after, asp, mask	ōō - true, cool, undo
uh - hut, butter, about	

A diphthong is a continuous blending of two vowel sounds to form one syllable. The first sound is the main one heard. Can you hear these diphthongs?

oi - oil, ploy, Roy
ou - ouch, pouch, bough

ī - ice, lice, buy

A consonant is produced when the breath stream is stopped, slowed, or diverted by articulators (lips, teeth, hard and soft palate, tongue, and glottis). Spoken English has twenty-four consonant sounds.

Stops

p - play, happy, tap
b - boot, abbot, cube
t - truck, attack, bat

d - dark, standing, red
k - cup, account, rake
g - got, burger, bug

Nasals

m - may, dump, tame
n - nuts, bent, grin

ng - swing, young

Liquids

w - wait, was, wear
l - lot, old, peal

y - yet, yeast, yesterday

Fricatives

f - fur, refute, cuff
v - vest, clover, stove
th - (voiceless) thin, faith, wealth
th - (voiced) this, weather, writhe
s - sap, feast, dress

z - zebra, frozen, please
sh - sheep, confession, blush
zh - treasure, beige, vision
h - has, rehearse, inhabit

Affricates

ch - cheat, rapture, beach

j - joy, reject, plunge

WORK OUT

- Turn to Appendix B and do numbers 1-5 of the breathing and relaxation exercises.
- Next, have a little fun while practicing the following voice and articulation drills:

> He killed the noble Mudjokivis,
> With the skin he made him mittens,
> Made them with the fur side inside,
> Made them with the skin side outside
> He, to get the warm side inside,
> Put the inside skin side outside:
> He, to get the cold side outside,
> Put the warm side fur side inside:
> That's why he put the fur side inside,
> Why he put the skin side outside,
> Why he turned them inside outside.

> *George A. Strong*

> The conductor when he receives a fare,
> Must punch in the presence of the passenjare;
> A blue trip slip for an 8-cent fare,
> A buff trip slip for a 6-cent fare,
> A pink trip slip for a 3-cent fare,
> All in the presence of the passenjare.
> Punch, brother, punch with care,
> Punch in the presence of the passenjare.

> *Isaac H. Bromley*

> A tutor who tooted a flute,
> Tried to teach two young tooters to toot.
> Said the two to the tutor,
> "Is it harder to toot, or
> To tutor two tooters to toot?

> *Carolyn Wells*

Betty Botter bought some butter,
"But," she said, "the butter's bitter;
If I put it in my batter
It will make my batter bitter,
But a bit of better butter
Will make my batter better."
So she bought a bit of butter
Better than her bitter butter,
And she put it in her batter
And the batter was not bitter.
So 'twas better Betty Botter
Bought a bit of better butter.

(Mother Goose)

Chapter 3

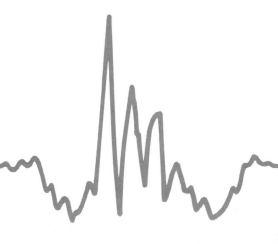

The Speaker
We See

What we love we shall grow to resemble.
—Bernard of Clairvaux

Our bodily actions often convey our message more clearly than our words. Daily, nonverbal communication replaces, supports, or contradicts what we say. For example, instead of saying *yes,* we sometimes simply nod; we also shrug our shoulders to show we are perplexed or wink to let a listener know our words are only in jest. A good speaker understands that what the audience sees is as important as what they hear.

Posture

Good posture helps establish credibility with your audience. If you appear tense or completely paralyzed with fear, your audience, though sympathetic, will give more attention to you and less to your message. On the other hand, if you listlessly stand with slumped shoulders, your sluggish appearance will give your audience the impression that you and your message are uninteresting. Even if your posture is not what it should be, it can be easily improved. All that's necessary is an awareness of what ought to be done and a willingness to put this knowledge into action.

Good posture results from proper relaxation and effective concentration. To achieve good posture, imagine that you are a marionette, suspended from two strings. One string is attached to the top of your head, and the other is attached to the top of your rib cage. Such "visualization" will help you keep your head up, your arms relaxed, and your chest high. Good posture will not only help you look better to the audience but will also help you feel more poised.

GUIDELINES FOR GOOD POSTURE

1. Stand comfortably balanced, one foot slightly ahead of the other. Be sure that your weight is evenly distributed on the balls of your feet. Do not shift your weight from foot to foot.
2. Keep your knees flexed. Do not lock them.
3. Keep your rib cage pulled up and away from your waist.
4. Keep your spine straight.
5. Keep your shoulders relaxed. Do not "stand at attention."
6. Keep your chin parallel to the floor.

Poise

A beginning speaker's tension often escapes through distracting mannerisms. If you catch yourself pulling at your sleeve, tapping your foot, or doing some other extraneous movement, consciously stop the distracting movement. Next, concentrate on relaxing the tense muscles. Be careful to *remove* the tension rather than *move* it to another group of muscles. If you find that controlling nervous movements is difficult for you, plan specific actions for your speech. Use a visual aid, for example. The principle is to direct your energies into your delivery.

Even before you speak, as you sit waiting or as you rise and walk to the platform, you are already giving the audience certain impressions. A speaker who slumps in his chair while waiting to speak and strolls to the platform studying the floor has already "spoken" to his audience before he opens his mouth. He will have to overcome his visual "speech" before his audience will listen to what he *says*. It is important, therefore, to consciously develop a physical and mental *alertness*. Your speech begins as soon as you enter the room and does not end until the next speaker begins or the meeting is adjourned.

Eye Contact

Establishing eye contact with your audience also helps to build your credibility. In our Western culture, we suspect dishonesty, insincerity, and fear in the person who refuses to "look us in the eye" during conversation. Certainly, many honest, sincere people are simply timid and find direct eye contact uncomfortable with those they don't know well. However, to be a good speaker you must overcome such shyness and use direct eye contact to establish a good rapport with your audience, maintain their attention, and observe their reactions to your presentation.

Try to establish eye contact with your audience during your approach to the speaker's platform by glancing toward them. Let them know that you are ready and eager to share your ideas and feelings with them. When speaking, do not look over their heads, out the window, at the ceiling, or down at the floor; instead, look directly at them. You will find that your audience will ignore you if you ignore them!

Facial Expression

Speakers frequently, for whatever reason, sound and look like robots. Too often their presentations seem born of drudgery, boredom, or worse yet, indifference. The lack of facial expression could come from stage fright; people sometimes hide their fear behind a stoical expression. To overcome monotonous presentation, decrease your rate of speaking and concentrate on your message and the needs of your audience.

Gestures

Gestures are used by the good speaker to accomplish specific purposes. Effective gestures are well timed, large enough to be seen, and harmonious with the idea being expressed. Wooden, mechanical gestures that draw attention to themselves and contradict your words are distracting. Match your actions to what you are saying and to the size of the room. For instance, pounding the lecturn for emphasis could seem ludicrous, even threatening, in a small room.

Grooming

Personal grooming is an important part of your nonverbal communication. You probably would agree that you are more likely to feel confident and poised if you know that you are dressed appropriately for the occasion and that you look your best. More important, however, is the effect of your dress on an audience.

Regardless of his physical appearance, a speaker who dresses appropriately is perceived as more trustworthy than one who does not. The neat, well-groomed speaker is more successful in persuading an audience and in sustaining his credibility.

Audience members tend to agree in their conclusions about a speaker based on his appearance. Their evaluations are also surprisingly accurate.

Men They should wear a coat and tie unless the speaking situation is obviously informal. Dark jackets worn with white or light blue shirts are recommended. The tie should be a conservative width, color, and print. Men should avoid inexpensive knit fabrics, loud plaids, bright primary colors, or inharmonious color combinations in their clothing.

Women They have greater freedom in choice of colors, but conservative suits or dresses of muted or darker colors lend greater authority to the female speaker. Simple, appropriate accessories, such as jewelry or scarves, are acceptable; however, such accessories must not attract attention. Skirts or dresses should always be worn when appropriate. Modesty is the major criterion for the Christian woman when dressing for any occasion.

Work Out

- Study the following photographs. Write a short description of what you think is happening in one of the pictures. Then tell what you have based your impression on.

The Speaker We See

UNIT TWO

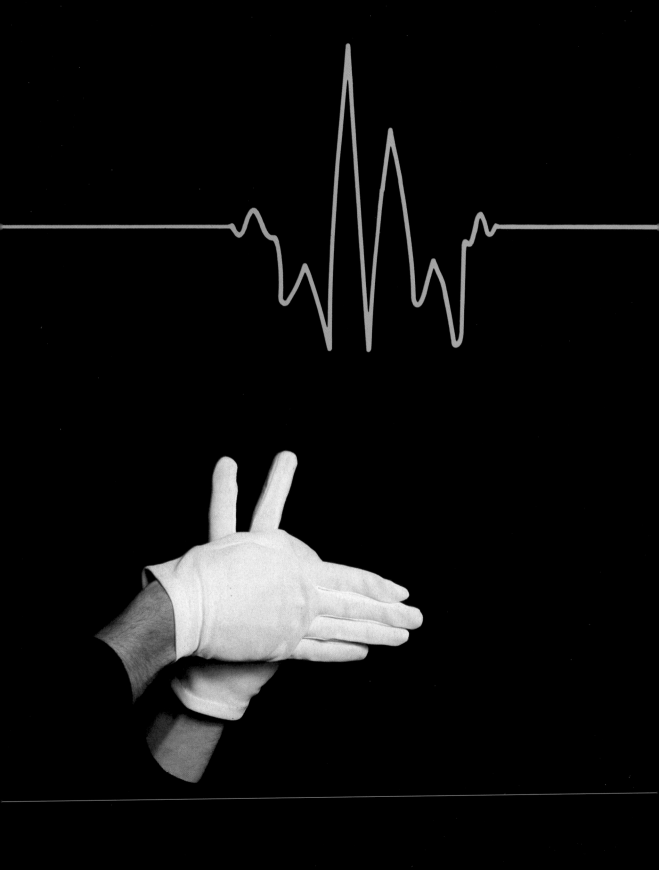

DR. EDWARD PANOSIAN

Profession: Professor of Church History
Professional Experience: Teaching, speaking at conventions, leading study tours in Europe
Hobbies: Dramatic acting

would be interesting and even disarming. I did not simply want to convey information about these men; I also wanted to subtly communicate their personalities. I found this approach effective for that purpose.

Interviewer: Did you find this method of presentation more challenging?

Edward Panosian: Frankly, I found it more comfortable. It was something I felt I could do. It didn't require notes; thus, it didn't create a physical barrier. It was unrehearsed and spontaneous, but it was a very misleading spontaneity. These performances were preceded by a great deal of study.

Interviewer: Obviously you were already familiar with these men, but how much extra research did you have to do?

Edward Panosian: Oh, a great deal. Somebody was once asked, "How long did you work on that lecture?" He said, "Twenty years and twenty minutes." The "twenty years" explains a little of the effort involved. I spent about thirty-five years of study but about three months of concentrated reading. Though I knew the general outline of the lives of all these men, I still needed to get the anecdotes and details of their lives which would increase interest in the actual presentation.

Interviewer: Did your method of presentation vary, or did you do each man much the same way?

Edward Panosian: As it turned out, I didn't find as much anecdotal material about John Calvin as I did about the others. So I had to resort to reading some estimates the historians have made of Calvin's life. Even people who disagreed with him had a remarkable sense of respect for him and his position. I also read his will in the presentation. We know so little about his conversion, and his will is a beautiful document of a spiritual autobiography, a spiritual testimony. It was, however, possible to read it and yet say it as if he were saying it.

Interviewer: Did you use costumes in your presentations?

Dr. Panosian recently prepared and presented a series of lectures on the three reformers: John Knox, Martin Luther, and John Calvin. These lectures provided opportunities for him to perform not only in his community but also in Europe.

Interviewer: What led to the invitation for you to speak in Ireland on the reformers?

Edward Panosian: It came about as a result of an opportunity I had here in Greenville. A local pastor who is interested in the reformers approached me with the idea of presenting the lives of these men to his congregation. I did so and a few weeks later Dr. Ian Paisley was at the church and heard the tapes. He invited me to go to Ireland and present them to his congregation as well, and I was thrilled with the opportunity.

Interviewer: Your major field is church history, so your interest and knowledge of the reformers is understandable. But why did you choose to use performance skills rather than a simple lecture method to present this historical information?

Edward Panosian: I was presenting the information to a lay congregation, not to a class of students; so I wanted to avoid a lecture. At the same time, I am not a preacher. So as a result of studying and thinking about it, I came up with the idea of "becoming" each individual reformer and presenting his ideas from that point of view. Because the approach was somewhat different, I thought it

Edward Panosian: No. I simply made an effort to divorce myself from the twentieth century, so I wore a black turtleneck longsleeved shirt which was not an intricate costume, just an attempt at something nondescript, nontwentieth century.

Interviewer: Do you think that your presentations helped you and your audience focus on Christ and His effect on the lives of men?

Edward Panosian: Yes. I think we know most of these men by a few books and a few main events; we tend to forget that they were men of like passions, men with feet of clay. All the evil of the flesh was in them too. They had trials and triumphs. Presenting these men as *men* helps Christian people to realize that they were not unique. They were uniquely used, but they were not men of semidivinity. They were human beings through and through. And I think that's helpful; it's been helpful to me. God used them, not because they were great, but because the greatness they had was God's doing. And after that, He used them because they were faithful and willing to be used.

Interviewer: You selected three reformers; if you had to capsule the most important principle that you learned from each man's life, what would it be?

Edward Panosian: For Luther, his entire life was an illustration of the Scripture, "I being in the way, the Lord led me." He was never sure of where he was headed, but he knew that the Lord was preparing him and leading him. He knew that God was the reason he ended up where he did. Calvin's life was an illustration of an unwavering confidence in God's sovereignty. God sees and knows all things in advance. Indeed, it may be better that we do not. The motto in Geneva was "After darkness, light." For Knox, God's providence stands out. God prepares in advance for us. For example, Knox was a prisoner of the French, aboard a galley for nineteen months. During that time he learned French in spite of himself. He found later that he needed the language in his service for God. Out of adversity God had prepared a future blessing.

Interviewer: In this particular unit we are discussing speaking to inform, to persuade, and to inspire. Though all of these men were obviously good speakers, can you give one example of the effective use of these skills?

Edward Panosian: As you said, all of these individuals were effective speakers. But more importantly, they all were good men. I strongly agree with the one who said, "A good speaker is a good man speaking well." Luther's bold speech at the famous Diet of Worms is one specific example. He was also very effective in a debate two years earlier. His success, however, was not due to bombast and oratory. He was very quiet while his opponent in the debate eloquently rambled, quoting widely from the church fathers. Luther in response simply cited a verse of Scripture from Paul and in a single sentence devastated the whole argument of his opponent. It wasn't the swaying oratory that moved his audience. That's a dangerous thing, in fact. A good speaker is a dangerous person unless he speaks the truth. He can manipulate and demagogically twist people. That is why what the person is saying is as important as how he says it. In any effective communication, it's not simply a loud voice and the ease of speech that is important. It is *what* you say and how you *use* the gifts God has given you.

Interviewer: What benefit have you gained from these presentations?

Edward Panosian: Oh, my! Much more than I know, probably. But one thing I think is the acquaintance with good language and quality literature. Though these opportunities are in a sense a form of relaxation for me, I am also very conscious of the character-developing quality in the literature. I've particularly enjoyed studying and reading for this because most of the sources are from the nineteenth century and before. During that time there was a sense of appreciation for good language and for choosing the most appropriate and colorful words to convey ideas. There was a sense of structural refinement in the way they spoke and wrote. They were also not at all hesitant to express their own appreciation for the subjects they were writing about. I enjoyed it, and I was conscious that the language, thoughts, and ideas were nourishing to a sensitive soul.

Chapter 4

Merchant of Venice, Shakespeare, Bob Jones University Classic Players.

Your Message

In all the world, there's no such thing as an uninteresting subject; there are only uninterested people.

—*G.K. Chesterton*

Choosing a Topic

As you sit down to write a speech, you may find that your mind is more averse to "training" than your body was. As you put your pen to the paper your mind asserts, "What in the world makes you think that you have anything of interest or of importance to say?" Don't cheat yourself. The Lord has given you many abilities and experiences that can be interesting—and beneficial—to others. The following guidelines will help you in the first step of choosing your topic.

You will need to have one of the following purposes in mind before you decide on a topic: to inform, to persuade, to inspire, or to entertain. In each case you want a specific response from your audience. For example, in an informative speech you may want to demonstrate wok cooking, to explain hang gliding, or to describe the cockpit of an airplane, but your goal is the same—to *inform* those who are listening. On the other hand, in a persuasive speech you want to move your audience to action. Your persuasive speech would provide information, of course, but the goal would be different. In your persuasive speech you want your audience to do more than understand; you want them to *act* on the information you give them.

- Draw speech topics from your interests and daily experiences. Do you like water-skiing, fishing, racquetball? What about your conversations with friends and family? Do you ever discuss current school problems? What are some solutions you and your friends have come up with? How about community problems? What do you think about the current issues you hear on the daily news?
- Talk about your unusual experiences. Has anything funny ever happened on a family vacation? Have you ever seen a tornado or a hurricane? Have you ever been stranded in a blizzard?
- What is your favorite subject in school? Do you like foreign languages, mathematics, poetry, or computers? If so, you might want to research and speak on foreign holidays and customs or the expanding field of computer graphics.

- Are you involved in a musical group in your community or church? Do you belong to clubs or other organizations? If so, why did you join, what is the purpose of these groups and organizations, and how have you benefited from them?
- You may also want to watch for possible speech topics while reading newspapers, magazines, and books. How do you react to the articles you read? Was the journalist fair in his assessment of the situation? Who is your favorite author? What lesson or idea did you glean from the last book you read? Could this idea be beneficial to others?

Narrowing the Topic

Your next step will be to narrow your topic to fit the time limit. For example, if you were doing a speech on John Newton, you would not be able to cover his entire life in a five-minute speech. However, you could focus on his final years as a slave trader and his subsequent conversion. Or you might want to talk about his ministry as a hymn writer and a preacher. Or you may want to be more specific and discuss only the circumstances surrounding the writing of his famous song, "Amazing Grace."

Once you have narrowed your topic and established your purpose or goal, you must identify a central idea. The central idea is a refinement of your stated purpose. It tells *how* you will achieve your purpose or goal. The following example may help to clarify this concept for you.

Purpose:	To explain what elements must be present to make a story an adventure story.
Central Idea:	The specific elements that create an adventure story are excitement, hazard, and suspense.

Notice that the purpose is to inform the audience—to give them information on how adventure stories are made. The central idea outlines the specific material that you will cover. A well-planned, well-stated central idea is essential in keeping your speech on track. As you prepare your speech, it would be wise to ask yourself frequently whether the information you intend to use relates directly to the central idea. Keeping to your central idea is like focusing a lens on a camera. Without this clear focus, the picture becomes fuzzy.

Doing Research

Once you have your central idea well in hand, it is time to do more investigation. The library, although not the only source of information, is a good place to begin. The library has many resources; the following discussion gives you a brief introduction to what is available.

A reference book like an encyclopedia is a good place to begin. When using this tool, notice the additional reference lists at the end of each entry. Collections of short biographies, yearbooks, and dictionaries are also valuable reference tools.

Don't forget the card catalog for locating books on your subject. Most card catalogs contain author, title, and subject entries. Each card is filed alphabetically and gives the author's name, the book title, call number, publication data, and a description of the book.

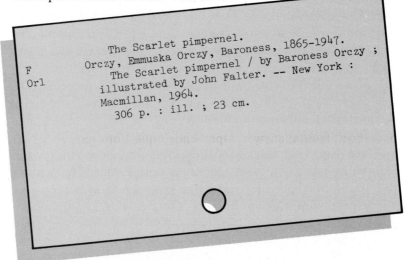

Periodicals are also a good source. Probably the most widely used index for locating specific articles is the *Reader's Guide to Periodical Literature.* This index lists articles from many popular magazines such as *Newsweek, National Geographic,* and *Sports Illustrated.* Similar indexes for specific disciplines include the *Education Index, Humanities Index,* and *Social Science Index.*

Other printed sources of information are government publications, newspapers, and statistical data. You may refer to the *Guide to U.S. Government Serials and Periodicals, The New York Times Index, Statistical Abstract,* and the *World Almanac.*

In addition to printed resources, you'll want to use nonprint sources, such as television, radio, films, tapes, and microfilm. You may also find it useful to conduct an interview with someone who is an expert on your topic. Before the interview, however, make certain that you have questions prepared to keep from wasting time. Basically there are two types of questions: open-ended and closed. Closed questions invite a yes-or-no answer or a short, factual answer. Open-ended questions require longer answers and are designed to allow the interviewee to do most of the talking. Make sure that your questions are well focused so that they require a concrete, specific answer.

Regardless of the type of research you do, you must devise a strategy to make the most efficient use of your time and energy. One way to make certain you do that is to take good notes and record the sources of your information on cards.

Taking good notes may seem to take time. But be patient. Disciplining yourself to be accurate and complete during your initial research will save you time later when you find you need specific information. When taking notes, remember the following pointers:

- Use cards of uniform size; 3″ x 5″ or 4″ x 6″ cards are usually best. Don't use large or irregularly shaped pieces of paper.
- Put only one idea on each card. If your material covers more than you can put on one card, you probably need a narrower subject heading.
- Check your notes against the source for accuracy.
- Never distort information by taking it out of context.

- Be sure you put a subject heading on the top line, beginning at the left margin. The heading should be short—one or two words. Then indicate the type of note you have taken by putting a code letter in the upper right corner. The following code letters may help you.

1. Most of your notes should be paraphrased—someone else's ideas stated in your words. Code them *P*.
2. Some of your notes may be a summary, or digest of longer works, such as a book, an article, or a speech. Code them *S*.
3. Some notes may be personal—taken from your own observations or experiences. Code them *M* (for mine).
4. A few of your notes may be quotations—someone else's ideas quoted word for word. Code them *Q*. It's usually best to use verbatim notes only when making a direct quotation. (Be sure to credit the person who made the statement at the time you quote him.)

- Indicate source and page number on the bottom line, beginning at the left margin.

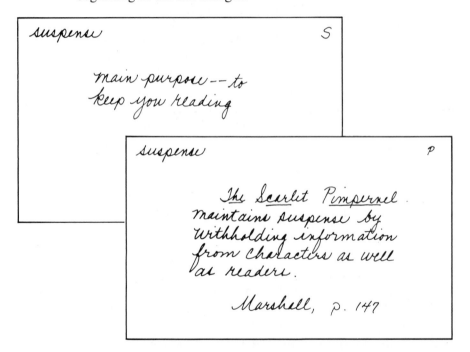

You will want to be certain to make a bibliography card for each source consulted. It is essential that each card have the name of the author with the last name listed first, the title of the work (underline [for italics] long works and enclose short works in quotations marks), and the publication data—place of publication, name of publisher, and date of publication.

> Marshall, Jonathan R. *The Best Adventures: Reading Stories.* New York: D. Meyer Press, 1981.

Do not underestimate the importance of good research skills. Taking notes and making bibliography cards properly will save time and will aid your investigation.

Supporting the Central Idea

Without valuable support material a speech can deteriorate into a mere recitation of uninteresting facts. Support material should lend interest, additional information, and insight. Make sure that the supports you choose are well adapted to your audience. If they are not, the dynamic effect you hoped for will be lost. Let's look at an example that was used on page 39. The central idea was stated as follows: "The specific elements of an adventure story are excitement, hazard, and suspense." How would you support that idea? One interesting way would be to take an excerpt from an adventure story and point out the elements you want to illustrate. For example, read through the following excerpt from *The Scarlet Pimpernel* by Baroness Orczy.

> They all looked a merry, even a happy party, as they sat round the table; Sir Andrew Foulkes and Lord Antony Dewhurst, two typical good-looking, well-born and well-bred Englishmen of that year of grace 1792, and the aristocratic French Comtesse with her two children, who had just escaped from such dire perils and found a safe retreat at last on the shores of protecting England.
>
> "Your leader, Monsieur?" said the Comtesse, eagerly. "Ah! of course, you must have a leader. But tell me where is he? I must go to him at once, and I and my children must throw ourselves at his feet, and thank him for all that he has done for us."

"Alas, Madame!" said Lord Antony, "that is impossible."

"Impossible?—Why?"

"Because the Scarlet Pimpernel works in the dark, and his identity is known only under solemn oath of secrecy to his immediate followers."

"Ah! Monsieur," sighed the Comtesse, "it all sounds like a romance, and I cannot understand at all."

"Why should you try, Madame?"

"But tell me, why should your leader—why should you all—spend your money and risk your lives for us French men and women, who are nothing to you?"

"Sport, Madame la Comtesse, sport," asserted Lord Antony, with his jovial, loud, and pleasant voice; "we are a nation of sportsmen you know, and just now it is the fashion to pull the hare from between the teeth of the hound."

But the Comtesse shook her head, still incredulously. To her it seemed preposterous that these young men and their great leader should for no other reason than sport run such great risks. With a shudder she recalled the events of the last few days, her escape from Paris with her two children, all three of them hidden beneath the hood of a rickety cart, and lying amidst a heap of turnips and cabbages, not daring to breathe, whilst the mob howled at that awful West barricade. Every moment under that cart she had expected recognition, arrest, herself and her children tried and condemned, and these young Englishmen under the guidance of their brave and mysterious leader, had risked their lives to save them all, as they had already saved scores of innocent people. And all for sport? Impossible!

The Scarlet Pimpernel

The threat of an innocent aristocratic family's being discovered, arrested, and sent to the guillotine definitely builds *excitement* in the story. Getting the Comtesse and her children away from a bloodthirsty Parisian mob and out of France in a death cart is certainly a *hazard*. Furthermore, an element of *suspense* is added to the story by the question, "Who is the brave and fearless Scarlet Pimpernel?" By the way, you don't find out who he is until the end of the story, and it is quite a surprise.

You could have opened the dictionary and given your audience the specific definitions for *excitement, hazard,* and *suspense.* Then you could have told them that they must keep these definitions in mind when writing an adventure story. However, by using *The Scarlet Pimpernel* as support material you have not only illustrated your point but also kept interest. Most listeners will remember a story long after they have forgotten a dictionary definition.

These specific supports will help you in collecting your own material for topics:

■ A story is a series of events arranged to achieve a certain goal. Factual stories from your experience or the experience of others are rooted in history. Fictional stories, on the other hand, may be drawn from literature or may be created by the speaker to fit the situation.

■ Sometimes events are listed but not described as they are in narratives. For example, a speaker giving a speech on God's dealing with sin may refer to the Flood, the Babylonian captivity, and the Tribulation. When stated in a list like this, the event must be familiar to the audience.

■ A testimony is limited to statements setting forth an individual's innermost convictions on a subject of much importance to him.

■ Quotations are expressions borrowed from someone else because they state exactly what you want to say. Some are used as sources of authority. Others are used because they have a self-contained message. This quotation, for example, does both: "Ask not what your country can do for you. Ask what you can do for your country." John F. Kennedy

■ Statistics and figures are factual supports. Statistics should be used with caution because it is often easy to distort the truth with them. Those you use should come from a reliable source. There is an old saying, "Figures don't lie, but liars can figure." It is also a good idea to round off figures to the nearest number and to associate dates with an era to aid comprehension. For example, you might tell an audience that the famous photographer Matthew Brady lived during the middle and late 1800s. Then you could go on to say that he was the most famous photographer of the American Civil War.

Photos by Mathew Brady during Civil War era

- Definition is a statement or explanation of what a word means or has meant. It is important that the audience understand the meanings of the terms you use. The classic method of defining a term uses four steps: tell what it is not like; tell what it is like; tell what it is not; tell what it is.
- Visual aids are charts, maps, graphs, diagrams, outlines, pictures, and models that are used in demonstrations. When preparing a visual, make sure that it is simple and that it can be seen from the back of the room. Also, do not pass a visual aid around the room while giving your speech; you want the attention of the audience on your speech.

Be looking for good support materials to put in a file for future speeches. Quotations, ideas, and interesting stories can be found in newspapers, magazines, and books; on television and radio; and even in conversations with friends.

Organizing the Material

Good organization helps to hold the attention of an audience. A disorganized speech does not build toward your specific goal, even if your information is good. If your speech is structured by a central idea, it will be easy to follow and will carry the audience along to the desired end.

Central Idea: An adventure story must have three basic elements: excitement, hazard, and suspense.

I. Element of excitement
II. Element of hazard
III. Element of suspense

Although a central idea can help, there are other tools that can help you organize. For example, the following standard patterns are often used to arrange ideas. Examine your research to decide which of these patterns is most useful to you.

The time or chronological pattern In the time or chronological pattern, the main points of the speech move in order either forward or backward in time. For example, here is an outline for a speech on dating.

Central Idea: The steps in choosing a date are selecting a victim, disguising your bad habits, and popping the question so that the person you're asking can't say "no" without feeling guilty.

I. Selecting a victim
II. Disguising your bad habits
III. Popping the question so that the person you're asking can't say "no" without feeling guilty.

The space pattern In the space pattern the main points are determined by physical placement. Take the following outline for example:

Central Idea: The three main storage areas in my bedroom are on the chair in the corner, under the bed, and on the floor of the closet.

I. On the chair in the corner
II. Under the bed
III. On the floor of the closet

The categorical or topical pattern In the categorical or topical pattern the speech is unified because the ideas are closely related, regardless of their order. The following is an example:

Central Idea: Three things that keep us from victorious Christian living are feeling guilty about mistakes made yesterday, doubting God's provision for today, and fearing what will happen tomorrow.

   I. Feeling guilty about mistakes made yesterday
  II. Doubting God's provision for today
III. Fearing what will happen tomorrow

The effect-cause or cause-effect pattern In the effect-cause or cause-effect pattern, you are either trying to show the results or find a cause. Notice the following example:

Central Idea: Speaking before thinking may cause such problems as foot-in-mouth disease, chickens-come-home-to-roost dilemma, and professing-oneself-to-be-wise syndrome.

   I. Foot-in-mouth disease
  II. Chickens-come-home-to-roost dilemma
III. Professing-oneself-to-be-wise syndrome

The problem-solution pattern The problem-solution pattern usually requires only two main points: a statement of the problem and a statement of the solution. Look at the following example:

Central Idea: The United States should establish a flat tax system.

   I. The current tax system is rife with loopholes and inequities.
  II. Establishing a flat tax system would eliminate these inequities.

Regardless of the type of organization, use at least two but no more than five main points.

Once you have organized your speech, you will want to think of transitions. Transitions are bridges between your main ideas. If you were to move from one main idea to the next without a good transition, you might lose your audience because of the abrupt change of thought. You may want to write these transitions into your outline while you are organizing your speech.

Writing Introductions and Conclusions

After finishing the basic organization for your speech, you will need to write an introduction and conclusion. It is best to write the conclusion before the introduction.

The conclusion gives the final punch to your central idea. There are three types of conclusions: the summary, the plea, and the illustration. The *summary* restates your central idea and briefly reviews the main points of your speech. Though not particularly dramatic, this conclusion can be effective especially for some informative speeches. For instance, if you were giving a demonstration speech, a summary would be very helpful. The *plea* for acceptance or action usually ends a speech of persuasion. In this case, you would restate the problem, the effect, and the solution. You would then encourage your listeners to take action on the solution you have proposed. An *illustration* summarizes or challenges indirectly. Here you would choose a quotation, a poem, or a human-interest story to give your speech a memorable ending.

The last step in preparing your speech is to write an introduction that will gain attention, arouse interest, and focus on your subject. Sometimes a *direct* introduction, which gets to the purpose of the speech immediately, is best. On the other hand, a *motivated* introduction may be better suited to your speech. The motivated introduction uses a relevant quotation, a comparison story, a personal reference, a striking statement, or a thought-provoking question to get the listener's attention. An *explanatory* introduction may be necessary for some speeches. In this introduction, you state your topic, the purpose of your speech, and then give any needed definitions or explanations.

The writing of your introduction and conclusion should be carefully considered. If you fail to gain the attention of the audience at the outset, your speech will fail. Or if you do not conclude the speech well, you will leave the audience with a dissatisfied feeling. You know how you feel when someone forgets the punch line of a joke or the end of a story; don't leave your audience with that same feeling.

Delivering Your Speech

There are four methods of delivery and composition used in public speaking: manuscript speaking, memorized speaking, extemporaneous speaking, and impromptu speaking. In manuscript speaking, the speaker reads his speech from the printed page. This method of delivery is useful when there are rigid time limits or when exact wording is essential. There are also times when a speaker must deliver someone else's speech; a press secretary must make an official announcement for the president, for example. In this case manuscript speaking is not only appropriate but also expected. Manuscript speaking usually lacks vitality and spontaneity. Because the speaker depends on the manuscript, he uses less bodily action, vocal variety, and effective eye contact.

A memorized speech keeps to exact wording and time limits. By memorizing a speech the speaker is freed to use more bodily action and eye contact. There are two disadvantages: a memorized speech does not allow the speaker to adjust to audience response, and the speaker may forget and be unable to improvise.

An extemporaneous speech is unmemorized but has been thoroughly prepared in advance. Adequate preparation includes research, writing, and rehearsal of the speech. Extemporaneous speaking is preferred by most public speakers because it frees them from the restrictions of a manuscript; it allows them to respond to the audience; and it helps them develop the ability to "think on their feet."

An impromptu speech is composed without advance preparation. For example, in your classes you may be called on to discuss the causes of World War II, define photosynthesis, describe the setting of an Edgar Allan Poe story, or state your opinion on arms control. In all of these cases, your response would take the form of an impromptu speech. Such speeches are valuable, but most of the time you should prepare your speech in advance.

 **Work Out**

- Use one of the following ideas and think of a speech topic.
  1. your personal interests
  2. some unusual experiences
  3. a current event or book

- After choosing a topic, establish a purpose and a central idea for your topic. Make sure that this purpose is clearly stated since it helps to organize your ideas.
- Use one of the following patterns, and organize your material into three to five main points.

1. chronological pattern
2. space pattern
3. categorical or topical pattern
4. effect-cause or cause-effect pattern
5. problem-solution pattern

- Use your topical central idea, and prepare an extemporaneous speech. To practice your speech, use the following guidelines.
  1. Read through your outline aloud at least five times. Read slowly and thoughtfully.
  2. Without your outline, practice your speech aloud. Practice as if you were speaking to your audience. Practice gestures, expressions, and projection. If you forget, don't stop; go on and finish the speech.
  3. Study your outline and note the details that you are forgetting. Some students find it helpful to tape record and later listen to their practice sessions.
  4. Without the outline, practice your speech aloud five to ten times.

Chapter 5

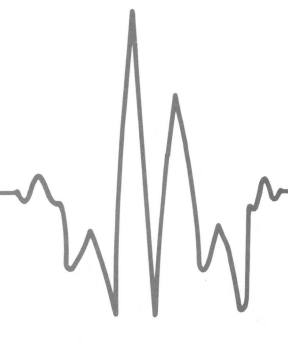

Your Audience

Think as wise men do, but speak as the common people do.

—Aristotle

It's your best friend's birthday. He hasn't said what he wants. But you go to the mall and come home with exactly the right gift. How do you know it's right? Because you know what he is like. In many ways, giving a speech is like choosing a gift: in both cases you must ask yourself, "Whom is this for?" and "Why am I giving it?" Understanding your audience and considering the occasion will help you in deciding what will best meet the needs of your listeners.

Will you be speaking to people your own age or will they be older or younger? Are all the people in the group the same age? Consider what is important to your listeners. Know what they like and dislike. Find out, if you can, what they already know about your topic. If they are not familiar with your topic, you will have to define your terms and explain key concepts. You must also determine whether they are sympathetic, neutral, or antagonistic toward what you have to say. Are they coming to be informed? Inspired? Or will your job be more difficult, demanding that you persuade them to your point of view? If you do not consider your audience, they may fail to consider your message.

Besides knowing your audience, it is also important to know the setting and the occasion of your speech. Is this a church gathering? A Christmas banquet? Or a graduation? Will you be outdoors? In a room that seats twenty? Or in an auditorium that seats five hundred? You ought to know if you will be the only speaker and when in the program you will speak. Decide whether you will need any equipment, such as a microphone, a lectern, or an overhead projector.

To illustrate the importance of these principles, let's go back to a Missouri courtroom one summer evening in 1870. The case of *Burden vs. Hornsby* was up for its last appeal. The suit had begun when Burden found his dog, Old Drum, dead from a bullet wound on his neighbor Hornsby's land. It was clear that Hornsby had shot the dog. The only question

was whether he should pay damages for the dog. In two previous hearings Burden had been denied his money. Confident of victory, Hornsby's lawyers were battering down this final appeal before a jury. They knew the facts; they were more experienced than Burden's lawyers. They believed "that it was ridiculous to make so much ado about a dog." They failed, however, to consider one thing—the jury.

Burden's lawyer, George Vest, did not forget them. He rose and delivered one of the most memorable courtroom speeches in history. Years later, the opposing lawyer still vividly recalled the scene: "I looked at the jury and saw they were all in tears. The foreman wept like one who had lost his dearest friend. The victory for the other side was complete. I said to Cockrell [his assistant] that we were defeated; that the dog, though dead, had won, and that we had better get out of the courthouse with our client or we would be hanged."

Audience

- Vest knew that he was speaking to men his own age and of his own community.
- Vest assumed that his audience believed in the fleeting nature of human affection and money.
- Vest knew that many there owned and liked dogs.
- Vest appealed to universal desires—such as the desire to be remembered.
- Vest knew that most of the spectators had come to see the confrontation of locally famous lawyers.

Occasion

- Vest knew that this was the last appeal.
- Vest knew he would be speaking in a crowded courtroom.
- Vest knew that he would speak last.

The following is the only existing portion of this famous speech.

A Man's Best Friend
George Vest

Gentlemen of the jury, the best friend a man has in this world may turn against him and become his enemy. His son or daughter whom he has reared with loving care may prove ungrateful. Those who are nearest and dearest to us—those whom we trust with our happiness and good name—may become traitors in their faith. The money that a man has he may lose. It flies away from him, perhaps when he needs it most. A man's reputation may be sacrificed in a moment of ill-considered action. The people who are prone to fall on their knees to do us honor when success is with us may be the first to throw the stone of malice when failure settles its cloud upon our heads. The one absolute, unselfish friend that man can have in this selfish world—the one that never proves ungrateful or treacherous—is his dog.

Gentlemen of the jury, a man's dog stands by him in prosperity and poverty, in health and sickness. He will sleep on the cold ground where the wintry winds blow, and the snow drives fiercely, if only he can be near his master's side. He will kiss the hand that has no food to offer; he will lick the wounds and sores that come in encounter with the roughness of the world. He guards the sleep of his pauper master as if he were a prince. When all other friends desert, he remains. When riches take wings and reputation falls to pieces, he is as constant in his love as the sun in its journey through the heavens.

If fortune drives the master forth an outcast in the world, friendless and homeless, the faithful dog asks no higher privilege than that of accompanying him to guard against danger, to fight against his enemies. And when the last scene of all comes, and death takes the master in its embrace, and his body is laid away in the cold ground, no matter if all other friends pursue their way, there by his graveside will the noble dog be found, his head between his paws, his eyes sad, but open in alert watchfulness, faithful and true even to death.

When George Vest sat down, Burden had his money and we had a famous proverb: "A man's best friend is his dog."

Work Out

- Read the following introduction for a speech on hospitality.

    "Not many sounds in life, and I include all urban and all rural sounds, exceed in interest a knock at the door." Like the famous essayist, Charles Lamb, I like to get company. Some people don't. Can you imagine that? These anticompany types say. . . .

- Complete the speech for an audience of your peers who agree with your position.
- Now, rework your speech as if presenting it to a group of men more interested in the football game on television than in getting company.

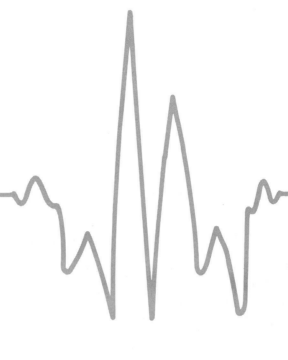

Chapter 6

Speaking to Inform

The greatest thing a human soul ever does in this world is to see something, and tell what it saw in a plain way.

—John Ruskin

Ruskin had a point. Plain speech is always best. For instance, how long would you remember the following proverb?

Homo sapiens abiding in structures of crystallized silicon dioxide should not traject lithospheres.

Not very meaningful, is it? How about this version?

People who live in glass houses should not throw stones.

The goal of an informative speaker is to communicate knowledge to the audience. However, even if *what* you have to say is valuable, your audience will not listen unless you are interesting, clear, and concrete.

BE INTERESTING	BE CLEAR	BE CONCRETE
In your presentation • be enthusiastic • be competent In your content • use a compelling introduction • use good support material	In organization • limit your points • move toward a goal • use transitions In language • be precise • be simple	In your support material • use charts • use diagrams • use models • use stories • use illustrations • use examples

Types of Informative Speeches

There are three kinds of informative speeches: demonstration, report, and instruction. These speeches are not far removed from your everyday experience. Have you ever shown somebody how to do something? Then you have given a demonstration speech. Or have you ever had to fill someone in on something he missed? That would have been a report. Or maybe you've had to give directions or explain the rules of a game. If you have, you already know something about giving an instructional speech.

Of course, these examples are informal. Formal situations require more structured presentations. Here are some tools that can help you structure your speech.

Tools for Informative Speeches

Description

Description sparks the imagination of the listener. When using description you create sensory images that establish mood, heighten interest, and clarify abstract ideas. Rather than using the word *patriotism,* describe the face of an old soldier as he sees his country's flag being raised. The description makes love of country easier to understand.

Narration

Narration tells a story. It helps give order, sustain interest, and support or illustrate your ideas. You could simply define ingratitude but this definition would be stronger if supported by a story about a girl who is rescued from a fire and later shuns her rescuer because he is scarred.

Exposition

Exposition explains, identifies, or classifies. Definitions, comparisons, contrasts, and examples are forms of exposition. Suppose you were giving a speech on friendship. You might begin with a definition, perhaps the dictionary one: "An alliance with one who is known, liked, and trusted." You could then compare friendship with a dogwood tree, which survives the harshest winter and yet is first to bloom in the spring. Using a contrast will make this idea even stronger. False friendship, for example, is like the mistletoe, which seems beautiful but is really deadly. You could then conclude your speech with the example of David and Jonathan.

Construction of an Informative Speech

Look at the following student's speech. Through description, narration, and exposition he helps us better understand the philosophy behind the British monarchy.

Fit for a Queen

Most people have heard the phrase "fit for a queen." But what exactly does the phrase mean? Well, if you're talking about the queen of England, it means a great deal. The British royal family today is one of the last great vestiges of monarchy in the twentieth century, representing the prestige, the influence, and especially the wealth of a bygone era.

Exposition

The queen is generally regarded as the world's richest woman. But where did all that money come from? There are two main sources. First, there is the Civil List, which is the official name for the queen's yearly salary. Each year she draws a salary in excess of 4.5 million U.S. dollars. Compare that to Ronald Reagan's $200,000-a-year salary, and you can see that in politics, at least, it pays to be British.

Exposition

While $4.5 million a year sounds like a lot to you and me, the Civil List is actually a rather minor source of income for the royal family. Much more important is direct inheritance. When Queen Elizabeth dies, she will leave an estimated $140 million in liquid assets to her heirs. That figure doesn't include such things as the crown jewels, the royal stamp and art collections, or the queen's ten castles and palaces with their hundreds of thousands of acres. One hundred and forty million dollars is a lot of money in any country, but in Great Britain, with its 75 percent inheritance tax, it's almost unheard of. If Prince Charles were an ordinary citizen receiving that inheritance, $105 million of it would go to the government. But since the royal inheritance has always been tax free, hundreds of millions of dollars have been kept in the family throughout hundreds of years.

Exposition

The queen's net worth has been estimated at about one billion dollars. We've seen that she makes $4.5 million a year in salary, and has $140 million in liquid assets. So where does the other $700 million or so come from? The answer is nonliquid assets. Let's look at two main areas: castles and palaces, and playthings.

Besides the White House, the queen's two official residences, Windsor Castle and Buckingham Palace, are probably the best-known homes in the world. The British government pays dearly for such worldwide recognition, spending almost $10 million every year just to maintain the two homes.

Exposition

Queen Elizabeth isn't the only member of the royal family with a penchant for nice houses. As a wedding present for his new bride, Prince Charles purchased a seventeenth-century mansion with nine bedrooms, four reception rooms, and a 346-acre estate. Should Princess Di get tired of her million-dollar mansion, she can always retreat to Charles' three-bedroom bungalow on one of the Scilly Islands. Three bedrooms may not sound that impressive until you realize that Charles doesn't own just the bungalow; he owns the entire island.

Exposition/
Description

It has been said that children never grow up, they simply acquire more expensive toys. If this is true, then the royal toy chest is surely the most expensive in the world. Take transportation, for example. Should the queen decide to go for a drive in the country, she can call up any car from her fleet of custom-made Rolls Royces with sterling-silver hood ornaments. If she finds that the traffic is heavy, she may summon the Royal Flight, which consists of three airplanes and two helicopters and costs over $5 million a year to maintain. Or if she really wants to go in style, she could take the Royal Yacht *Britannia*. At 413 feet in length, the *Britannia* is generally considered the world's largest private yacht. Built in the 1950s at a cost of $5 million, it is a floating Windsor Castle, with a formal dining room to seat 60 guests and a ballroom for another 200.

Narration

A little closer to home, the queen is expected to throw sumptuous parties for visiting dignitaries. She succeeds royally. Many people are surprised to learn that the queen doesn't even have a sterling-silver table service. But don't feel too sorry for her—her table service is solid gold. It takes three weeks to polish for a state banquet, and it weighs over five tons!

Exposition

To us Americans, it seems ridiculous to spend this kind of money on a figurehead. But to most of the British, the queen is much more than just a figurehead. She is a symbol of all the history, the stability, the hospitality, the power, and the grandeur of Great Britain. On her foreign tours, she represents friendship rather than power, the people rather than official government. To millions around the world, the queen *is* Great Britain. As such, say the British, she must live in a style fit for a queen.

Description

Speaking to Inform

The following outline will now help you see how the speaker used the principles we learned in Chapter 4 to structure his speech.

Sample Outline for Informative Speech

Introduction Everyone has heard the phrase "fit for a queen." But what exactly does the phrase mean? Well, if you're talking about the queen of England, it means a great deal. The British royal family today remains as the last great vestige of monarchy in the twentieth century, representing the prestige, the influence, and especially the wealth of a bygone era.

Transition The queen is generally regarded as the world's richest woman. But where did that money come from?

  I. The British royal family fortune is limited in its source.
    A. There is government support through the Civil List.
      1. The queen makes $4.5 million a year.
      2. The president makes only $200,000 a year.

Transition Four-and-one-half million dollars sounds good to you and me, but to the royal family it's minor compared to direct inheritance.

    B. There is family support through inheritance.
      1. The amounts are staggering.
      2. The money is tax free.

Transition The queen's estimated net worth is about one billion dollars. We've seen that she makes $4.5 million per year and has 140 million dollars in liquid assets. So where does the 700 million come from?

II. The British royal family fortune is awesome in its scope.

Transition First, there are the castles and palaces.
  A. They own many castles and palaces.
    1. Windsor Castle and Buckingham Palace are the official state residences of the Queen.
    2. Fine houses are not limited to the Queen.
      a. Prince Charles bought a one-million-dollar mansion for Lady Di.
      b. Prince Charles also owns an island bungalow (complete with island).

Transition It's been said that children never grow up, they just acquire more expensive playthings.

  B. They own many playthings.
    1. The family owns a fleet of Rolls-Royces, a fleet of airplanes, and the royal yacht *Britannia*.
    2. The royal table service (in gold, not silver) weighs five tons.

Conclusion To us Americans, it seems ridiculous to spend this kind of money on a figurehead. But to the British, the queen is much more than a figurehead. She is a symbol of all the history, the stability, the hospitality, the power, and the grandeur that is Great Britain. To millions around the world, the queen *is* Great Britain. As such, say the British, she must live in a style fit for a queen.

Work Out

■ Use the chart on page 60 to show how "Fit for a Queen" was made interesting, clear, and concrete.

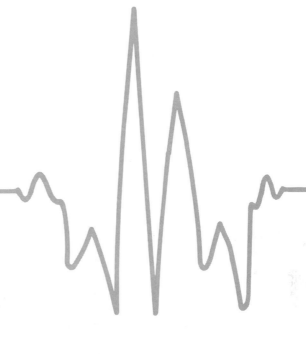

Chapter 7

Speaking to Persuade

For I will give you a mouth and wisdom, which all your adversaries shall not be able to gainsay nor resist.

—Luke 21:15

Your goal as a persuasive speaker is to move your audience to action. However, in moving toward this goal do not neglect the most important principle in persuasive speaking: make the audience think before they act. Ethical persuasion is the combination of argumentation and motivation. Argumentation is directed toward the mind. Motivation is directed toward the emotions. Used together they operate on the will.

ARGUMENTATION	+	MOTIVATION	=	PERSUASION
(directed toward mind)		(directed toward emotions)		(directed toward will)

A speech that bypasses argumentation and deals *only* with motivation is propaganda, not persuasion.

PERSUASION	−	ARGUMENTATION	=	PROPAGANDA

Suppose you wanted to persuade someone who knew nothing about skydiving to try it. You would first convince him that it is a safe sport by giving him statistics and professionals' statements to support your point. Then you could describe the thrill of free fall and the delight of floating to earth. If, however,

your main point was that "skydiving is a sport only for the courageous," you would be trying to move your listener to action solely on the basis of emotion—and that is propaganda. The chart below will help you see how argumentation and motivation function.

	ARGUMENTATION	MOTIVATION
Goal	belief	action
Process	rational	nonrational
Basis	logic	emotion

To build an effective persuasive speech, you need to understand the tools of argumentation and motivation.

Argumentation

To convince, we appeal to the rational. We do so by using logic, the process of reasoning to a conclusion. The two most common types of reasoning are deductive and inductive.

Deduction *Deduction* is reasoning from a general truth to a specific conclusion. Probably the most famous example of deduction is this:

> All men are mortal;
> Socrates is a man;
> Therefore, Socrates is mortal.

This form is called a *syllogism.* It begins with a general truth, or a major premise, and is followed by a specific truth, or a minor premise. It then ends with a conclusion.

Deduction will work every time, provided that the premises are true and that the form is valid. If either premise is false, the conclusion probably will be too:

major premise: All men are green;
minor premise: Socrates is a man;
conclusion: Therefore, Socrates is green.

major premise: All men are mortal;
minor premise: God is a man;
conclusion: Therefore, God is mortal.

As you can see, a false premise will often lead to a false conclusion. But sometimes you can end with a false conclusion even when the premises are true. How? By combining the premises in the wrong way. When this happens, we say the syllogism is invalid even though the premises themselves may be true.

There are three kinds of syllogisms: categorical, hypothetical, and disjunctive. (For explanations and examples of these syllogisms, see Appendix C.)

Induction *Induction* is simply the opposite of deduction; it is reasoning from specific examples to a general conclusion. But keep in mind that induction is not certain, like deduction. If a syllogism has true premises and its form is valid, then it is safe to assume the conclusion is correct. But induction doesn't work that way; it is tentative. You can come up with valid conclusions, but you usually can't be absolutely certain that they are true. There are three kinds of induction: enumeration, analogy, and scientific analysis.

Enumeration is listing specific examples and drawing a general conclusion by extrapolation. The most common example of this is the public-opinion poll. We hear that "x percent of all Americans favor [or oppose] the death penalty." How do the pollsters know this? Did they ask you what you think? Probably not. They asked a certain number of people for their opinions, and then they extrapolated the results: that is, they assumed that the entire public believed pretty much as their "sample" believed. This method is enumeration.

> Jane votes democratic; Elaine votes democratic; Paula votes
>   democratic; etc.
> Therefore, women tend to vote democratic.

Note that the conclusion is tentative: "tend to vote." This is a sign of induction.

Analogy is the second type of induction. In this type two things are alike in many ways, so you conclude that they are alike in others. Here is what Benjamin Franklin concluded and what led to his famous kite experiment:

> Electricity gives off sparks;
> Lightning looks much like sparks;
> Perhaps lightning is a form of electricity.

Scientific analysis, or "scientific method," is the third type. Any properly conducted experiment is a form of induction. The scientist proposes a hypothesis and then tests it. If the test is successful, then he assumes that his hypothesis is true. Again, he cannot be certain, for he is dealing in induction. Perhaps his hypothesis will later be disproved.

Inductive Fallacies Induction, too, has fallacies—many more than deduction. Since induction depends on proper interpretation of proper evidence, most of the fallacies result from improper gathering of evidence or improper interpretation.

Below are four of the most common inductive fallacies.

Slanted selection bases a conclusion on a biased representation:

> According to the students, the teacher assigns too much homework.

Red herring bases a conclusion on an unrelated fact:

> How can you give me a failing grade on the test when I have two sisters who are at home starving?

Post hoc is the assumption that two things are related just because one follows the other:

> Every time I wash my car, it rains.

Hasty generalization is a conclusion based on insufficient evidence:

> My survey of these four women has yielded several conclusions about American women in general.

Study these forms of reasoning until you know them well. You should know not only how to use them, but how *not* to use them. Most of the enemies of truth succeed by using one or more forms of these fallacies.

Motivation

Once convinced, the listener can then be moved to action through nonrational appeals. Here are four commonly used nonrational appeals.

Connotation "His uncle was notorious." "His uncle was famous." There is actually very little difference between the literal meanings of *notorious* and *famous*. *Notorious* literally means "generally known or talked of." It is the frequent use of the word in a negative context that gives us an unfavorable impression of a "notorious" person. We say, then, that the connotative meaning of notorious is "infamous" rather than "famous."

Association "Baseball is as American as motherhood and apple pie." All of us realize that people in other countries have mothers and that apple pie is not exclusively American. However, we have come to associate our feelings of "home" with the concept of motherhood and the taste of apple pie; hence the phrase.

Moving stories and illustrations These are also commonly used as motivational appeals. Such appeals help make the reasoning both personal and concrete. It is one thing to tell an audience that we need to improve the educational standards. But the argument is more persuasive if we can tell a specific story about an illiterate man who, though intelligent, could not feed his family because no one would hire a man who could not fill out an application.

Humor and wit These are also effective motivational appeals. A comic effect can be produced by the intentional violation of expectation. Humor often uses exaggeration, or over-statement. It gives more emphasis than is expected to the subject.

W. H. Auden once said of Sigmund Freud, "To us he is no more a person now but a whole climate of opinion."

Wit uses an understatement that gives less emphasis to the topic than is expected.

After reading his obituary in the newspaper, Mark Twain sent this cable to the Associated Press: "The reports of my death are greatly exaggerated."

These motivational appeals can not only establish rapport with the audience but also reinforce your arguments.

Procedure

The following steps will help you balance logic and emotion in your persuasive speech.

BALANCING YOUR PERSUASIVE SPEECH

1. Gain attention; state the problem.
   (argumentation and/or motivation)
2. Analyze the problem.
   (argumentation)
3. Show how the problem affects the listener.
   (motivation)
4. Propose a solution and show how it will affect the listener.
   (argumentation and motivation)
5. Call for a specific response from the listener.
   (motivation)

Although all persuasion aims at generating action, the way you structure your speech to achieve that goal will vary according to your audience. If your audience does not believe as you do, you will need to devote more of your speaking time to convincing them through logical appeals. However, if they already agree with you, you are free to spend more time on motivational appeals. Speeches that emphasize the rational are speeches to convince. Those that emphasize the nonrational are speeches to inspire. Following are three sample speeches: one, a speech to convince and the others, speeches to inspire.

Speech to Convince

For Medicine or Money
Student Speech

1) gaining attention and stating the problem

Every ninety seconds one American dies of cancer. This disease has reached epidemic proportions, and we still have only the "cut, burn, and poison" ways of combating it. Alan Stang, author of *American Opinion,* says that these orthodox treatments have done little to curb the spread of cancer. He claims these methods have a success rate of less than 10 percent. Why is the survival rate so low? Some have been made to believe that there is not enough money for research. Others have been convinced that extensive research has simply produced no answers. It may be, however, that the American medical profession could give us a more plausible reason for why they have failed to pursue new treatments.

The American Medical Association seems to be prejudiced against research on alternative cancer treatments. For instance, the California Cancer Commission, when doing some tests on the effectiveness of Laetrile, did not completely examine the patients treated. Despite the incomplete examination, the commission explained the patients' improvement as the delayed result of early orthodox treatment, the result of natural body reactions, or the discovery that the patients never had cancer. Furthermore, the National Cancer Institute, one of the foremost cancer research organizations in the country, refuses to study Laetrile, saying that it is worthless and harmful. How is it that the institute is able to come up with such a startling discovery before it even begins to study Laetrile? The only answer is prejudice.

2) analyzing the problem

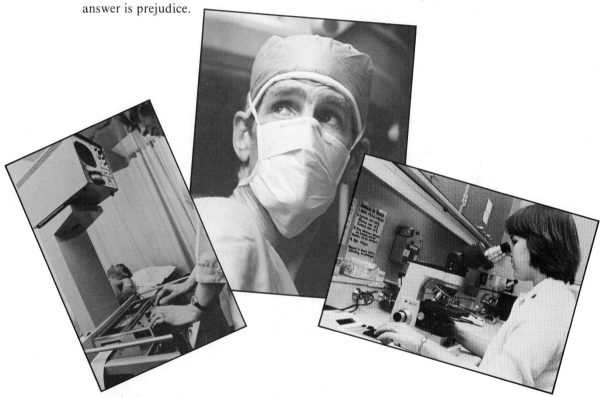

Prejudice may keep the medical administrations from accepting new treatments, but it can only be pride that makes them reject new findings that would make their orthodox methods seem obsolete. Wilhelm C. Hueper, a researcher for the National Cancer Institute, made discoveries about occupational and chemical cancer causes. But the Federal Food and Drug Administration silenced his discoveries, covered his

3) showing how the problem affects the listener

reports, and discredited his ability because he disagreed with the administration's public stand. How do you feel about the deliberate suppression of information that might help save someone you love? Is this not a horrible price to pay for anyone's professional pride?

It is inexcusable to allow prejudice to thwart research for alternative treatments. It is contemptible to withhold valuable medical information because of pride. But it is inhuman to prey on suffering for profit. Modern orthodox treatments are financially profitable for all involved—all, that is, except the patient. In 1975, cancer therapy reaped a profit of over 20 billion dollars. One wonders where all this money goes. As early as 1922, the American Medical Association has been accused of forming a financial empire. The *Illinois Medical Journal* published an article that year entitled "The AMA Becomes an Autocracy," which scolded the association for its desire to build a "financial empire." Even the American Cancer Society can be accused of empire building. The society holds the patent rights to one of the most effective and often-used chemicals in chemotherapy, and thus it receives huge sums of money in royalties. In fact, these royalties compose one of the largest sources of income for the Society. It would indeed be a disadvantage, then, were Laetrile to replace, even partially, chemotherapy. Certainly it is better to stamp out new treatments that threaten profits than to lose a financial empire.

4) proposing a solution and showing the benefits

To say that the medical profession is more interested in its image and pocketbook than in people is a serious charge, and one not readily believed. But the evidence cannot be denied: the FDA, the AMA, and the ACS have deliberately withheld information that the American people have a right to know. And some Americans are fighting back. Glen L. Rutherford, an advocate of freedom of choice in cancer therapy, is appealing to the Supreme Court, charging the American Medical Association with allowing 4 million Americans to suffer and die needlessly. Other groups are calling for strict regulations to be imposed on medical associations, requiring full accounts on donations and expenditures.

5) calling for a response

There is something you can do too. Write to your congressman, asking him to initiate investigations into the practices of the FDA. Also encourage him to vote for legislation that would allow experiments on new drugs. By writing your representatives, you can help force medical officials to face up to their moral responsibilities. Do not sit idly by while greedy men force others to die an agonizing death.

Speeches to Inspire

July 29, 1588—Queen Elizabeth I's speech to her army during the peril of the Armada

Let tyrants fear; I have always so behaved myself that, under God, I have placed my chiefest strength and safeguard in the loyal hearts and good will of my subjects. And therefore I am come amongst you at this time, not as for my recreation and sport, but being resolved, in the midst and heat of the battle, to live or die amongst you all; to lay down, for my God, and for my kingdom, and for my people, my honor and my blood. I know I have but the body of a feeble woman; but I have the heart of a king, and of a king of England too. I myself will take up arms; I myself will be your general, judge, and rewarder of every one of your virtues in the field. I know already, by your forwardness, that you deserve rewards and crowns; and we do assure you, on the word of a prince, they shall be duly paid to you.

June 6, 1944—King George VI's speech on the D-Day invasion

Four years ago our nation and empire stood alone against an overwhelming enemy with our backs to the wall—a testing such as never before in our history—and by God's providence we survived that test. After nearly five years of toil and suffering, we must renew that crusading impulse on which we entered the war and met its darkest hour. We and our allies are sure that our fight is against evil and for a world in which goodness and honor may be the foundation of the life of men in every land. That we may be worthily matched in this summons of destiny, I desire, solemnly, to call my people to prayer and dedication. We are not unmindful of our own shortcomings, past and present. We shall ask not that God may do our will but that we may be enabled to do the will of God. And we dare to believe that God has used our nation and empire as an instrument for fulfilling His high purpose. I hope that throughout the present crisis of the liberation of Europe there may be offered up earnest, continuous, and widespread prayer. We who remain in this land can most effectively enter into the suffering of our subjugated Europe by prayer, whereby we can fortify the determination of our sailors, soldiers, and airmen who go forth to set the captive free.

Work Out

- Make up your own valid syllogism.
- Exchange your syllogism for a classmate's. Use the conclusion of his syllogism as your major premise, and construct an invalid syllogism.
- Exchange syllogisms another time. Identify the problem in the syllogism you receive and correct it.

Chapter 8

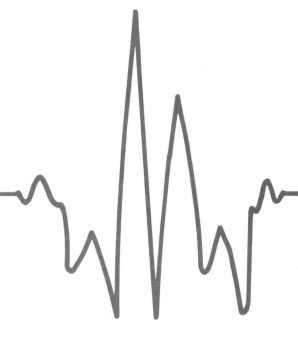

Speaking in Special Situations

A word fitly spoken is like apples of gold in pictures of silver.

—Proverbs 25:11

Why begin a discussion of special speaking situations with this verse? Because a stirring speech is like a beautiful painting. Both are carefully designed and skillfully fashioned. And both give pleasure. Tribute speeches, courtesy speeches, and after-dinner speeches require of the speaker artistic care and skill.

Tribute Speeches

Presentations, dedications, farewells, nominations, and eulogies are tribute speeches. The purpose of these speeches is either to show appreciation or to give honor. However, each has a unique structure. The following guidelines and sample speeches will help you know what specific information should be included in each type of speech.

Presentation Speech

If you are ever called on to present an award, you need to follow these guidelines:

1. Comment on any special features of the occasion and on the purpose of the occasion.
2. Describe the award and what it represents.
3. List the recipient's achievements.
4. Present the award, prize, or gift and congratulate the recipient.

Dedication Speech

November 19, 1863—Lincoln's Gettysburg Address

Four score and seven years ago our fathers brought forth on this continent, a new nation, conceived in Liberty, and dedicated to the proposition that all men are created equal.

Now we are engaged in a great civil war, testing whether that nation, or any nation so conceived and so dedicated, can long endure. We are met on a great battle-field of that war. We have come to dedicate a portion of that field, as a final resting place for those who here gave their lives that the nation might live. It is altogether fitting and proper that we should do this.

But, in a larger sense, we cannot dedicate—we cannot consecrate—we cannot hallow—this ground. The brave men, living and dead, who struggled here, have consecrated it, far above our poor power to add or detract. The world will little note, nor long remember what we say here, but it can never forget what they did here. It is for us the living, rather, to be dedicated here to the unfinished work which they who fought here have thus far so nobly advanced. It is rather for us to be here dedicated to the great task remaining before us—that from these honored dead we take increased devotion to that cause for which they gave the last full measure of devotion—that we here highly resolve that these dead shall not have died in vain—that this nation, under God, shall have a new birth of freedom—and that government of the people, by the people, for the people, shall not perish from the earth.

1) Mention the significance of the dedication.

2) State the purpose of the dedication.

3) Describe past hardships.

4) Suggest future goals.

5) Some dedication speeches would also include a thank-you to those who worked on the project and a presentation of the item being dedicated.

Farewell Speech

February 11, 1861—Lincoln's Farewell Address to Springfield

No one, not in my situation, can appreciate my feelings of sadness at this parting. To this place, and the kindness of these people, I owe everything. Here I have lived a quarter of a century, and have passed from a young to an old man. Here my children have been born and one is buried. I now leave, not knowing when or whether ever I may return, with a task before me greater than that which rested upon Washington. Without the assistance of the Divine Being who ever attended him [who always watched over George Washington], I cannot succeed. With that assistance, I cannot fail. Trusting in Him who can go with me, and remain with you, and be everywhere for good, let us confidently hope that all will yet be well. To His care commending you, as I hope in your prayers you will commend me, I bid you an affectionate farewell.

1) Express regret at leaving.

2) Mention future plans.

Nomination Speech

June 15, 1876—Robert Ingersoll's "The Plumed Knight"
Nomination of Senator James G. Blaine for President

1) List the qualifications for the office.

The Republicans of the United States demand as their leader a man of intelligence, a man of integrity, a man of well-known and approved political opinions. They demand a statesman. They demand a politician in the highest, broadest, and best sense—a man of superb moral courage. They demand a man whose political reputation is spotless as a star. The man who has all these splendid qualifications is James G. Blaine.

2) Show how the candidate meets qualifications.

Like an armed warrior, like a plumed knight, James G. Blaine marched down the halls of the American Congress and threw his shining lance full and fair against the brazen foreheads of the defamers of his country and the maligners of his honor. For the Republicans to desert this gallant leader now is as though an army should desert their general upon the field of battle.

James G. Blaine is now, and has been for years, the bearer of the sacred standard of the Republican party. I call it sacred, because no human being can stand beneath its folds without becoming and without remaining free.

3) Make the nomination.

Gentlemen of the convention, in the name of the great republic, the only republic that ever existed upon the earth; in the name of all her soldiers living; in the name of all her soldiers dead upon the field of battle; and in the name of those who perished in the skeleton clutch of famine at Andersonville and Libby, whose suffering he so vividly remembers, Illinois—Illinois nominates for the next president of this country that prince of parliamentarians, that leader of leaders, James G. Blaine.

Eulogy Speech

April 17, 1945—Winston Churchill's "A Bitter Loss to Humanity"
A tribute to Franklin D. Roosevelt

1) Comment on the occasion.

As the saying goes, he died in harness, and we may well say in battle harness like his soldiers, sailors, and airmen who died side by side with ours and are carrying out their tasks to the end all over the world. What an enviable death was his.

Chapter 8

He had brought his country through the worst of its perils and, happiest of all, its trials. Victory had cast its sure and steady beam upon him. He had broadened and stabilized in days of peace the foundations of American life and union. In war he had raised the strength, might, and glory of a great republic to a height never attained by any nation in history. On her left hand she was leading the advance of our conquering Allied Armies into the heart of Germany. On her right, on the other side of the globe, she was irresistibly and swiftly breaking the power of Japan.

2) Make tribute to the specific occasion.

And all the time ships, munitions, food, and supplies of every kind were on every side aiding on a gigantic scale her allies in the course of the struggle. But all this was no more than worldly power and grandeur had it not been that the causes of human freedom and social justice to which so much of his life had been given, had added a luster quite of its own which will long be discernible among men.

3) Build respect for the person honored.

He left behind him a band of resolute, able men handling numerous interrelated parts of the vast American war machine. He has left a successor who comes forward with firm steps and sure conviction to carry on the task to its appointed end. For us it remains only to say that in Franklin Roosevelt there died the greatest American friend we have ever known and the greatest champion of freedom who has ever brought help and comfort from the New World to the Old.

4) Set forth worthwhile principles for others to follow.

Courtesy Speeches

The word *courtesy* comes from the old French word for *court* and originally referred to the behavior expected of a courtier. *Courtesy* now means gracious and polite in manner. Introductory, welcoming, and acceptance speeches should be nobly phrased and graciously delivered.

Introductory Speech

A speech of introduction should do the following:

1. Tell the speaker's qualifications.
2. Announce the topic or title of the presentation.
3. Show how the topic is significant for the audience.

Welcoming Speech

A speech to make guests feel welcome should do these things:

1. Say how much you appreciate the guests' coming.
2. Announce any activities of interest to the visitors.
3. If appropriate, give the agenda for the meeting.
4. Ask the visitors to stand.
5. Suggest that the members of the audience personally greet the visitors later.

Acceptance Speech

When accepting an award, a nomination, or a gift, you should remember to do the following:

1. Thank whoever presented the award, etc.
2. Recognize the value of the award, etc.
3. Tell what it means to you.
4. If appropriate, say what you plan for yourself or the organization.

After-Dinner Speeches

After-dinner speeches are speeches to entertain or to edify. The following are two sample after-dinner speeches.

Entertainment Speech

Kinfolk and Cubby Lockers
Student Speech

1) Center on a theme.

In the musical "My Fair Lady," Henry Higgins poses a pointed question for the English population when he asks, "Why can't the English teach their children how to speak? Norwegians learn Norwegian; the Greeks are taught their

Greek!" Obviously the English did teach their children how to speak. But problems arose when the English language changed so much and so fast that the parents couldn't keep up with their children. Over the years, the gap became so wide that nowadays if one of us tried to communicate with an Englishman, we might find the task a bit difficult.

For example, in Great Britain you don't buy your groceries from a grocer, you get them from a greengrocer. If it's fish that you want, go see the fishmonger. But don't get confused, if you want fresh fish, see the wet fishmonger. Cooked fish is prepared only by the dry fishmonger. Are you thirsty? Have a mineral—a fizzy mineral if it's carbonated. And after dinner we don't have dessert, we have afters!

2) Use interesting, light examples to develop theme.

In America a vehicle is equipped with a hood, four fenders, two bumpers, and a glove compartment. But in Great Britain a car has a bonnet, four wings, two overriders, and a cubby locker. If these terms sound unusual or even ridiculous to you, it should be clear that the English don't speak the same English that we do.

When you were growing up, your mother may have told you to clean your room, sweep it out, "red it up," or get it squared away. Do you prefer hoagies, subs, poorboys, or grinders? Depending on which part of the country you come from, you may swim in a creek or a "crik," and in that "crik" you're likely to run across a crab, a crawfish, a crawdad, or a craw.

When my family moved, we encountered some situations that were rather amusing. People in Florida just don't speak the same English that people in Pennsylvania do. I'll never forget the day an elderly lady rushed up to me after church and announced that she was "fixin' to carry my sister up yonder." I was shocked! I wasn't sure whether to thank her for her services or go get my dad. But a quick interpretation by a friend of mine set my mind at ease, and I realized that the lady was "getting ready to take my sister to the school."

In reality, I guess it doesn't matter whether you raise your kids, rear your children, or fetch up yer yung'ins. And I suppose it makes no difference whether you have relatives, kinfolk, or relations. Just remember, not everybody speaks your English. So, you can snip out on a short errand, but don't take off too far because the people around you may not catch what you're lookin' to say.

Devotional Speech

Extraordinarily Ordinary

1) Begin with an interesting fact, question, or anecdote.

Let's begin with a question. What is the essence of godliness? Or, how did our Lord impress on His disciples that He was indeed God?

Some of the most interesting passages in the Gospels to me are those where the Holy Spirit tells us what our Lord was thinking before He said or did something. Jesus reflects on the situation, and then He acts. Studying these passages is a humbling experience. What Christ does or says is often the opposite of what I would say or do.

One of the most striking examples of this concept is found in John 13:3. "Jesus *knowing* that the Father had given all things into his hands, and that he was come from God, and went to God," rose up and did something. What do you think it was He did? How did He demonstrate that He knew who He was? Jesus rose from His seat, took a towel, and washed His disciples' feet. Not spectacular, was it? Didn't draw a crowd. Impressive? Not really. Mundane and ordinary—He simply did what a servant would do. Our Lord chose to demonstrate godliness through humility and gentleness—through meeting an ordinary need of His disciples. As the psalmist says, "Thy gentleness [literally, 'thy stooping down'] hath made me great."

2) Identify and discuss passage on which central idea is based.

3) Show how the central idea relates to the listener.

I think too often we think that God wants us to be spectacular for Him—to be always doing something impressive—something exceptional. He doesn't. He wants us to be unnoticed—to be so enraptured with Him that we forget all about ourselves. He wants us to be involved in the ordinary—to serve the needs of others, to be unobtrusive. I often think that the small deeds done in devotion to Christ are more precious in His sight than the most eloquent sermon or the most stirring testimony. Those little things demonstrate Christ in us.

The best example—other than our Lord—might be the man Enoch. Enoch never did anything spectacular—no miracles, no stupendous acts of faith—he simply "walked with God." How ordinary! The testimony of Enoch's faith was not what he did in exceptional times, but what he did in the humdrum of everyday life.

4) Support the central idea with other specific illustrations and/or examples.

What happened to Enoch? We know the story; God took him home. And even that wasn't done in a spectacular way. Nobody saw him go. Nobody knew he was going. Hebrews tells us that they looked for him and couldn't find him. But, when they couldn't find Enoch, they came to a remarkable conclusion. They determined that God must have taken him, because Enoch pleased God. If you or I were to disappear today, what would people conclude? That God took us? I often wonder what the world will think of the disappearance of the church at the Rapture. "God must have taken them"? Or, "I haven't the faintest idea what happened to them"?

Enoch made an extraordinary impression, don't you think? Yet he did it in the ordinary things. He walked with God

daily, and God was so moved He took him to heaven—and the world was not surprised that God would do so. By the way, Enoch's testimony didn't cease when God took him home. He had a great-grandson who had this testimony: "Noah walked with God."

5) Make a general application.

The Devil doesn't worry so much about the Christian who simply goes to church every time the doors are open, sings in the choir, and gives his testimony every opportunity he gets. Those things may be good and profitable. But, the man who walks with God everyday—in the Word, in prayer, and in "stooping down"—this is the man the Devil fears. These Enochs demonstrate the omnipotence of God in the ordinary things—as the Saviour did. How desperately the world—and the church—needs such men.

Work Out

- Use your imagination to prepare a humorous courtesy or after-dinner speech.
- Make an outline for a tribute speech.

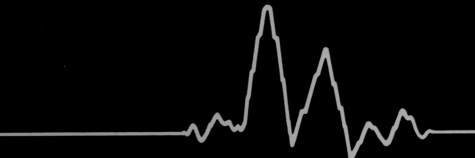

INTERVIEW

JOYCE PARKS

Profession: Professor of Public Speaking and Parliamentary Procedure
Professional Experience: Served as a delegate to the 1984 Republican National Convention, currently serves as a professional consultant on parliamentary procedure
Hobbies: Reading, miniatures, travel, swimming

work. Then he appeared before local clubs to enlist their support for a larger state appropriation. Finally, he ended up in Washington, D.C. before a Congressional committee, defending and explaining the value of his proposals. So, when it comes to the future usefulness of speech skills or their effect on your work, you just never know.

Interviewer: How do these skills help the Christian in his daily life?

Joyce Parks: First of all, they help him reason effectively. In a day when situation ethics saturates modern decision making, it is particularly important that Christians reason carefully, starting from a base of biblical truth. First we must establish our core values, beginning by asking ourselves questions, such as "What is the nature of God?" "What is the nature of man?" and "What is the source of truth?" These answers establish absolutes— positions for which no further proof can be given.

Our core values form the basis of our total value-belief-attitude system: values spring from core values; beliefs are formulated from values; attitudes or judgments are dictated by relevant facts or are built from our values and beliefs; opinions derive from attitudes, and our communication stems from our opinions. This diagram may help:

Interviewer: What specific careers would you say demand a mastery of the skills taught in debate and parliamentary procedure?

Joyce Parks: Any career that involves analysis. For instance, you would need analytic skills for the pastorate, for a pastor must be able to speak, to think on his feet, to decide issues, to organize his thoughts, and to make judgments. Public speaking gives you a foundation for performing these responsibilities. Furthermore, no pastor can function in his church without some knowledge in parliamentary procedure, for, as the leader of the church, he would need to conduct business meetings. In such meetings, certainly, a knowledge of parliamentary rules helps avoid unnecessary tensions and mistakes.

Teachers, salesmen, business executives, managers—in essence, anyone who must discuss and solve problems needs a basic knowledge of this field.

I remember reading about a man who went into forestry so that he wouldn't have to deal with people—something he was uncomfortable doing. Yet, after a year or so he developed some ideas that could be tried to make his work more effective. First, he spoke at the County Foresters' meeting to defend his proposals and explain how they would

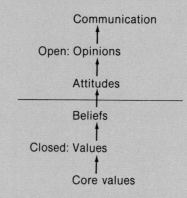

You can see why it is so important for us to rely on God's Word as the source of absolute truth. We cannot trust senses alone.

Situation ethicists maintain that the whole value-belief-attitude system should be open for negotiation and they object to the fact that many "religious" people have a totally closed system. Personally, I contend that the three lower levels—core-values, values, and beliefs—should be closed. Open-core values lead to the devastation of the Christian life.

In teaching persuasion, I tell my students, "Know the facts. Know the situation under discussion better than your opponent and from all points of view. Have a solid foundation of information; do not simply spout personal bias." Our biblical bias, however, is not personal. It rests on what God said, and He alone is all-knowing and gives never-changing, eternal truth. When trying to convince someone of something, it is insufficient simply to say, "Well, my opinion is. . . ." Few people care what our opinions are. Consequently, we must know not only what we believe but why we believe it. We cannot formulate truth just because some person said something. Everything we think or do should be examined in the light of what Scripture says. That is our personal responsibility. If we allow others to do our thinking, we place ourselves in the tenuous position of yielding to the last person who did a particularly good selling job—not just with products but, even more dangerously, with ideas. God expects more of us than that.

Interviewer: As a result of your knowledge in this field, what specific opportunities have you had?

Joyce Parks: There have been many speaking and writing opportunities that the Lord has sent my way, but not because I sought them. Specifically, I was elected a board member of an international organization of parliamentarians. During my service on the board, I was requested to set up a professional parliamentarians' bureau, and I contributed to a new parliamentary textbook for colleges and law schools, as well as helping revise a popular parliamentary manual. I also give advice on procedure to elected officials and attorneys of city and county government. I serve the state Republican Party as their parliamentarian and was chosen as delegate-at-large to the Republican National Convention at which I had opportunity to talk to leaders from all over the country.

Interviewer: Have these opportunities provided you any occasions to witness?

Joyce Parks: The Lord has provided many opportunities for presenting the gospel. One specific occasion I remember was at a luncheon for a professional organization. Those I was eating with began talking about evolution and creation. Someone said how stupid it was that there are still creationists in the world. I said, "I'm one." They were taken aback. In a brief statement, I explained my belief and stood pleasantly for the truth.

Interviewer: You have at times been called upon to work with those who do not have a Christian philosophy. Has this ever caused a conflict?

Joyce Parks: A Christian will always have conflict because people resent Christ. However, even if people disagree with you, you will find that they respect you if they find you competent and gracious.

Interviewer: How do you handle such conflict?

Joyce Parks: I find it is always best to reduce confrontation and try to get the person you're dealing with to think. That is what a debater does—he finds out what the opposition believes which is inconsistent with what he is trying to prove or suggest. We can learn from the way Christ approached men and women. He spoke to the rich young ruler, for instance, probing and analyzing so that the young man could see his own inconsistencies.

It is interesting to note that the word *persuasion* comes from the Latin word *persuado.* The prefix means "through," and the stem of the word means "sweetness." Persuasion is not battering down your opponent; it is graciously presenting your view in such a way that your opponent will acknowledge the premise to be valid or will accept it. Often, unfortunately, we try ramming something down the throat of a listener rather than persuading him. We need to listen and understand the point of view of the other person, to "get inside his skin." When we speak from the viewpoint of the audience, we understand what a person's needs are.

Of course, in our convictions we must be unflinching but gracious, competent but personally unambitious, courageous but unselfish.

Chapter 9

Debate

Be ready always to give an answer to every man that asketh you a reason of the hope that is in you.

—I Peter 3:15b

How would you define *debate?* Would you say that it is two presidential candidates vying for political support on national television? Or would you define it as an organized argument in which two people talk fast and sound intelligent? These definitions may not be incorrect, but they are incomplete. Debate is more than a formal argument; it is a way of looking at both sides of an issue, a practical method of problem solving that you probably use every day. For example, you might ask yourself, "Could I keep my grades up if I got a job after school?" In considering this question, you would have to use the same reasoning skills a formal debater uses. You would gather information, organize it logically, analyze it, and then draw a conclusion. This example points out that you already know more about debating than you may have thought you did.

Of course, debating with yourself has its limitations—it's hard to lose your case. But there will be times when your opponent will be more formidable and the topic more serious. Studying formal debate will help you sharpen the reasoning and persuasive skills that you will need to "give a reason of the hope that is in you."

Choosing a Topic

The topic must be significant. To be significant, a formal debate topic must either involve a large number of people or seriously affect a few. Topics such as teenage driving, dating, and taking required classes are significant and could be debated because they affect many people. Topics of national concern, such as nuclear armament, however, may be easier to research. A life-threatening disease that strikes only one in ten thousand people would also be considered a "significant" problem, not because it affects many but because it affects a few greatly.

The topic must also be debatable. Good men on both sides of the issue should be able to find substantial evidence. Take, for instance, the topic of space travel. You could debate the usefulness of the space shuttle. However, you could not debate whether astronauts should wear space suits during space walks.

Stating the Resolution

Once you've decided that the topic or problem is significant and debatable, you are now ready to frame the resolution. There are three types of resolutions—fact, value, and policy.

A fact resolution It is a statement that must be proved either true or false.

> Resolved: The Loch Ness monster lives.

A value resolution It says that one thing is better than another.

> Resolved: Soccer is better than football.

A policy resolution It advocates a change in the way things are done.

> Resolved: All college-preparatory high school students take a year of foreign language.

Here only policy resolutions will be discussed. To be well stated, these resolutions follow certain criteria.

1. The resolution must contain only one idea.

Incorrect: To improve their health, all high school students should jog to school and eat hamburgers for lunch.

Correct: To improve their health, all high school students should jog to school.

2. The resolution must advocate a change from the present system, or status quo.

Incorrect: The Social Security System should be maintained. (Unless the Social Security System has been recently abolished, this example is invalid.)

Correct: The Social Security System should be abolished.

3. The resolution must be free of ambiguous terms.

Incorrect: High school administrators should encourage scholastic achievement.

Correct: High school administrators should organize science fairs.

4. The resolution must be timely and interesting.

Incorrect: Members of the basketball team should wear one blue and one red sock.

Correct: Members of the basketball team must have a *B* average.

Gathering Information

In Chapter 4 we discussed how to use library resources and how to take notes. The following questions will help you focus the research you do on your debate topic.

- What is the cause of the problem?
- Why does the problem need to be corrected immediately?
- What will happen if nothing is done?
- What harms does the problem cause?
- Are the harms significant?
- Are there other causes of the problem?
- How is the present system attempting to correct the problem?
- Why is the present system failing to solve the problem?
- Are other solutions available?
- Are other solutions less costly?
- Are other solutions more efficient?
- Are there any disadvantages to your solution?

As you read, you should take notes on answers to the preceding questions. When taking notes, use a subheading that tells what the card is about, and label the information *pro* or *con.* Also be sure to include on your card not only the author's name but also his qualifications. His qualifications will help establish the validity of your argument.

"Carding" your evidence makes it easier to find information in the "heat of battle." You will never win any rounds by saying, "I have several cards in my file box that prove my point, but I just can't find them right now."

Sometimes beginning debaters find an article on their topic and get fifty cards from this one source. Such diligence may be commendable, but it is weak debate strategy. The other team has only to bring into question the author's qualifications or contradict his findings with other studies. The best plan is to have evidence from many sources.

There are two types of sources: primary and secondary. Primary evidence comes directly from the author of a book, a researcher, or some other expert on your topic. It is considered the most reliable. On the other hand, secondary evidence reports, explains, or analyzes what the experts have said or done. Almost all news magazines—such as *Time, Newsweek,* and *U.S. News & World Report*—fall into this category.

Writing Your Case

Once you have compiled a sufficient number of cards (somewhere between two and two thousand), you are ready to write the case.

Affirmative Team

Before the debate really begins, the affirmative team states the resolution and defines its terms, establishing common ground to avoid useless arguments.

> Resolved: The federal government should require an individual
>   to protect his own health and safety.

The terms necessary to define in this resolution would be *require, protect, health,* and *safety.* Good sources for definitions are *Webster's International Dictionary,* the *Oxford English Dictionary, Words and Phrases,* and *Black's Law Dictionary.* Once these preliminaries are out of the way, you are ready to begin the actual debate.

If you are on the affirmative team you must first show that a problem exists in the present system. There are three ways to do this: by testimony, by quality-of-life issue, and by the weight of empirical evidence.

Testimony Experts say there is a problem. For example, Joe Schmuck says that 98 percent of all persons killed in traffic accidents were not wearing seat belts. (Remember, however, if Joe Schmuck is not a traffic safety engineer or an expert in some related field, our case is in big trouble.)

Quality-of-life issue People are seriously affected by this problem. The statistic above is important not only because *so many* people are affected but also because they are affected *so greatly*.

The weight of empirical evidence Many experiments have confirmed the same conclusion. For example, fourteen studies have confirmed this statistic for every state and for every model of car.

You must then prove that the problem is harmful. The harms may be either physical or psychological. Ideally, you should "quantify" this evidence. You should say that *6 million* rather than *many* are homeless. There is, however, one word of caution here. Any harms you point out you must also provide a solution for later.

The next step is to prove that the problem is caused by the present system and that your plan is designed to correct that flaw in the system.

Once you have established these points, you then show why the problem must be solved immediately by proving that any delay in adopting your plan would result in severe loss (loss of life, money, or opportunities).

Your next task will be to show how your solution to the problem is more effective and more efficient than the status quo's solution. For example, there is adequate funding, competent personnel, and sufficient power to implement the plan you have suggested, and according to your evidence the status quo cannot make these claims.

Finally, you must show any other advantages that will result from the adoption of your plan. These advantages are the "icing on the cake." You have already shown how your solution will solve the problem and diminish the harms. Now you show that there are even more advantages than the essential two.

Affirmative Team Review

1. State the resolution and define necessary terms.
2. Identify the problem and establish its significance.
3. Show that the problem is harmful.
4. Show that the problem is caused by the present system.
5. Show that the problem must be solved immediately.
6. Show how your plan will solve the problem.
7. Show any additional advantages of your plan.

Negative Team

The negative team's job is a bit more difficult because they do not know what solution the affirmative team will offer. Fortunately, if you are on the negative team there are some stock arguments that you can use against your opponents.

Presumption This is one of the strongest of the arguments. It means that the burden of proof rests on the affirmative team. They must prove that the change in the current system is justified. Your job, then, is to prove that it is not. Some common arguments used by the negative team are the following:

1. The affirmative team's statistics of significance are flawed.

2. The harms pointed out by the affirmative team are not caused by the present system.

3. The solution the affirmative team suggests treats only the symptoms of the problem, not the root cause.

Topicality This argument asserts that the affirmative team's solution must meet the needs of all those mentioned in the resolution and that every service promised in the resolution must be supplied. The following example might help clarify this point:

> Resolved: That the federal government should provide all high school students with dental floss.

Under this resolution, the affirmative team would have to show how the federal government could provide dental floss to *all high school students*. Your job would be to show either that all students would not receive the service or that the service could not be provided.

Status quo and repairs This argument allows you to agree that a significant problem exists. Your team maintains, however, that the solution is to correct the present system rather than to accept the radical change in the affirmative's new plan. The affirmative team might counter with "Isn't giving the status quo more money like pouring water into a sieve?" Your team then could respond by saying, "The affirmative side would have us buy a new car because the tires on our present car are out of alignment." And so goes the debate.

A counterplan This is any major alternative solution. Unlike the status quo and repairs argument, which suggests minor changes, the counterplan requires you to propose a totally new solution. You then assert that your solution is better than the affirmative's.

Straight refutation It denies everything the affirmative says. You say there is no problem. It is not significant, and it is not harmful. Of course, you must substantiate these claims. Mere denial will never convince a judge. You must give him proof. Show him that your evidence is more up to date, that your source is more qualified, or that you have more evidence.

Plan objections These are workability, solvency, and disadvantages.

> Workability—You claim that the affirmative plan will not work. Some of the reasons might be that their plan is too hard to enforce, too costly, too complex, or too simplistic.

> Solvency—You charge that the affirmative has not provided solutions for all the harms that they have cited.

> Disadvantages—You show that adopting the affirmative's plan will cause more problems than it solves. You would use this

argument when the affirmative can indeed solve the problem under debate.

> **Negative Team Review**
> 1. Show that a change in the system is unjustified.
> 2. Show that the affirmative's plan is not topical.
> 3. Show that the present system can be adequately repaired.
> 4. Offer an alternative solution.
> 5. Deny all the affirmative's claims.
> 6. Charge that the affirmative's plan is unworkable, incomplete, or inadvisable.

Participating in the Debate

Constructive and Cross-Examination Speeches

First Affirmative: Constructive (five minutes)

1. State the resolution.
2. Define the necessary terms.

3. Identify the significant problems.
4. Identify the cause for which you will provide a solution.
5. Identify the harms.
   a. Give specific numbers to support your claim.
   b. Show that the harms are serious.
6. Show that the problem is inherent in the current system.

Second Negative: Cross-examination (two minutes)

1. Question the significance of the problem.
2. Question the definitions (only if they are unreasonable).
3. Ask if there are other causes for the problem.
4. Question the seriousness of the harms.
5. Ask whether the affirmative plan will remove or greatly reduce the harms.

First Negative: Constructive (five minutes)

1. Accept or reject definitions. (If you reject their definitions, say why and offer others.)
2. Show that the problem is not significant.
3. Show that the harms are not as serious as the affirmative claims.

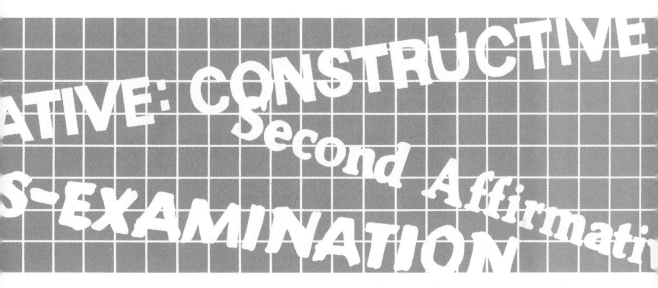

4. Assert that the present system is solving the problems.
5. Offer a counterplan.
6. Show that there may be other causes of the problem.

First Affirmative: Cross-examination (two minutes)

1. Question his evidence.
   a. Are his sources more recent than the affirmative's?
   b. Are his sources more reliable?
2. Question his charges about the seriousness of the harms.
3. Question his arguments.

Second Affirmative: Constructive (five minutes)

1. Read the plan.
2. Read your advantages.
   a. Show how your plan solves the problem.
   b. Show how your plan reduces or removes the harms.

First Negative: Cross-examination (two minutes)

1. Ask questions about the workability of the plan.
2. Question the solvency of the plan.
3. Show another cause they have not identified or solved.
4. Ask if there are any disadvantages to their plan.

Second Negative: Constructive (five minutes)

1. Attack the affirmative plan.
   a. Say it won't work.
   b. Say it won't solve the problems.
   c. Say it is inadvisable to adopt.
2. If time allows, attack the significance and the harms of the affirmative's case.

Second Affirmative: Cross-examination (two minutes)

1. Ask for specific arguments against workability, solvency, and disadvantages.
2. Question the authority of sources they use to discredit your plan.
3. Ask for the dates of their sources.

Rebuttal Speeches

(Rebuttal speeches summarize each speaker's arguments and respond to the opponents' arguments. You should not reread evidence unless it has been contested. Spend more time in analyzing than in repeating evidence. Below are some guidelines for rebuttal speeches. Of course, a speaker will not necessarily use all the points under any one speech.)

First Negative Rebuttal (three minutes)

1. Concisely restate your arguments.
   a. Say that the problem is not significant.
   b. Show that other causes exist.
   c. Show that the affirmative plan won't work.
   d. Prove that repairs in the present system will solve the problem.
   e. Prove that your counterplan is better.
2. Show that your evidence is more recent and reliable.

First Affirmative Rebuttal (three minutes)

1. Rebuild entire case and plan. (You must deal with every argument that has been raised against your side.)
2. Respond to any *major* negative argument.
3. Group negative arguments. (An example of grouping arguments would be this: if your opponents have read statistics from five studies to prove that there is no significant problem, you should take the lowest figure they have read and show how even that figure is significant.)

Second Negative Rebuttal (three minutes)

1. Review workability, solvency, and advisability.
2. Summarize your reasons for believing that the negative team has a better case.
3. Point out any of your arguments that the affirmative rebuttal overlooked.

Second Affirmative Rebuttal (three minutes)

1. Review workability, solvency, and advisability.
2. Summarize your reasons for believing that the affirmative team has a better case.

Hints for Cross Examination

Cross examination is probably the most terrifying part of debate. The best way to prepare is to know your arguments and to listen carefully when the questioner is speaking. Whether you are questioning someone or being questioned, remember you are attacking ideas, not individuals.

When You Are Being Questioned

1. Look at the judge. Try to be relaxed. Be polite.
2. Answer the questions—ask questions only for clarification.
3. Answer any fair or reasonable question.
4. Briefly state any qualification of your answer *before* you answer.
5. Be on your guard.
6. Don't defend the indefensible.
7. Don't volunteer information.
8. Don't argue.
9. Take your time.

When You Are Doing the Questioning

1. Ask simple, direct questions.
2. Arrange your questions to progressively reveal your goals.
3. Get admissions.
4. Expose weak evidence.
5. Expose faulty reasoning.
6. Expose lack of preparation.
7. Expose contradictions.
8. Expose unfounded assertions.
9. Get information for your partner.
10. Stay in control of the cross examination. Be polite, but firm.
11. Ask one question at a time and require an answer.
12. Use a quiet, moderate style.
13. Avoid questions that you don't know the answer to.

• Read the following resolution.

Resolved: Exams should be abolished.

- Divide the class into two teams, affirmative and negative.
  1. Take five minutes to marshal evidence for your case.
  2. Elect a spokesman for your team.
- Have the affirmative team state their case.
- Have the negative team state their case.
- Have the spokesmen return to their groups and take three minutes to prepare cross-examination questions.
- Have the spokesmen cross examine each other (two minutes apiece), the affirmative going first.
- Have the spokesmen return to their groups for three minutes to prepare the rebuttals.
- Have the spokesmen give the rebuttals, the negative going first.
- When you have finished, critique the debate as a class and choose a winner.

Chapter 10

Parliamentary Procedure

Let all things be done decently and in order.
—I Corinthians 14:40

Imagine this scene in the United States Senate: on an especially busy afternoon with all one hundred senators present, every single one of them decides he has something to say. Each of them is allowed to talk as long as he wants to, on any subject he chooses, and at the same time everyone else is talking. How much work do you think this group of distinguished lawmakers would get done? Would they ever listen to each other, much less agree on anything? What would happen if a few disagreed with the general opinion? Would this minority be listened to, or would they be bound, gagged, and dumped in the hallway?

Without rules for operating, almost anything can happen in a meeting. Parliamentary procedure is a code of manners to insure that meetings are conducted "decently and in order."

What Is Parliamentary Procedure?

Originally, parliamentary law was the code of customs and rules the English parliament used to conduct business. This centuries-old code was the main source for Thomas Jefferson's *Manual of Parliamentary Practice,* which he wrote as a guide for the United States Senate.

Today we still conduct orderly meetings by parliamentary procedure. Parliamentary procedure can work for almost any organization from the United Nations to your writers' club. It is based on the idea of democracy, and its purpose is to save time and keep order while it protects the rights of individual members.

Thumbing through a manual of parliamentary procedure is a good way to confuse yourself if you do not understand the subject. But as complicated as it seems, the hundreds of rules listed there all rest on a few principles, and understanding the principles will help you to comprehend the whole process. These are the principles:

Equality and dignity Every member of the group has the same right to speak and to vote, both in making decisions and in choosing those who will hold power. Each is also entitled to understand, at all times, what question is being discussed.

Freedom of speech The right of free debate says that all members can argue for what they think is right until they are ready to stop. Debate can be limited only when it strays from the subject, and then only when the group agrees (votes) to stop it.

The rule of the majority with fairness to the minority Until the group votes on a subject, the minority has just as much right to participate as the majority. After the vote, however, the minority must cooperate with the decision of the majority. Some types of action require a two-thirds vote to make sure that the minority's rights are respected.

How Does Parliamentary Procedure Work?

Parliamentary practice has one primary rule: only one main *motion* at a time. A *motion* is a proposal offered to the members. An organization run on parliamentary law does all of its business by means of motions. A motion is essentially a request for some action from the group, including action that affects the way the meeting is run. Take for instance the following examples:

"I move that our class hold a spring festival to help raise money for the new gym."

"I move that we refer this matter to a committee for study."

"I move to adjourn the meeting."

Many motions must be *seconded* because the group cannot consider a question if only one member is interested in it. At least one other member must show some interest by saying, "I second the motion."

To make a motion, you must first raise your hand or stand to be recognized by the *chair*—not a piece of furniture, but the person in charge of the meeting, usually the president.

(Except in special circumstances, members talk to the chair rather than to each other.) After you have been recognized or "given the floor," you may state your motion: "I move that we set a date for the Christmas party."

Notice the correct form for making a motion: "I move that (or "I move to") . . ." rather than "I make a motion . . . ." Notice, too, that a motion is worded positively whenever possible. You would say, "I move that nominations cease," rather than, "I move that we not have more nominations."

There are also rules that state when certain motions can be made and in what order they can be voted on. For instance, if someone moves to amend the motion already on the floor, the motion to amend must be voted on first before the main motion can be discussed. Handbooks of parliamentary procedure list this order (referred to as "the precedence of motions") in detail.

Who Is Responsible for What?

Parliamentary process assumes that everyone involved will do his job. Both officers and members have specific responsibilities.

The president is addressed during sessions by a legal title, "Mister (or Madame) President" or "Madame (or Mister) Chairman." This officer keeps the meeting running smoothly and makes sure that everyone is treated fairly. He cannot take sides while holding the chair, and if he wants to introduce business or take part in a discussion, he must give up the chair to do so. He regains the chair after the motion has come to a vote. The president has two primary duties: to achieve the organization's general objectives and to administer parliamentary law.

The vice president takes charge at the president's request or if the president is absent. If the president cannot continue his office for some reason, the vice president takes over those powers and duties until another election is held.

The recording secretary has an important duty: keeping the minutes, the official record of the organization. The office of secretary is sometimes combined with the office of treasurer. The treasurer's job is to receive and pay out money for the organization. This officer keeps a complete record of all money transactions and is always ready to give a financial report.

The officers perform their duties to help the group function smoothly, but the members play an even more important role

in keeping things running. No matter how carefully the rules are followed or how diligent the leaders are, a group will fail if the members are unwilling to do their part. The following guidelines will help you to understand your responsibilities as a member of a group:

Be faithful. If your group is to accomplish its goals, each member must be willing to devote both time and effort. Faithful attendance is a necessity.

Be prepared. As much as possible, prepare for each meeting in advance. For example, if you are a member of a committee responsible for raising funds for the senior trip, you could do some preliminary research on how other schools have conducted their fund-raising projects and take this information with you to the meeting.

Be open-minded. Listen without prejudice. We must be careful that our own preconceived ideas do not keep us from accepting alternative suggestions. Such objectivity is especially important when a proposal is offered by someone we do not admire. Our responsibility is to weigh the proposal apart from the person.

Be discerning. We must also be careful not to *accept* an idea simply because we esteem the person who presents it. We should always evaluate what we hear and make wise judgments based on that evaluation. (Prov. 18:13)

Be single-minded. Keep your mind on the problem being discussed. In any group situation it is easy to get side-tracked by minor issues. You can help avoid this problem by contributing only pertinent information and by being brief when you do speak. (James 1:19)

Be courteous. A courteous participant is one who can disagree without bruising egos. Proverbs 15:1 reminds us that "A soft answer turneth away wrath: but grievous words stir up anger."

Be encouraging. A good participant not only contributes ideas but also encourages others to do so. Sometimes another member can get someone to talk when the chairman hasn't been able to. Once a group decision has been made, you should be willing to support it even though you may not have voted for it.

Be enthusiastic. Nothing kills a discussion faster than someone's half-hearted participation or negative attitudes. Statements like "That won't work" or "That's no good" are destructive.

The member who believes that others have value and that their opinions are worthwhile will find these guidelines easy to follow. "Let nothing be done through strife or vainglory; but in lowliness of mind let each esteem other better than themselves." (Phil. 2:3)

Work Out

- As a class, do some preliminary research on the long and heated senatorial debate known as the Webster-Hayne debate.
- Appoint the vice president (who in a senatorial debate is supposed to maintain order).
- Act out the most exciting moments of this debate, trying to be true to the research you have done.
- After the dramatization, critique the debate on how well the participants followed parliamentary procedure. You may begin the critique by asking questions like these:
  1. Did the debaters break any parliamentary rules?
  2. Did the vice president remain impartial during the debate?
  3. Did the vice president maintain proper order?
  4. Did the participants maintain proper parliamentary etiquette?
  5. How did the various "diversions" from proper procedure affect the issues being discussed?

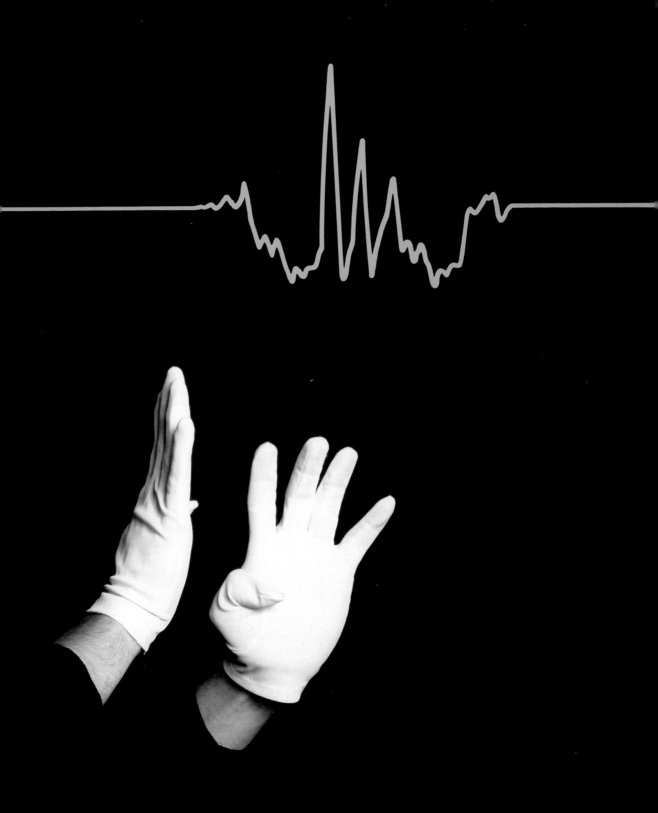

ELIZABETH EDWARDS
Profession: Professor of Oral Interpretation
Professional Experience: Performing, directing
Hobbies: Reading, sewing

beyond our own small world and prepares us for understanding the thoughts and experiences of others. Such knowledge can give us a greater perspective and better enable us to share our knowledge of God with other men whose experiences may be very different from our own.

A second inherent value comes from the pleasure we can experience through our involvement in the arts. Now in my mind there is a difference between being entertained and experiencing pleasure. Entertainment tends to be mere escape. On the other hand, pleasure can come from having attained something that demands a conscious effort. I think that is true of any of the arts if they are to give true pleasure. Whether I am performing a good piece of prose or listening to another perform, there must be an effort to convey or to grasp the rich meaning. That takes work, but it also affords a great deal of pleasure.

The performing arts can also help a student develop personally. For example, all of us need to develop poise and flexibility. Poise will help us to communicate our message effectively, and flexibility will help us get along well with others so that they will desire to accept the message we give.

Finally, studying speech (especially interpretation of literature) can help develop our voice. I'm sure you've heard that voice is one indicator of personality. Our communication depends not just on what we *say* but how we *sound*.

Interviewer: Due to your knowledge in speech, what opportunities have opened up for you that you might not have had otherwise?

Elizabeth Edwards: Of course, here at the university where I teach, I've had opportunities to perform both on stage and in films. However, my training has given me opportunities to become involved in my community as well. I've performed in surrounding churches, in ladies' clubs, local auditoriums, and even in private homes. For example, this past Christmas a friend and I went to a woman's club to perform some Christmas material. Those older women were moved to tears by

Interviewer: How did you first become interested in performance?

Elizabeth Edwards: While in elementary school, I took "expression" lessons, and that is where my interest in speech was first kindled. We did recitations and plays for both school and church activities. So actually I grew up performing, and by the time I was ready for college, I knew that I wanted to major in the field.

Interviewer: What would you say to someone who believed that training in the performing arts was not valuable for the Christian?

Elizabeth Edwards: First, I would stress that knowledge and appreciation of the arts is a vital part of becoming a well-rounded individual. William Phelps, a noted speaker and writer has said, "It is curious that many people believe in the importance of what they call vocational and practical courses but regard the study of literature as merely ornamental." He goes on to say, however, that in reality "nothing is more essential to the proper furnishing of a man's mind than a knowledge of the world's best literature. Literature is the immortal part of history." When an individual performs a good piece of literature, he opens up that part of history and helps his audience understand not only *what* others have done but also *why* they have done it. Such knowledge helps us see

some of the pieces. I never lose the excitement of the response you get to good literature. This particular occasion provided us with a witnessing opportunity.

For twelve years I also had the opportunity of producing and directing a community program called "The Singing Christmas Tree." The project was started by Dr. Hollis, a Greenville educator. His idea was to promote the best in fine arts for the local young people. I felt that I had a real opportunity of witness before many of these students. They were selected through auditions from the county public schools. It was a unique privilege to give my testimony to them, to have prayer with them, and to help them understand their dependence on the Lord. For those twelve years I endeavored to influence the quality of the music as well as the overall quality of the program. There are still many opportunities not only in the surrounding areas but in other states as well.

Interviewer: How do you feel your interpretative skills have better equipped you to influence others for Christ?

Elizabeth Edwards: I think of a story I once heard about Charles Laughton, a man famous for his roles on stage and on screen. He was becoming bored with what he was doing when he encountered two wounded men in a hospital. He asked them what they did in the evenings, and they said that they had nothing much to do. So he asked if he might each night come and read to them. He said, "I read Dickens, Aesop, Shakespeare, Whitman, Thurber, Hans Anderson, and Washington Irving. Then one day I picked up a Bible. The men protested. They did not want to hear anything from a dull book. The Bible was not dull to me, but I had to prove to them that it was not dull to me. I had to use every trick I'd learned and they liked it and asked for more." That's a perfect example. Here was a man who wasn't even a Christian, but made the Scripture come alive for those men—and who knows, the Scripture implanted in their hearts may have changed their lives. Those of us who truly believe the Word of God should desire even more than Charles Laughton to use every opportunity to make the Word "live" for others.

Interviewer: What character qualities do the rigors of performance develop?

Elizabeth Edwards: First of all, I would say discipline. You need to discipline your mind, body, and time when you participate in any production. A facet of this discipline is concentration. In any role, the ability to concentrate is essential. There is also the development of attention to detail. All of these three, of course, can be transferred into every other area of life. One other major character quality that I touched on earlier is flexibility—the ability to work well with others. Years ago I worked with a student on a production crew who later went to the mission field. When he returned for a visit he came to me and said that what he had learned from the rigors of production put him in good stead for the mission field. Working on the stage crew had taught him how to get along with others, an invaluable lesson for anyone who wants to serve the Lord successfully.

Interviewer: Would you encourage those entering an unrelated field, such as business, to take a performance class? If so, why?

Elizabeth Edwards: In any business or industry the ability to communicate effectively is important. I recently read that an executive will probably spend fourteen hours per week communicating in informal conferences. My son is a managing partner of a large professional practice. There are seven hundred in his organization, and he is constantly using his speech skills. Hardly a week goes by when he is not called upon to present his ideas before corporate executives. He has even been to Europe to present a speech on marketing to the firm's partners there. You'll find that many organizations are paying high prices for speech teachers to help their employees. This shows the value put on speech skills by these professionals.

Interviewer: In advising a beginning performer, what one pitfall would you caution him to avoid?

Elizabeth Edwards: I would tell them to avoid being "arty." Artificiality is never becoming. What you must do is take that which is right and use it in a way that is natural for you. Speech is communication; and any artificiality in voice, mannerisms, or behavior will create a barrier between you and your audience. As Christians, all we do should be done for the glory of God. Consequently, anything that would mar our message or would bar others from understanding what we have to say should be discarded.

Chapter 11

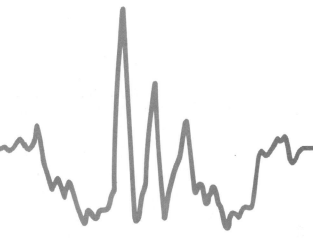

Understanding Literature

Good literature continually read for pleasure must, let us hope, do some good to the reader: must quicken his perception though dull [provide insight], and sharpen his discrimination though blunt [develop discernment], and mellow the rawness of his personal opinions [help refine and educate].
—*A. E. Housman*

The Masque of the Red Death

by Edgar Allan Poe

The "Red Death" had long devastated the country. No pestilence had ever been so fatal, or so hideous.[1] Blood was its Avatar and its seal—the redness and the horror of blood. There

[1] The last great plague was in the early 1600s. Since

the masqueraders'
costumes are of
this period as well,
it is possible that
Poe was basing his
"Red Death" on
this historical
epidemic. He does,
however,
exaggerate the
horrors of the
disease in order to
create a more
terrifying
atmosphere.

[2]Prosperous (irony in name)

were sharp pains, and sudden dizziness, and then profuse bleeding at the pores, with dissolution. The scarlet stains upon the body and especially upon the face of the victim, were the pest which shut him out from the aid and the sympathy of his fellow-men. And the whole seizure, progress and termination of the disease, were the incidents of half an hour.

But the Prince Prospero[2] was happy and dauntless and sagacious. When his dominions were half depopulated, he summoned to his presence a thousand hale and light-hearted friends from among the knights and dames of his court, and with these retired to the deep seclusion of one of his castellated

abbeys. This was an extensive and magnificent structure, the creation of the prince's own eccentric yet august taste. A strong and lofty wall girdled it in. This wall had gates of iron.[3] The courtiers, having entered, brought furnaces and massy hammers and welded the bolts. They resolved to leave means neither of ingress or egress to the sudden impulses of despair or of frenzy from within. The abbey was amply provisioned. With such precautions the courtiers might bid defiance to contagion. The external world could take care of itself. In the meantime it was folly to grieve, or to think. The prince had provided all the appliances of pleasure. There were buffoons, there were improvisatori [entertainers who compose extemporaneously], there were ballet-dancers, there were musicians, there was Beauty, there was wine. All these and security were within. Without was the "Red Death."

It was toward the close of the fifth or sixth month of his seclusion, and while the pestilence raged most furiously abroad, that the Prince Prospero entertained his thousand friends[4] at a masked ball of the most unusual magnificence.

It was a voluptuous scene, that masquerade. But first let me tell of the rooms in which it was held. There were seven—an imperial suite. In many palaces, however, such suites form

[3]Symbolic of the prince's
futile effort to physically
"wall out" death.

[4]Biblical allusion
to Daniel 5
(Belshazzar's
feast).

a long and straight vista, while the folding doors slide back nearly to the walls on either hand, so that the view of the whole extent is scarcely impeded. Here the case was very different; as might have been expected from the duke's love of the *bizarre*. The apartments were so irregularly disposed that the vision embraced but little more than one at a time.[5] There was a sharp turn at every twenty or thirty yards, and at each turn a novel effect. To the right and left, in the middle of each wall, a tall and narrow Gothic window looked out upon a closed corridor which pursued the windings of the suite. These windows were of stained glass whose color varied in accordance with the prevailing hue of the decorations of the chamber into which it opened. That at the eastern extremity was hung, for example, in blue—vividly blue were its windows. The second chamber was purple in its ornaments and tapestries, and here the panes were purple. The third was green throughout, and so were the casements. The forth was furnished and lighted with orange—the fifth with white—the sixth with violet. The seventh apartment was closely shrouded in black velvet tapestries that hung all over the ceiling and down the walls, falling in heavy folds upon a carpet of the same material and hue. But in this chamber only, the door of the windows failed to correspond to the decorations. The panes were scarlet—a deep blood color. Now in no one of the seven apartments was there any lamp or candelabrum, amid the profusion of golden ornaments that lay scattered to and fro or depended [hung down] from the roof. There was no light of any kind emanating from lamp or candle within the suite

[5]Rooms symbolize life. (We cannot see ahead in life.) Colors symbolize the different stages of life: blue—birth, innocence, spring; purple—the deepening of blue, experience; green—youth, growth, summer; orange—maturity, ripeness, autumn; white—old age, winter; violet—darker experience (see reference for purple); black with red panes—the "Red Death."

of chambers. But in the corridors that followed the suite, there stood, opposite each window, a heavy tripod, bearing a brazier [a metal pan for holding burning coals] of fire that projected its rays through the tinted glass and so glaringly illumined the room. And thus were produced a multitude of gaudy and fantastic appearances. But in the western or black chamber the effect of the fire-light that streamed upon the dark hangings through the blood-tinted panes, was ghastly in the extreme, and produced so wild a look upon the countenances of those who entered, that there were few of the company bold enough to set foot within its precincts at all.

It was in this apartment, also, that there stood a gigantic clock of ebony.[6] Its pendulum swung to and fro with a dull, heavy, monotonous clang; and when the minute-hand made the circuit of the face, and the hour was to be stricken, there came from the brazen lungs of the clock a sound which was clear and loud and deep and exceedingly musical, but of so peculiar a note and emphasis that, at each lapse of an hour, the musicians of the orchestra were constrained to pause, momentarily, in their performance, to hearken to the sound; and thus the waltzers perforce [by necessity] ceased their evolutions; and there was a brief disconcert of the whole company; and while the chimes of the clock yet rang, it was observed that the giddiest grew pale, and the more aged and

sedate passed their hands over their brows as if in confused reverie or meditation. But when the echoes had fully ceased, a light laughter at once pervaded the assembly; the musicians looked at each other and smiled as if at their own nervousness and folly, and made whispering vows, each to the other, that the next chiming of the clock should produce in them no similar emotion; and then, after the lapse of sixty minutes (which embrace three thousand and six hundred seconds of the Time that flies,) there came yet another chiming of the clock, and then were the same disconcert and tremulousness and meditation as before.

But, in spite of these things, it was a magnificent revel. The tastes of the duke were peculiar. He had a fine eye for colors and effects. He disregarded the *decora* of mere fashion. His plans were bold and fiery, and his conceptions glowed with barbaric lustre. There are some who would have thought him mad. His followers felt that he was not.

He had directed, in great part, the moveable embellishments of the seven chambers, upon occasion of this great féte; and it was his own guiding taste which had given character to the masqueraders. Be sure they were grotesque. There were much glare and glitter and piquancy [pleasant odor] and phantasm [something apparently seen but not a reality]. There were arabesque [a position of a ballet dancer] figures with unsuited limbs. There were delirious fancies such as the madman fashions. There was much of the beautiful, much of the wanton, much of the *bizarre,* something of the terrible, and not a little of that which might have excited disgust. To and fro in the seven chambers there stalked, in fact, a multitude of dreams. And these—the dreams—writhed in and about, taking hue from the rooms, and causing the wild music of the orchestra to seem as the echo of their steps. And, anon, there strikes the ebony clock which stands in the hall of velvet. And then, for a moment, all is still, and all is silent save for the voice of the clock. The dreams are stiff-frozen as they stand. But the echoes of the chimes die away—they have endured but an instant—and a light, half-subdued laughter floats after them as they depart. And now again the music swells, and the dreams live, and writhe to and fro more merrily than ever, taking hue from the many-tinted windows through which stream the rays from the tripods. But to the chamber which lies most westwardly of the seven, there are now none of the maskers who venture; for night is waning away; and there flows a ruddier light through the blood-colored panes; and the blackness of the sable drapery appalls; and to him whose foot falls upon the sable carpet, there comes from the near clock of ebony a muffled peal more solemnly emphatic than any which reaches their ears who indulge in the more remote gaieties of the other apartments.[7]

But these other apartments were densely crowded, and in them beat feverishly the heart of life. And the revel went whirlingly on, until at length there commenced the sounding

[7]The futile efforts of those who fear death to lose their fears in self-indulgence.

of midnight upon the clock. And then the music ceased, as I have told; and the evolutions of the waltzers were quieted; and there was an uneasy cessation of all things as before. But now there were twelve strokes to be sounded by the bell of the clock; and thus it happened, perhaps, that more of thought crept, with more of time, into the meditations of the thoughtful among those who revelled. And thus, too, it happened, perhaps, that before the last echoes of the last chime had utterly sunk into silence, there were many individuals in the crowd who had found leisure to become aware of the presence of a masked figure which had arrested the attention of no single individual force. And the rumor of this new presence having spread itself whisperingly around, there arose at length from the whole company a buzz, or murmur, expressive of disapprobation and surprise—then, finally, of terror, of horror, and of disgust.

In an assembly of phantasms such as I have painted, it may well be supposed that no ordinary appearance could have excited such sensation. In truth the masquerade license of the night was nearly unlimited; but the figure in question had out-Heroded Herod,[8] and gone beyond the bounds of even the prince's indefinite decorum. There are chords in the hearts of the most reckless which cannot be touched without emotion. Even with the utterly lost, to whom life and death are equally jests, there are matters of which no jest can be made. The whole company, indeed, seemed now deeply to feel that in the costume and bearing of the stranger neither wit nor propriety existed. The figure was tall and gaunt, and shrouded from head to foot in the habiliments [grave clothes] of the grave. The mask which concealed the visage was made so nearly to resemble the countenance of a stiffened corpse that the closest scrutiny must have had difficulty in detecting the cheat. And yet all this might have been endured, if not approved, by the mad revellers around. But the mummer [masked actor] had gone so far as to assume the type of the Red Death. His vesture was dabbled in blood—and his broad brow, with all the features of the face, was besprinkled with the scarlet horror.

When the eyes of Prince Prospero fell upon this spectral image (which with a slow and solemn movement, as if more fully to sustain its role, stalked to and fro among the waltzers) he was seen to be convulsed, in the first moment with a strong shudder either of terror or distaste; but, in the next, his brow reddened with rage.

"Who dares?" he demanded hoarsely of the courtiers who stood near him—"who dares insult us with this blasphemous mockery? Seize him and unmask him—that we may know whom we have to hang at sunrise, from the battlements!"

[8]Biblical allusion to Herod's unbridled extravagances (See Mark 6:14-29.)

It was in the eastern or blue chamber in which stood Prince Prospero as he uttered these words.[9] They rang throughout the seven rooms loudly and clearly—for the prince was a bold and robust man, and the music had become hushed at the waving of his hand.

It was in the blue room where stood the prince, with a group of pale courtiers by his side. At first, as he spoke, there was a slight rushing movement of this group in the direction of the intruder, who at the moment was also near at hand, and now, with deliberate and stately step, made closer approach to the speaker. But from a certain nameless awe with which the mad assumptions of the mummer had inspired the whole party, there were found none who put forth hand to seize him; so that, unimpeded, he passed within a yard of the prince's person; and, while the vast assembly, as if with one impulse, shrank from the centres of the rooms to the walls, he made

[9]Notice that death is present throughout life (see the symbolic reference to the blue room), but it is ignored until the very end.

his way uninterruptedly, but with the same solemn and measured step which had distinguished him from the first, through the blue chamber to the purple—through the purple to the green—through the green to the orange—through this again to the white—and even thence to the violet, ere a decided movement had been made to arrest him. It was then, however, that the Prince Prospero, maddening with rage and the shame of his own momentary cowardice, rushed hurriedly through the six chambers, while none followed him on account of a deadly terror that had seized upon them all. He bore aloft a drawn dagger, and had approached, in rapid impetuosity, to within three or four feet of the retreating figure, when the latter, having attained the extremity of the velvet apartment, turned suddenly and confronted his pursuer. There was a sharp cry—and the dagger dropped gleaming upon the sable carpet, upon which, instantly afterwards, fell prostrate in death the Prince Prospero. Then, summoning the wild courage of despair, a throng of revellers at once threw themselves into the black apartment, and, seizing the mummer, whose tall figure stood erect and motionless within the shadow of the ebony clock, gasped in unutterable horror at finding the grave-cerements [cloth coated with wax, formerly used for wrapping the dead] and corpse-like mask which they had handled with so violent a rudeness, untenanted by any tangible form.

And now was acknowledged the presence of the Red Death. He had come like a thief in the night. And one by one dropped the revellers in the blood-bedewed halls of their revel,[10] and died each in the despairing posture of his fall. And the life of the ebony clock went out. And the flames of the tripods expired. And darkness and Decay and the Red Death held illimitable dominion over all.

[10]Biblical allusion (This allusion provides a frame for the story, death came to the revelling Belshazzar—see first allusion in the second paragraph—so death comes to the Prince Prospero. And as Belshazzar's guests were doomed to death by the fall of this Babylonian king and his kingdom, so the followers of Prospero were doomed at the death of their leader.)

The Elements of a Story

Would you say that this is a good story? If so, what do you mean by *good*? Do you mean that it is enjoyable? Enjoyment is part of what makes a story "good"—but only part. Literature teaches as well as delights. So, before you call a piece of literature good, you must understand what it teaches. Understanding will come from careful observation of conflict, character, action, and resolution. These elements work together to produce the theme—the message of the story. Let's see if "The Masque of the Red Death" is really a good story.

Conflict

Every good story has a conflict, a struggle between opposing forces. This clash creates movement and drives a story toward its resolution. Without such opposition in it, a story would be static and uninteresting. A conflict can be one man fighting with another, one man combating a larger force, or even one man struggling with himself. In Poe's story the conflict is Prospero against the Red Death, one man combating a cosmic force.

Character

Characters are imaginary people or animals, or personified abstractions (for example, the Red Death). All characters are caught up in the conflict either directly or indirectly. How close they are to the conflict determines whether they are central or secondary characters. In "The Masque of the Red Death" Prospero and the Red Death are central and the masqueraders secondary.

Plot

Characters move through a series of events. The arrangement of these events is the plot. A plot must have a beginning, a middle, and an end and can usually be outlined on a chart like the following:

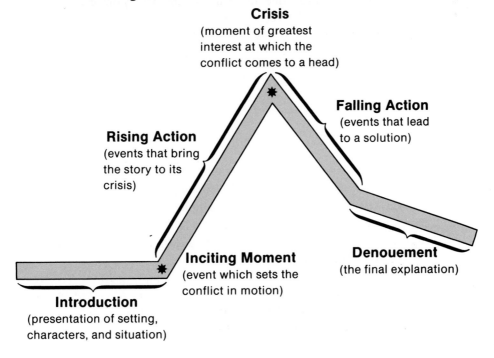

Crisis
(moment of greatest interest at which the conflict comes to a head)

Falling Action
(events that lead to a solution)

Rising Action
(events that bring the story to its crisis)

Inciting Moment
(event which sets the conflict in motion)

Denouement
(the final explanation)

Introduction
(presentation of setting, characters, and situation)

From the opening of Poe's story to the appearing of the Red Death is the *introduction.* This introduction describes the castle, Prospero and his friends, the terrors of the plague, and the revellers' attempt to escape danger. The *inciting moment* is the arrival of the Red Death. The *rising action* is Prospero's desperate flight through the six chambers of the castle in pursuit of the unwelcome visitor. The *crisis* occurs when Death turns on Prospero in the seventh chamber. During the *falling action* a few brave revellers try to unmask Death, finding the "grave-cerements and corpse-like mask . . . untenanted." The last paragraph of the story is the *denouement,* the final outcome of events.

Resolution

The resolution is the solution for the conflict, and it occurs during the falling action and the denouement. It solves the conflict, settles the fate of the characters, and completes the action. A story without a resolution is only an episode. In "The Masque of the Red Death" Death wins, solving the conflict; the fate of the characters is thus decided, and the action stops.

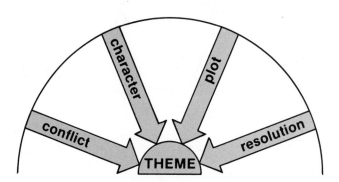

Theme

As the chart illustrates, all elements of a good story support the theme. Follow the steps listed below, and see if you can discover the theme of "The Masque of the Red Death."

- Identify the conflict.
- Identify the central and the secondary characters, and answer the following questions.
  1. On which side of the conflict is each character?
  2. What are each character's goals?
  3. How does each character respond to events and to the other characters?

- What is the order of events?
  1. What causes each event?
  2. What are the results of each event?
- How is the conflict resolved?
- What one idea do most of the details of the story support?
- State this idea, the theme, in one sentence.

This is the theme of Poe's story: Man's attempt to escape death is futile.

The Moral Tone of the Story

You now know what the story teaches, but until you evaluate this message you cannot be sure if the story is good. You must determine the moral tone. Moral tone is the overriding philosophy of the story.

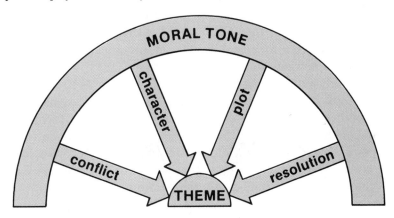

This philosophy influences how all the elements we have discussed—conflict, characters, plot, resolution, and theme—are presented. To determine the moral tone of a story, ask yourself the following questions:
- Are the characters that you like noble?
- Does the action cause you to desire virtue and reject vice?
- Does the resolution reward good and punish evil? Does it honor wisdom and scorn foolishness?
- Does the theme conflict with God's truth? If it does, how and where is the flaw?

We are not drawn to Prospero and his friends in Poe's story, and rightfully so, for they are foolish. We do not desire their revelry because of Poe's melancholy description of its futility. The end of such foolishness is revealed in the resolution, and the theme supports the truth that man cannot escape death by his own schemes. This evaluation confirms our first impression: "The Masque of the Red Death" is indeed a good story.

Elements of Poetry

Although its elements differ, poetry, like prose, must meet certain standards if we are to call it good. Poetry is generally more rhythmic and is more concerned with sound and imagery than prose. It is also more compressed. Because poetry tries to state a great deal in a few words, those words must be carefully chosen. They are usually chosen first for what they mean and then for how they sound. The poet's craft is to arrange his choice words in pleasing images and rhythms. But a poem needs more than well-chosen words. It also needs concrete images— a description of a still lake is clearer than the abstract word *serenity*. Robert Frost's poem about making decisions would not be nearly so memorable without his concrete images of two roads diverging in an autumn wood.

All well-written poetry has a definite pattern of stressed and unstressed syllables. Some poems follow established patterns, like iambic pentameter, and some use the free-verse form. But whether the poem is traditionally metered or free-verse form, rhythm should help unify the work, support the main idea, or condense the expression of that idea. For example, in Ezra Pound's free-verse poem, "In the Station at the Metro," the rhythm and the sounds combine to create the impression of a train's slowing to a stop in a subway station.

Look at the following poem. It presents a concrete image— a man bending down to stroke his dog's head—and the title gives the setting for this action. Notice how the sounds of the words help unify the poem.

By A Milking Gate

I like to see a farmer stoop
To cup between his coarsened hands
A silky collie head. That droop
Of shoulder shores against demands
Of chores or ruin of a drought,
And shows me something in the man
Necessity cannot wear out.

Dawn Watkins

Hard *c* sounds (ll. 2-3) underscore hardness of life.

Repetition of *sh* sounds (l. 4) and rhyme of *shores* and *chores* tie lines together. Rhyme scheme is *ababcbc*.

All these details may show that the poem could be recommended on technical merits, but they do not fully answer the question, "Is the poem good?" You must ask whether the poem has a good message, whether the idea supported by its word choice, rhythm, and imagery is worthy. What does "By a Milking Gate" say to the reader? It commends (the narrator says "I like" at the outset) a man who does not let the monotony of chores or the threat of disaster make him unkind. This a worthy theme.

How to Understand a Poem

1. Read the poem several times.
2. Look up any words you don't know.
3. Look for repetition of sounds. Try to discover why those sounds are repeated. Do they make the mood stronger? Do they make a line read more smoothly? Do they tie lines together?
4. See if there is a rhyme scheme. If there is, see how it unifies or intensifies the work. Does the rhyme come naturally?
5. Think about the images. Do they appeal to your senses?
6. Mark the stressed and unstressed syllables. Does the poem have a regular meter or is it free verse? How does the rhythm contribute to the effect of the poem?
7. Discover what all the details seem to suggest about the meaning of the poem.

• Choose one of the following stories in Appendix D to read.

   1. "Dr. Heidegger's Experiment" by Nathaniel Hawthorne
   2. "The Bit of String" by Guy de Maupassant
   3. "The Last Leaf" by O. Henry (William S. Porter)
   4. "Rip Van Winkle" by Washington Irving

• Evaluate the story and in *one* sentence state the theme.

Chapter 12

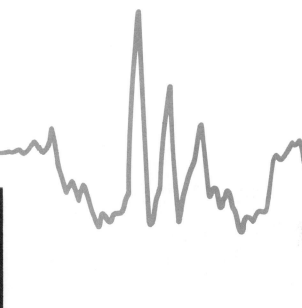

Performing Literature

Good, the more communicated, the more abundant grows.

—John Milton

You now understand "The Masque of the Red Death" and have judged it worthy. How then would you communicate its message to others? Let's look at the story again, not as readers but as performers. As a performer you must study the images and the structure of the piece.

Prose

Images

An image is a word picture, a description of something that you can perceive through your senses. In our story, then, we will look for details of sight, sound, taste, touch, and smell. Some sense images are so vivid that they become physiological.

To help clarify the definition and uses of imagery, let's look at a few of the images in "The Masque of the Red Death."

> The "Red Death" had long devastated the country. No pestilence had ever been so fatal, or so hideous. Blood was its Avatar and its seal—the redness and the horror of blood. [*sight image*] There were sharp pains, and sudden dizziness, and then profuse bleeding at the pores, with dissolution. [*physiological image*]

The images in the first paragraph set the mood of the entire piece. Even when Prospero and his revelers are described, the eerie melancholy first established hangs over all their "masquerading." Of course, the overall mood fluctuates throughout the piece. For example, Poe gives several descriptions of "magnificent revel," but he always brings back the "dark imagery" to renew our dread.

Poe also uses sound images to reinforce his theme. Look at the following example.

> It was in this apartment, also, that there stood a gigantic clock of ebony. Its pendulum swung to and fro with a dull, heavy, monotonous clang; and when the minute-hand made the circuit of the face, and the hour was to be stricken, there came from the brazen lungs of the clock a sound which was clear and loud and deep and exceedingly musical, but of so peculiar a note and emphasis that, at each lapse of an hour, the musicians of the orchestra were constrained to pause, momentarily, in their performance, to hearken to the sound; and thus the waltzers perforce ceased their evolutions; and there was a brief disconcert of the whole company; and while the chimes of the clock yet rang, it was observed that the giddiest grew pale, and the more aged and sedate passed their hands over their brows as if in confused reverie or meditation.

Notice that by the end of this paragraph the sound images have become physiological.

Some of the images also serve to subtly give us a message which contradicts the words of the story. For example, look at the following illustration.

> The tastes of the duke were peculiar. He had a fine eye for colors and effects. He disregarded the decora of mere fashion. His plans were bold and fiery, and his conceptions glowed with barbaric lustre. [*sight image*] There are some who would have thought him mad. His followers felt that he was not.

The sight image indicates that the Duke *is* mad, in spite of the fact that the narrator says that his "followers felt he was not."

Structure

Phrasing This is a way of grouping words held together by a single thought. A reader can be guided by punctuation marks, but the listener does not have this advantage. As a performer you are to help him by using proper phrasing. Look first at the punctuation. A comma usually indicates a pause, without which the sentence would be unclear. A semicolon normally divides two distinct thoughts that are related, and sometimes it separates long phrases. A single dash or a colon often indicates that a restatement or a capping of previous ideas follows. Look at the following example from our story, first as a reader:

And the rumor of this new presence having spread itself whisperingly around, there arose at length from the whole company a buzz, or murmur, expressive of disapprobation and surprise—then, finally, of terror, of horror, and of disgust.

Now look at the example as a performer:

And the rumor of this new presence having spread itself
  whisperingly around,/
there arose at length from the whole company a buzz, or
  murmur,/
expressive of disapprobation and surprise—/
then finally,/
of terror, of horror, and of disgust.

Stress and subordination To give specific words their appropriate emphasis in the phrase, use stress and subordination. Nouns and verbs generally get the greatest stress. Adjectives and adverbs are usually secondary, and the other parts of speech are almost always subordinate. Let's look at the same example, adding stress and subordination. Words needing the greatest emphasis are in boldface; words needing secondary emphasis are in italics.

And the **rumor** of this **new presence** having **spread** itself
  whisperingly around,/
there **arose** at length from the **whole company** a **buzz,** or
  murmur,/
expressive of **disapprobation** and **surprise—**/
then finally,/
of **terror,** of **horror,** and of **disgust.**

Sound This is the means for communicating your phrasing and emphasis. Sound involves your pitch, your volume, and your voice quality. In Chapter 2 we discussed the importance of these elements in expression; those principles apply here.

Pacing A variation in tempo is pacing. This change in rate, like a change in pitch or volume, helps sustain interest. Without it your listeners will be unable to discern between important and unimportant action. As a story nears a crisis, the pace will quicken. If it is not the major crisis, the pace will slow down and pick up again. The major crisis is the crescendo of pacing and emphasis. Likewise, the falling action is slower, winding down to the denouement. Let's look at the second half of Poe's story. Of course, these are only major pacing divisions. There are, however, variations in pacing even in a single paragraph. The major pacing divisions are marked. Once you

have scanned these, you may want to examine the separate paragraphs to discover the pace changes in each.

In an assembly of phantasms such as I have painted, it may well be supposed that no ordinary appearance could have excited such sensation. In truth the masquerade license of the night was nearly unlimited; but the figure in question had out-Heroded Herod, and gone beyond the bounds of even the prince's indefinite decorum. There are chords in the hearts of the most reckless which cannot be touched without emotion. Even with the utterly lost, to whom life and death are equally jests, there are matters of which no jest can be made. The whole company, indeed, seemed now deeply to feel that in the costume and bearing of the stranger neither wit nor propriety existed. The figure was tall and gaunt, and shrouded from head to foot in the habiliments of the grave. The mask which concealed the visage was made so nearly to resemble the countenance of a stiffened corpse that the closest scrutiny must have had difficulty in detecting the cheat. And yet all

moderate pace

this might have been endured, if not approved, by the mad revellers around.

But the mummer had gone so far as to assume the type of the Red Death. His vesture was dabbled in blood—and his broad brow, with all the features of the face, was besprinkled with the scarlet horror.

slight increase in pace

When the eyes of Prince Prospero fell upon this spectral image (which with a slow and solemn movement, as if more fully to sustain its role, stalked to and fro among the waltzers) he was seen to be convulsed, in the first moment with a strong shudder either of terror or distaste; but, in the next, his brow reddened with rage.

pace quickens a little more

"Who dares?" he demanded hoarsely of the courtiers who stood near him—"who dares insult us with this blasphemous mockery? Seize him and unmask him—that we may know whom we have to hang at sunrise, from the battlements!"

crisis point (fast pace)

It was in the eastern or blue chamber in which stood Prince Prospero as he uttered these words. They rang throughout the seven rooms loudly and clearly—for the prince was a bold and robust man, and the music had become hushed at the waving of his hand.

pace drops again

It was in the blue room where stood the prince, with a group of pale courtiers by his side. At first, as he spoke, there was a slight rushing movement of this group in the direction of the intruder, who at the moment was also near at hand, and now, with deliberate and stately step, made closer approach to the speaker. But from a certain nameless awe with which the mad assumptions of the mummer had inspired the whole party, there were found none who put forth hand to seize him; so that, unimpeded, he passed within a yard of the prince's person; and, while the vast assembly, as if with one impulse, shrank from the centres of the rooms to the walls, he made his way uninterruptedly, but with the same solemn and measured step which had distinguished him from the first, through the blue chamber to the purple—through the purple to the green—through the green to the orange—through this again to the white—and even thence to the violet, ere a decided movement had been made to arrest him.

pace quickens

It was then, however, that the Prince Prospero, maddening with rage and the shame of his own momentary cowardice, rushed hurriedly through the six chambers, while none followed him on account of a deadly terror that had seized upon them all. He bore aloft a drawn dagger, and had approached, in rapid impetuosity, to within three or four feet of the retreating figure, when the latter, having attained the extremity of the velvet apartment, turned suddenly and confronted his pursuer.

There was a sharp cry—and the dagger dropped gleaming upon the sable carpet, upon which, instantly afterwards, fell prostrate in death the Prince Prospero. Then, summoning the wild courage of despair, a throng of revellers at once threw themselves into the black apartment, and, seizing the mummer, whose tall figure stood erect and motionless within the shadow of the ebony clock, gasped in unutterable horror at finding the grave-cerements and corpse-like mask which they had handled with so violent a rudeness, untenanted by any tangible form.

crescendo (pace at a peak)

falling action (pace slows)

And now was acknowledged the presence of the Red Death. He had come like a thief in the night. And one by one dropped the revellers in the blood-bedewed halls of their revel, and died each in the despairing posture of his fall. And the life of the ebony clock went out. And the flames of the tripods expired. And darkness and Decay and the Red Death held illimitable dominion over all.

denouement (pace winds down)

Poetry

Image and structure are also important in poetry. You study the images in poetry the same way you do in prose. But poetry

has different elements in its structure. Traditional verse has rhyme and meter, two things rarely found in prose. Free verse, although it does not use rhyme, does have a distinct pattern in its rhythm. A good performer needs to know how these elements support what the poem says.

Rhyme The repetition of like sounds is rhyme. It unifies the poem and pleases the ear. Perfect rhyme, sounds that are exactly

alike, is most often used. Slant rhyme, sounds that are nearly alike, is usually used to create a sense of uneasiness or incompleteness. A performer should never emphasize rhyme for its own sake, but rather let its music subtly add interest and harmony.

Rhythm The purposeful arrangement of stressed and unstressed syllables in a poem is rhythm. Traditional verses follow one of several established patterns, such as iambic tetrameter. One iamb is an unstressed syllable followed by a stressed syllable (often marked). Four iambs together make iambic tetrameter. "By a Milking Gate" uses this pattern.

I like to see a farmer stoop
To cup between his coarsened hands
A silky collie head. That droop
Of shoulder shores against demands
Of chores or ruin of a drought,
And shows me something in the man
Necessity cannot wear out.

Lines 1 and 3, 2 and 4, and 5 and 7 rhyme perfectly. Lines 4 and 6 make a slant rhyme.

The regular meter in the poem supports the mood of daily monotony a farmer may face:

$$\breve{I} \text{ líke} \, / \, t\breve{o} \text{ sée} \, / \, \breve{a} \text{ fárm} \, / \, \breve{e}r \text{ stóop}$$

Free verse, despite how it may look on the page, is not simply broken-up prose. While such poetry is not in a traditional meter, it does have a distinct pattern of stressed and unstressed syllables which supports the message or unifies the work. Whether you are performing traditional or free verse, you need to recognize and respond to the flow of the words.

The principles that you have studied in this chapter and the preceding one apply to both solo and group performance. In both types of performances you must first see the images and then communicate these mental images with your voice and body. The equation below illustrates this process.

Concentration + Control = Communication
(mind)   (voice + body)

In group performance you are still directly communicating to the audience, but you also need to be aware of the others performing with you. Try to visualize their actions and responses, still keeping your focus toward the audience. In the next chapter are two scripts that you may like to perform. (You may want to review Chapters 2 and 3 and do some of the exercises in Appendix A to help you get your voice and body ready for performance.)

- Read the following poem.
- On a piece of paper, write the images and label them.
- Make two columns on a piece of paper. Label one *primary stress words* and the other *secondary stress words*. Then list each stress word in its proper column.

To Autumn

Season of mists and mellow fruitfulness,
Close bosom-friend of the maturing sun;
Conspiring with him how to load and bless
With fruit the vines that round the thatch-eaves run;
To bend with apples the mossed cottage-trees,
And fill all fruit with ripeness to the core;
To swell the gourd, and plump the hazel shells
With a sweet kernel; to set budding more,
And still more, later flowers for the bees,
Until they think warm days will never cease,
For Summer has o'er-brimmed their clammy cells.

Who hath not seen thee oft amid thy store?
Sometimes whoever seeks abroad may find
Thee sitting careless on a granary floor,
Thy hair soft-lifted by the winnowing wind;
Or on a half-reaped furrow sound asleep,
Drowsed with the fume of poppies, while thy hook
Spares the next swath and all its twined flowers:
And sometimes like a gleaner thou dost keep
Steady thy laden head across a brook;
Or by a cider-press, with patient look,
Thou watchest the last oozings hours by hours.

Where are the songs of Spring? Ay, where are they?
Think not of them, thou hast thy music too,—
While barred clouds bloom the soft-dying day,
And touch the stubble plains with rosy hue;
Then in a wailful choir the small gnats mourn
Among the river shallows, borne aloft
Or sinking as the light wind lives or dies;
And full-grown lambs loud bleat from hilly bourn;
Hedge-crickets sing; and now with treble soft
The red-breast whistles from a garden-croft;
And gathering swallows twitter in the skies.

John Keats

Chapter 13

Scripts for Performance

The Master Speaker is the Tear: it is the Great Interpreter.

—*Ridgely Torrence*

As you perform the following two scripts, remember the principles you have studied in Chapters 11 and 12.

My Father's Hands

An essay by Calvin R. Worthington
Scripting by Karen Duncan

Narrator: How different our lives would be without the "small" abilities we almost take for granted—

Woman:	Like singing . . .
Man:	Or telling time . . .
Woman:	Or seeing colors . . .
All:	Or reading and writing.
Man:	Most of us read and write often and easily, without thinking much about it.
Woman:	We learned how when we were five or six,
Narrator:	And now we read all the time.
Woman:	Not just books for school or pleasure or information,
Man:	Or newspapers,
Narrator:	Or comic books—
Woman:	But stop signs and cereal boxes.
Man:	We also write all the time.
Woman:	Do you remember a time when you couldn't sign your name?
Narrator:	. . . Or write a note or letter?
Woman:	These skills enrich our lives and sometimes save our lives—
Man:	And living without the ability to read and write can hold its own special tragedy.
Woman:	In his story "My Father's Hands," Calvin R. Worthington tells of his father's struggle to live without being able to read or write.
	(All open scripts and take places. Narrator is the voice of Cal, Man is Father, and Woman is Mother.)
Narrator:	His hands were rough and exceedingly strong. He could gently prune a fruit tree or firmly wrestle an ornery mule into harness. He could draw and saw a square with quick accuracy. But what I remember most is the special warmth from those hands soaking through my shirt as he would shake me by the shoulder and, hunkering down beside my ear . . .
Father:	. . . point out the glittering swoop of a blue hawk, or a rabbit asleep in its lair.

Narrator: They were good hands that served him well and failed him in only one thing: they never learned to write. My father was illiterate. The number of illiterates in our country has steadily declined, but if there were only one I would be saddened, remembering my father and the pain he endured because his hands never learned to write. He started in first grade. For some reason, shapes, figures, and recitations just didn't fall into the right pattern inside his six-year-old towhead. Maybe he suffered from some learning handicap such as dyslexia. His father took him out of school after several months and set him to a man's job on the farm. Years later . . .

Wife: . . . his wife, with her fourth-grade education, would try to teach him to read.

Narrator: And still later I would grasp his big fist between my small hands and awkwardly help him trace the letters of his name. He submitted to the ordeal, but soon grew restless. Flexing his fingers and kneading his palms, he would declare that he had had enough and depart for a long solitary walk. Finally, one night . . .

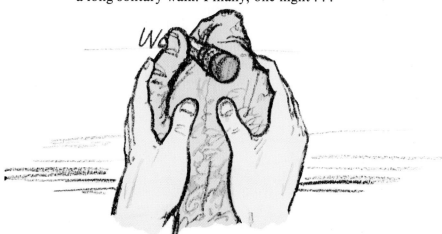

Father: . . . when he thought no one saw, he slipped away with his son's second-grade reader and labored over the words, until they became too difficult. He pressed his forehead into the pages and wept.

Narrator: Thereafter, no amount of persuading could bring him to sit with pen and paper. From the farm to road-building and later factory work, his hands served him well.

Father: His mind was keen, his will to work unsurpassed. During World War II, he was a pipefitter in a shipyard and installed the complicated guts of mighty fighting ships. His enthusiasm and efficiency brought an offer to become line boss—until he was handed a qualification test. His fingers could trace a path across the blueprints while his mind imagined the pipes lacing through the heart of the ship. He could recall every twist and turn of the pipes. But he couldn't read or write. After the shipyard closed, he went to the cotton mill, where he labored at night and stole from his sleeping hours the time required to run the farm. When the mill shut down, he went out each morning looking for work—only to return night after night and say to Mother . . .

Father: They just don't want anybody who can't take their tests.

Narrator: It had always been hard for him to stand before a man and make an *X* for his name . . .

Wife: . . . but the hardest moment of all was when he placed "his mark" by the name someone else had written for him, and saw another man walk away with the deed to his beloved farm.

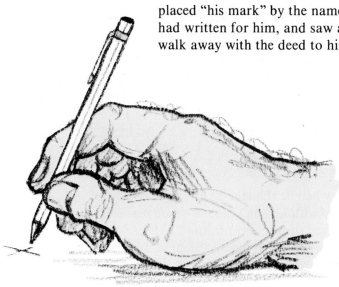

Narrator: When it was over, he stood before the window and slowly turned the pen he still held in his hands—gazing, unseeing, down the mountainside. I went to the springhouse that afternoon and wept for a long while. Eventually he found another cotton-mill job, and we moved into a millhouse village with a hundred look-alike houses. He never quite adjusted to town life. The blue of his eyes faded; the skin across his cheekbones became a little slack. But his hands kept their strength, and their warmth still soaked through when he would sit me on his lap and ask that I read to him from the Bible. He took great pride in my reading and would listen for hours. When mother left once for a weekend visit with her sister, Dad went to the store and returned with food for dinner. After the meal . . .

Father: . . . he said he had a surprise for dessert . . .

Narrator: . . . and went out to the kitchen, where I could hear him opening a can. Then everything was quiet. I went to the doorway, and saw him standing before the sink with an open can in his hand.

Father: The picture looked just like pears . . .

Narrator: . . . he mumbled. He walked out and sat on the back steps, and I knew he had been embarrassed before his son. The can read "Whole White Potatoes," but the picture on the label did look a great deal like pears. Years later, when mom died, I tried to get him to come live with my family . . .

Father: . . . but he insisted on staying in his small house on the edge of town with a few farm animals and a garden plot.

Narrator: His health was not good. He was in and out of the hospital with several mild heart attacks. Old Doc Green saw him weekly and gave him medication, including nitroglycerin tablets to put under his tongue should he feel an attack coming on. *(Father pantomiming suggested*

action that follows) My last fond memory of
Dad was watching as he walked across the
brow of a hillside meadow, with those big
warm hands—now gnarled with age—resting
on the shoulders of my two children. He
stopped to point out, confidentially, a pond
where he and I had swum and fished years
before. That night, my family and I flew to a
new job and a new home, overseas. Three
weeks later, he was dead of a heart attack.
(Father out)

I returned alone for the funeral. Doc Green
told me how sorry he was. In fact, he was
bothered a bit because he had just written Dad
a new nitroglycerin prescription and the
druggist had filled it. Yet the bottle of pills had
not been found on Dad's person. Doc Green
felt that a pill might have kept him alive long
enough to summon help.

An hour before the chapel service, I found
myself standing near the edge of Dad's garden,
where a neighbor had found him. In grief, I
stooped to trace my fingers in the earth where
a great man had reached the end of his life. My
hand came to rest on a half-buried brick,
which I aimlessly lifted and tossed aside, before
noticing underneath it the twisted, battered, yet
unbroken, soft plastic bottle that had been
beaten into the soft earth. As I held the bottle
of nitroglycerin pills, the scene of Dad
struggling to remove the cap and in
desperation trying to break the bottle with the
brick flashed painfully before my eyes. With
deep anguish I knew why those big warm
hands had lost in their struggle with death. For
there, imprinted on the bottle cap, were the
words, "Child-Proof-Cap—Push Down and
Twist to Unlock."

The druggist later confirmed that he had
just started using the new safety bottle. I knew
it was not a purely rational act, but I went
right downtown and bought a leather-bound
pocket dictionary and a gold pen set. I bade

Dad good-bye by placing them in those big old hands, once so warm, which had lived so well, but had never learned to write.

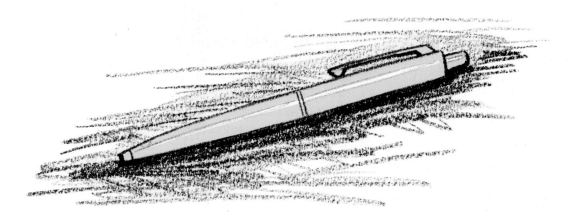

The Reader's Dilemma
Scripting by Karen Duncan

Cynic: Listen to this:
"'Tis the good reader that makes the good book; . . . the profit of books is according to the sensibility of the *reader.*
This was written by Ralph Waldo Emerson, a great American writer—someone who *ought* to know what he's talking about, right?

Woman: Uh—what's wrong with that? What you get out of a book does depend on how carefully you read.

Cynic: Yes, but don't you see? Everybody blames us *readers* for trouble in communication—and I just don't think the problems are all our fault.

Man: All right, then, who or what *does* cause the problem?

Cynic: I maintain the trouble lies in what the reader is given to read. The reading *material* causes dilemmas.

Woman: I'm not convinced. Explain some more.

Cynic: I thought you'd never ask. As I see it, reading dilemmas fall into two categories. First, reading that is too difficult. Take this sentence for instance: "If I believed that Mammonism with its adjuncts was to continue henceforth the one serious principle of our existence, I should reckon it idle to solicit remedial measures from any Government, the disease being insusceptible of remedy." *(Listeners look pained)* Did you understand that? *(Others shake heads)* Do you think the problem was with you? *(Shake heads again)* Right! Thomas Carlyle had the problem when he wrote that— and it's been giving readers trouble for over one hundred years!

Man: We see your point. Sometimes the reading material is too hard. But what else could be wrong with it?

Cynic: That brings us to category two: reading that is too simple.

Woman: How can *that* be a problem?

Cynic: Allow me to illustrate. *(Hands out scripts)*

(For this segment, the cynic becomes the Narrator, Woman Reader becomes Voice of OSHA #1, and Man Reader becomes Voice of OSHA #2. All address the Audience.)

Narrator: Here is an actual unedited extract from the Congressional Record:

Both 1 and 2: OSHA is the Occupational Safety and Health Administration.

Voice 1: OSHA helps people. OSHA helps people to be safe.

Voice 2: OSHA wants farmers to be safe. OSHA made a little book for farmers.

Voice 1: What does the little book say?

Both 1 and 2: This is what it says—*(Readers sit)* Be careful around the farm. . . .

Voice 1: Hazards are one of the main causes of accidents.

Voice 2: A hazard is anything that is dangerous.

Voice 1: Be careful when you are handling animals. Tired or hungry or frightened cattle can bolt and trample you. Be patient. Talk softly around the cows. Don't move fast or be loud around them. If they are upset, don't go into the pen with them.

Voice 2: Keep pets and children away too.

Voice 1: Don't fall!

Voice 2: Be careful that you do not fall into the manure pits. Put up signs and fences to keep people away. These pits are very dangerous.

Voice 1: Put away tools, equipment, and feed when not using them.

Voice 2: If your ladder is broken, do not climb on it.

Both 1 and 2: Wear clothes that fit right.

Narrator: Then comes more advice from the Omaha World Telegram:

(Voice 1 becomes Voice of O.W.T.; Voice 2 becomes Farmer.)

O.W.T.: See the farmer. See the farmer go to the mail-box. See the farmer get the little book.

Farmer: The farmer can read. The farmer can read big words. The farmer can read long sentences. The farmer knows about cows. The farmer knows about manure pits.

O.W.T.: See the farmer read the little book.

Farmer: Now the farmer knows about OSHA.

O.W.T.: See the farmer kick the mail-box. See the farmer throw the little book into the manure pit. See OSHA. See OSHA print. See OSHA write. See OSHA throw money into the manure pit.

Farmer: That's it—I've had enough of OSHA.

O.W.T.: We've all had enough!

All: . . . of The Reader's Dilemma.

UNIT FIVE

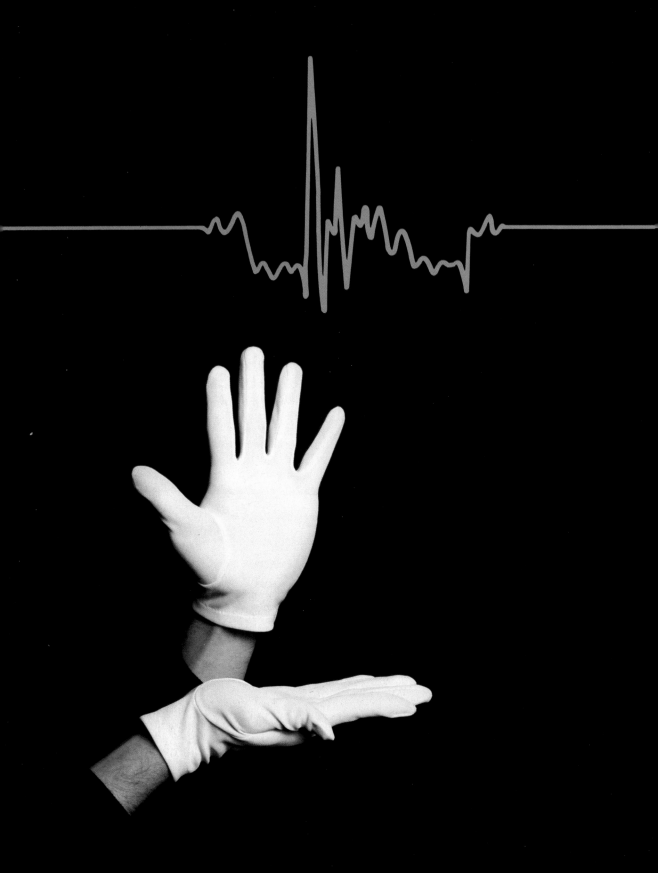

BILL MOOSE

Profession: College and high school speech teacher
Professional Experience: Fine arts coordinator, program director, puppeteer, and actor
Hobbies: Writing poetry, music, reading

DORIS MOOSE

Profession: Christian Education Director, writer, teacher
Professional Experience: Writing and directing children's productions and puppet plays
Hobbies: Music and art

BILL PINKSTON

Profession: Head of high school science department, teacher
Professional Experience: Acting, play directing, writing
Hobbies: Directing college productions and reading children's literature

Interviewer: As a Christian director or performer, you must be able to analyze a play. What are some guidelines you use?

Bill Pinkston: First of all, the message of the play must conform to biblical standards. As a Christian, I can't be in or direct a play if the message or philosophy conflicts with God's Word.

Bill Moose: When an audience sees you performing in a play, they assume you condone the play's philosophy. Acting is different from simply analyzing a piece of literature.

Interviewer: So you can study or analyze a play that you cannot perform.

Bill Moose: Exactly. You are not by your association condoning it if you are just reading or studying it. I think that the material needs to be carefully considered before you advocate it by using it.

Bill Pinkston: This is not to say, however, that *all* the characters in the play have to be "good characters." If the overall philosophy of the play is good, you can learn something even from the negative characters.

For example, I once played a character in a Shakespearean play who was comic because of being strait-laced. His flaunting his strict standards of behavior in a haughty manner was mockable to the other characters. I think Shakespeare was mocking the external trappings of this arrogant character. That role caused me to do a lot of thinking about myself and my testimony. It caused me to change some things in my life. This is one example of how good literature actually can help a person's life. This character helped me to see clearly how undesirable a false testimony really is.

Interviewer: Mrs. Moose, how do you choose material for children?

Doris Moose: Mostly, I tell a Christian-conduct story or a Bible story. I am especially careful not to choose anything that would cheapen the Scripture or go against biblical principles. For example, when using puppets, I do not portray Christ. Nor would I have a story in which a child got away with disobedience or where the disobedience was viewed as humorous.

Interviewer: How do you think involvement in performance, either in the church or school, can help the high school student develop either spiritually, emotionally, or socially?

Doris Moose: Young people can grow spiritually while preparing a lesson or story. For instance, we often have teenagers helping us in our puppet ministry. If the young person looks on his performance as a ministry, he can grow spiritually by preparing the material to help others through his performance.

Bill Moose: As a teacher, I have seen many students "bloom" by being involved in performances. Just the experience of being before an audience is invaluable in developing poise.

Interviewer: How could a Christian student use his talents in this field of Christian service?

Doris Moose: There is a great need for good Christian plays and programs, and dramatic training is invaluable in helping someone know how to write well in this field. Churches always need good scripts with sound biblical principles.

Interviewer: What advice would you give someone interested in this field?

Bill Moose: You must do what you do well; you've got to be sharp. Otherwise, you will lose the audience and fail to communicate your message.

Bill Pinkston: Doing things as well as we can is an important part of our testimony. We're in a competition, really. Television, films, and videos have captured the sight and hearing of the people. As Christians, we can't use the same material they do, but what we perform can be done exceptionally well—with as much poise and polish as is possible for any performer.

Interviewer: What pitfalls would you warn them against?

Doris Moose: We must also be careful not "to get stars in our eyes." For example, we once had a friend who had always talked about becoming a foreign missionary, but he began to develop his talents in the acting field and lost his burden for the unsaved. We feel he forfeited a great privilege.

Bill Pinkston: I would advise young people against being carried away with what seems fun and exciting. Unless a drama meets scriptural standards, it is not the Lord's will for any young person to be involved in it—no matter how fun and exciting it seems.

Doris Moose: You also want to be careful not to become artificial or unnatural.

Bill Moose: I agree. I think that artificiality will alienate a listener or an observer more quickly than anything else. The whole idea of performance is communication. Your technique should never detract from your message. I remember a teacher who told us that if after we performed we heard comments like, "My, didn't he perform well," or "Wasn't that good"; then we had failed. However, if they [the audience] couldn't remember the performer but only the message performed, then we had been successful.

Chapter 14

Understanding a Play

Thou also, son of man, take thee a tile, and lay it before thee, and pourtray upon it the city, even Jerusalem: and lay siege against it, and build a fort against it, and cast a mount against it; set the camp also against it, and set battering rams against it round about. Moreover take thou unto thee an iron pan, and set it for a wall of iron between thee and the city: and set thy face against it, and it shall be besieged, and thou shalt lay siege against it. This shall be a sign to the house of Israel.

—*(Ezekiel 4:1-3)*

In this passage of Scripture the Lord instructs Ezekiel to build a set; "take thee a tile, and lay it before thee, and pourtray upon it the city." God then tells the prophet to dramatize the siege of Jerusalem so the children of Israel might see their sin and recognize the consequences of rebellion. This passage shows that drama can be used to teach God's truth. As you know, the Christian's speech should bring glory to God and benefit to others. Drama is no exception to this rule.

Analysis

The principles used in judging prose are also used in judging drama. A play, too, must have conflict, characters, plot, and resolution that produce a worthy theme. Using *The Tragical History of Dr. Faustus,* let's look at how these principles apply to drama.

Conflict

The conflict in this play is between man and authority. Faustus recognizes only the authority of his own desire; anything interfering with that inspires his rebellion. In his pride, he refuses the authority of God in order to delve into the forbidden realm of magic. To do so, he must make a pact with Satan.

Characters

The characters in the scene we will study are Faustus, Mephistophilis, Lucifer, Belzebub, Wagner, and two scholars.

Faustus He is a scholar who, with seemingly boundless energy, has mastered all fields of human knowledge. His immense pride will not allow him to be content with his achievements but causes him to eye the forbidden realm of magic. Since pleasure is his only goal, he believes magic will give him everything he wants: "A sound magician is a demigod."

Mephistophilis This character is a demon who answers Faustus' conjuring. He pretends to be the scholar's servant, only to control him. He keeps Faustus on his way to hell by providing him with every pleasure.

Lucifer He is the prince of the demons. He appears when Mephistophilis cannot control Faustus. As ruler of hell, Lucifer knows well how to play upon human weakness. He uses both terror and bribery on Faustus and arrives in the last scene to gloat over his victory.

Belzebub He is one of the chief demons who assists Mephistophilis.

Wagner Faustus' personal servant is Wagner. Although he is a rough and unlearned man, he is totally loyal to Faustus. This loyalty is rewarded: Faustus draws up a new will, leaving everything to Wagner.

The two scholars The friends and followers of Faustus in all but the occult are the two scholars. They try to persuade Faustus to return to God. When they cannot, they leave to pray for his soul.

Plot

The following major scenes clearly show this conflict. Let's look briefly at a synopsis of these scenes.

Act I, scene 1 We see in this opening segment an intelligent but overly ambitious man. Here Faustus has the first of several debates with himself and the Good and Bad Angels. The scene ends with his fatal decision: "This night I'll conjure though I die. . . ."

Act II, scene 2 The crisis occurs in this scene. Here Faustus makes his last true consideration of repentance, coming to the point of crying, "O Christ, my Savior, my Savior!/ Help to save distressed Faustus' soul." But Lucifer appears to threaten and bribe him, and Faustus gives over thoughts of God in favor of worldly pleasure and plunges headlong into his career as Satan's subject. He makes a contract with the Devil and sells his soul. His desperate cries of mercy in the final scene which we will study are borne of fear rather than of a desire to be righteous.

Act V, scene 1 Faustus, his contract nearly expired, carouses with the scholars and is rebuked by an old man. He now begins to fear the consequences of his deed, but Mephistophilis has no trouble turning his mind back to the pleasures of evil by making the beautiful Helen of Troy appear.

Act V, scene 2 The expiration of Faustus' contract is but an hour away. His final agony is expressed in some of the most powerful poetry found in Elizabethan drama. This is the scene we will study.

Resolution

Faustus' rebellion against God and his contract with Satan seal his ruin and make the resolution inevitable. As he is dragged to hell, there is no doubt that his own choices have brought this tragic end.

Theme

The theme of the play is that man should abide within the realm of the lawful knowledge of God and not be fooled by the futility of earthly pleasure. Faustus' loss of salvation is clearly not worth the knowledge and pleasure it was traded for.

Moral Tone

The theme of Marlowe's play conflicts with what we know of his personal beliefs. Marlowe was an atheistic humanist, and as one critic pointed out, it is ironic that such a man should write a play so edifying to the saints and terrifying to sinners. But does Marlowe's personal belief make his play unworthy? Only if his philosophy corrupts the moral tone of the piece. From what you know of the play, how would you evaluate it? Does the action cause you to desire virtue and reject vice? Surely you would have to say that it does. Does the resolution reward good and punish evil? Clearly. Does it honor wisdom and scorn foolishness? Yes. Faustus, as the rich fool in Luke 12, forfeits eternal joy for temporal wealth. Does the theme conflict with God's truth? Faustus' tragic story reflects rather than conflicts with God's truth by vividly illustrating the following scriptural truths: the human soul is of more value than wealth, prestige, or cunning; the Devil delights in destroying men's souls; and hell is a terrifying reality for those who reject God to serve Satan.

Performance

As we discussed in the last unit, in oral interpretation the interpreter communicates directly with the audience. His focus is on the literature and on helping his audience understand the story or poem. The actor, however, directly interacts with other characters. His intention is not to focus on a piece of literature but to present an "imitation" of life. To do so, he must create a believable character that acts and reacts with other characters.

Of course, to accomplish this goal of communicating a character, an actor will draw on his interpretative skills. He will look for specific images in the play, and he will note the phrasing, the stress/subordination, and the pacing of each scene. Then he will use his voice and body to reveal his character to the audience.

Dividing the dialogue into beats and verbing lines are two specific methods that help an actor to understand the thought of each scene and the motivations of the characters within the scene. A beat is much like a paragraph in a story. It expresses a unit of thought and can be made up of one or several lines of dialogue. Verbing is defining the motivation for each speaker's lines. The examples in the following scene may help clarify these two ideas. The scene is divided into beats, and verbing for the dialogue is marked.

(*Enter* **Lucifer, Belzebub,** and **Mephistophilis**)

Lucifer: to claim a soul

Lucifer: Thus from infernal Dis [Hades] do we ascend
To view the subjects of our monarchy,
Those souls which sin seals the black sons of hell.
'Mong which as chief, Faustus, we come to thee,
Bringing with us lasting damnation
To wait upon thy soul. The time is come
Which makes it forfeit.

Mephistophilis and Belzebub: to gloat over Faustus' ruin

Mephistophilis: And this gloomy night
Here in this room will wretched Faustus be.

Belzebub: And here we'll stay
To mark him how he doth demean himself.

Beat 1

Mephistophilis: to mock Faustus' efforts of escape

Mephistophilis: How should he but with desperate lunacy?
Fond worldling, now his heart blood dried with grief,
His conscience kills it, and his laboring brain
Begets a world of idle fantasies
To overreach the devil; but all in vain:
His store of pleasure must be sauced with pain!
He and his servant Wagner are at hand.
Both come from drawing Faustus' latest will.

Beat 2

See where they come.

(*Enter* **Faustus** and **Wagner**)

Faustus: to draw comfort from Wagner's approval

Faustus: Say, Wagner, thou hast perused my will;
How dost thou like it?

Wagner: to show gratitude

Wagner: (*Kneeling to Faustus*) Sir, so wondrous well
As in all humble duty I do yield

Beat 3

My life and lasting service to you.

(**Faustus** *makes* **Wagner** rise; **Scholars** *enter.* **Wagner** *exits.*)

Beat 4

Faustus: Welcome, gentlemen.

Scholars: to show concern

1 Scholar: Now, worthy, Faustus, methinks your looks are changed.

Faustus: Ah, gentlemen!

2 Scholar:	What ails Faustus?	Beat 5
Faustus:	Ah, my chamber-fellow, had I lived with thee [had I chosen thy company rather than Mephistophilis'], then had I lived still!—But now must die eternally. Look, sirs, comes he not, comes he not?	Faustus: to hide from Mephistophilis

Beat 6

1 Scholar: Oh, my dear Faustus, what imports this fear?

2 Scholar: Is all our pleasure turned to melancholy?

1 Scholar: He is not well with being over-solitary.

1 Scholar: to find reason for Faustus' change
2 Scholar: to restore Faustus

2 Scholar: If it be so, we'll have physicians, and Faustus shall be cured.

1 Scholar: 'Tis but a surfeit [discomfort resulting from some form of excess], sir; fear nothing.

Faustus: A surfeit of deadly sin that hath damned both body and soul!

Beat 7

2 Scholar: Yet Faustus, look up to heaven and remember God's mercies are infinite.

Faustus: But Faustus' offense can ne'er be pardoned; the serpent that tempted Eve may be saved, but not Faustus! Ah, gentlemen, hear me with patience and tremble not at my speeches.

Faustus: to pour out his
agony

Though my heart pants and quivers to
remember that I have been a student these
thirty years, O would I had never seen
Wittenburg, never read a book.—And what
wonders I have done all Germany can witness,
yea, all the world, for which Faustus hath lost
both Germany and the world,.yea heaven
itself—heaven the seat of God, the throne of
the blessèd,
the kingdom of joy—and must remain in hell
forever! O hell forever! Sweet friends, what
shall become of Faustus, being in hell forever?

Beat 8

1 Scholar: Yet Faustus, call on God.

Faustus: to lament his
forfeited redemption

Faustus: On God, whom Faustus hath abjured
[renounced]? On God, whom Faustus hath
blasphemed? O my God, I would weep, but the
devil draws in my tears! Gush forth blood
instead of tears, yea life and soul! O, he stays
my tongue! I would lift up my hands, but see,
they hold 'em, they hold 'em!

Scholars: to grasp the horror
of Faustus' act   Beat 9

All: Who, Faustus?

Faustus: Why, Lucifer and Mephistophilis.
O gentlemen, I gave them my soul for my
cunning.

Scholars: to express horror
Faustus: to confess his evil

All: God forbid!

Faustus: God forbade it indeed, but Faustus hath done
it. For vain pleasure of four and twenty years
hath Faustus lost eternal joy and felicity. I writ
them a bill with mine own blood. The date is
expired. This is the time. And he will fetch me.

Beat 10

Scholars: to grieve over
Faustus' wretched state

1 Scholar: Why did not Faustus tell us this before, that
divines might have prayed for thee?

Faustus: to deny
responsibility

Faustus: Oft have I thought to have done so, but the
devil threatened to tear me in pieces if I named
God—to fetch both body and soul if I once
gave ear to divinity; and now 'tis too late.
Gentlemen, away, lest you perish with me.

Beat 11

2 Scholar: O, what may we do to save Faustus?

Faustus: Talk not of me but save yourselves and depart.

2 Scholar: God will strengthen me. I will stay with Faustus.

1 Scholar: Tempt not God, sweet friend, but let us into the next room and pray for him.

Faustus: Ay, pray for me, pray for me. And what noise soever ye hear, come not unto me, for nothing can rescue me.

Scholars: to intercede for Faustus
Faustus: to face his fate alone

	2 Scholar:	Pray thou, and we will pray that God may have mercy upon thee.
	Faustus:	Gentlemen, farewell! If I live till morning, I'll visit you. If not, Faustus is gone to hell.
Beat 12	**All:**	Faustus, farewell.

(*Exit* **Scholars;** *enter* **Mephistophilis.**)

Mephistophilis: to torment his prey	**Mephistophilis:**	Ay, Faustus, now thou hast no hope of heaven. Therefore, despair! Think only upon hell. For that must be thy mansion, there to dwell.
Faustus: to revile his tempter	**Faustus:**	O thou bewitching fiend, 'twas thy temptation hath robbed me of eternal happiness.
	Mephistophilis:	I do confess it Faustus, and rejoice. 'Twas I, that when thou wert i' the way to heaven Dammed up thy passage. When thou took'st the book To view the Scriptures, then I turned the leaves And led thine eye. What, weep'st thou! 'Tis too late, despair, farewell! Fools that will laugh on earth, must weep in hell.

Beat 13		

(**Mephistophilis** *exits; clock strikes eleven.*)

Faustus: to gain a stay of execution	**Faustus:**	O Faustus! Now hast thou but one hour to live And then thou must be damned perpetually. Stand still, you ever-moving spheres of Heaven, That time may cease and midnight never come; Fair nature's eye, rise, rise again and make Perpetual day, or let this hour be but a year, A month, a week, a natural day—
Beat 14		That Faustus may repent and save his soul. The stars move still, time runs, the clock will strike: The devil will come, and Faustus must be damned!
Faustus: to flee from hell		O, I'll leap up to my God! Who pulls me
Beat 15		down? See, see, where Christ's blood streams in the

firmament!—
One drop would save me. O my Christ!—
Rend not my heart for naming of my Christ!
Yet will I call on him ! O spare me, Lucifer!—

Faustus: to plead with Lucifer   Beat 16

Where is it now? 'Tis gone; and see where God
Stretcheth out His arm and bends His ireful
brows!
Mountains and hills, come, come and fall on
me
And hide me from the heavy wrath of God!
No?
Then will I headlong run into the earth.

Faustus: to flee from the wrath of God	Gape earth! O no, it will not harbor me.
	You stars that reigned at my nativity,
	Whose influence hath allotted death and hell,
	Now draw up Faustus like a foggy mist
	Into the entrails of yon laboring cloud
	That when they vomit forth into the air,
	My limbs may issue from their smoky mouths—
	But let my soul mount and ascend to heaven!

Beat 17   (*Clock strikes half past the hour.*)

O half the hour is past! 'Twill all be past anon!
O God,

Faustus: to bargain with God

If thou wilt not have mercy on my soul,
Yet for Christ's sake whose blood hath ransomed me,
Impose some end to my incessant pain!
Let Faustus live in hell a thousand years,
A hundred thousand, and at last be saved!

Beat 18

No end is limited to damnéd souls!
Why wert thou not a creature wanting soul?
Or why is this immortal that thou hast?
All beasts are happy, for when they die
Their souls are soon dissolved in elements.

Beat 19

But mine must live still to be plagued in hell!

Faustus: to shift his blame

Cursed be the parents that engendered me!

Faustus: to blame self and Satan   *Beat 20*

No Faustus, curse thyself, curse Lucifer
That hath deprived thee of the joys of heaven.

(*Clock strikes twelve*)

It strikes, it strikes! Now body, turn to air,
Or Lucifer will bear thee quick to hell!

(*Thunder and lightning*)

O soul, be changed to little water-drops
And fall into the ocean, ne'er be found.
My God, my God! Look not so fierce on me!

Beat 21   (*Enter Devil*)
Faustus: to vent his desperation; to tear himself from Satan's grasp

Adders and serpent, let me breathe awhile!
Ugly hell, gape not! Come not Lucifer!

Beat 22

I'll burn my books—O Mephistophilis!

Work Out

■ Mark the beats and verb the lines of the following excerpt from *Doctor Faustus.*

Mephostophilis: But tell me, Faustus, shall I have thy soul—
And will I be thy slave and wait on thee
And give thee more than thou hast wit to ask?

Faustus: Ay Mephostophilis, I'll give it.

Mephostophilis: Then, Faustus, stab thy arm courageously
And bind thy soul that at some certain day
Great Lucifer may claim it as his own.
And then be thou as great as Lucifer!

Faustus: Lo, Mephostophilis, for love of thee
Faustus hath cut his arm and with his proper blood
Assures his soul to be great Lucifer's,
Chief lord and regent of perpetual night.
View here this blood that trickles from mine arm
And let it be propitious for my wish.

Mephostophilis: But Faustus,
Write it in manner of a deed of gift.

Faustus: Ay so I do—But Mephostophilis,
My blood congeals and I can write no more.

Mephostophilis: I'll fetch thee fire to dissolve it straight. *Exit*

Faustus: What might the staying of my blood portend?
Is it unwilling I should write this bill?
Why streams it not that I may write afresh:
"Faustus gives to thee his soul?" O there it is stayed.
Why shouldst thou not? Is not thy soul thine own?
Then write again: "Faustus gives to thee his soul."

Chapter 15

Producing
a Play

"A playwright admits materials to a drama only because he chooses them. His choices—both in his art and in his life—comprise his vision."
—*Sam Smiley,* Playwriting: The Structure of Action

Now that you know how to choose a play, you are ready to undertake the production of a drama. You will be relieved to know that producing a play is hardly a one-man show. A successful drama requires the cooperation and talent of many individuals. The following chart gives a quick overview of the production personnel and their basic roles.

Production Staff

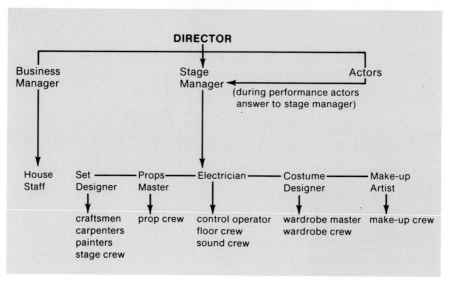

Figure 15a

Production Staff Roles

Director

The director is, in theory, responsible for overseeing all phases of production. In practice, however, such responsibility is overwhelming for one person. Consequently, the director delegates some of his authority to other competent individuals. These individuals work with the director to bring the play from script to stage, freeing the director to focus his attention on the following specifics.

Analysis The director's first responsibility is to analyze the play, using the criteria already discussed in Chapter 14.

Rehearsal Schedule Once he has completed this analysis and chosen his drama, he may want to set up a tentative rehearsal schedule. By informing potential cast members of this schedule, the director can discover and avoid scheduling conflicts.

Tryouts During tryouts the director looks for general acting ability. He does not yet focus on the specific needs of the play. Consequently, those trying out are often free to perform a piece they have chosen themselves.

Callbacks The director is now ready to focus on the needs of the play, and individuals are called back to read for specific parts. Following callbacks, the director will make his final casting decisions.

Table Reading During this first rehearsal the cast members read through the play to gain an overall feel for the drama. This is also the time when the director presents valuable background information. (Such information is especially helpful when producing a historical drama.) He may also want to give a brief description of each major character and provide a time for actors to ask any specific questions they may have about their roles.

Blocking The first problem to be solved once the actors begin rehearsing on stage is who moves where when. However, blocking involves more than simple logistics. It also involves picturization and composition or *how* the actors are grouped on stage. Composition and picturization are essential, for these elements visually reinforce what is spoken in the dialogue. Figure 15.1 shows some of the specific principles of picturization and composition.

Figure 15.1

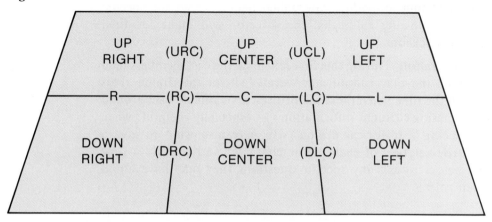

Stage Areas and Composition

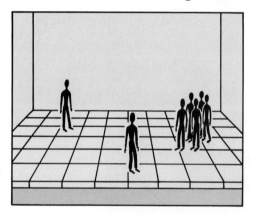 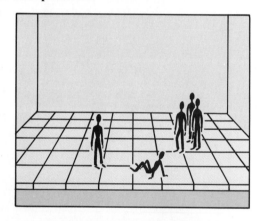

Characterization/Motivation During these rehearsals the director guides the performers in understanding what the characters are like, why they do what they do, and how they interact with one another.

Business and Properties By this time in the rehearsal schedule, those who have the major speaking parts should have their lines memorized. Now it is time to incorporate the walk-ons and to work on timing for sword fights, crowd scenes, etc.

Pacing In every drama there are "fast" and "slow" scenes. For example, as a play nears the climax, the pace usually quickens, and it is the director's responsibility to see that it does. Plotting the drama during analysis (see page 133 of Chapter 11) is helpful in determining the pace of each scene.

Polishing The remainder of the rehearsals will be to put the finishing touches on the performance.

To help you visualize what we have been discussing, take some time to examine Figure 15.2. This schedule and accompanying photographs were taken during an actual preparation of a dramatic production. They may help you when planning your own schedule. Notice that the scenes are not always rehearsed in order. This arrangement is for the convenience of your cast members. For example, if several of the same performers were in scenes 3 and 8, you would want to block these scenes at one rehearsal. Of course, when your rehearsals reach the polishing stage, you would want to run the scenes in order.

Date	Time	Location	Scenes	Objectives/Instructions
1-14	7:00-9:00	P.H.	Entire Play	Read Through
1-19	8:00-9:00	P.H.	Scene 1	Blocking
	9:00-9:30	P.H.	Scene 2	
1-22	7:00-8:30	P.H.	Scene 3	Blocking
	8:30-9:00		Scene 4	
	9:00-9:30	P.H.	Scene 8	Blocking
1-25	7:00-8:30		Scene 5	
	8:30-9:00		Scene 6	
	9:00-10:00	P.H.	Scene 7	Characterization
1-26	7:00-8:00		Scene 1	
	8:00-8:20		Scene 2	
	8:20-9:00		Scene 3	
	9:00-9:30	P.H.	Scene 8	Characterization
1-28	7:00-8:00		Scene 4	Characterization
	8:00-9:30	P.H.	Scene 5	
1-30	7:00-8:15		Scene 1	Characterization
	8:15-9:30	P.H.	Scene 6	
1-31	7:00-8:15		Scene 5	
	8:30-9:30	P.H.	Scene 6	Run Through of Play (lines memorized)
2-2	6:45-10:00	P.H.	Entire Play	Motivation
2-4	7:00-7:45		Scene 1	
	7:45-8:00		Scene 2	
	8:00-8:45		Scene 3	
	8:45-9:30	P.H.	Scene 8	Motivation
2-6	7:00-7:30		Scene 4	
	7:30-8:15		Scene 5	
	8:15-8:45		Scene 6	
	8:45-9:30	P.H.	Scene 7	
2-8	7:00-9:30	P.H.	*TBA	TBA
		P.H.	Entire Play	Technical Rehearsal (Add technical elements to all rehearsals)
2-11	7:00-10:00	P.H.	Entire Play	Add all extras (walk ons, props, etc.)
2-12	7:00-10:00	P.H.	Entire Play	Pacing
2-16	7:00-10:00	P.H.	Entire Play	*Costume Parade
2-18	6:30-10:00	P.H.	Entire Play	TBA
2-19	7:00-10:00	P.H.	Entire Play	Costumes & Make-up Check
2-20	5:30-10:00	P.H.	Entire Play	Polishing
2-22	7:00-10:00	P.H.	Entire Play	Polishing (Costumes but no Make-up)
2-25	5:30-10:00	P.H.	Entire Play	Run Through of Play
2-28	7:00-9:30	P.H.	Entire Play	

Figure 15.2
Sample Rehearsal Schedule

*TBA: Abbreviation for *to be announced*. The director will usually have one or two of these rehearsals to work on problem scenes.

*Costume Parade: During this rehearsal the performers simply try on their costumes and the director and the costume designer discuss any changes needed for individual costumes.

Business Manager

The business manager and his crew are responsible for publicity, ticket sales, programs, and general house maintenance (ushering, cleanup, etc.). The business manager is also responsible for keeping an accurate record of all expenditures (see Figure 15.3) and for making certain that bills are paid promptly.

Sample Business Report

Figure 15.3

INITIAL BALANCE: $000.00

BILLS:	Amount Spent
Item	$00.00
Royalties	$00.00
Costumes	$00.00
Make-up	$00.00
Props	$00.00
Publicity & Tickets	$00.00
Set Construction	$00.00
Technical Crew	$00.00
Miscellaneous	Total
ASSETS:	$000.00
Ticket Sales	
	$000.00
NEW BALANCE:	

Stage Manager

The stage manager is responsible for overseeing several crews. Aside from the director, the stage manager carries the greatest organizational burden of the preproduction time, for

he must be sure that all the following crews are working together and effectively implementing the director's plans. The following breakdown will give an idea of the various roles.

Set Designer and Crew
- Determine how many sets are needed (being careful to use as few as possible and to overlap set pieces from scene to scene when appropriate).
- Draw thumbnail sketch of each scene (see Figure 15.4).

Sample Thumbnail Sketch

Figure 15.4

Producing a Play

Sample Floor Plan

Figure 15.5

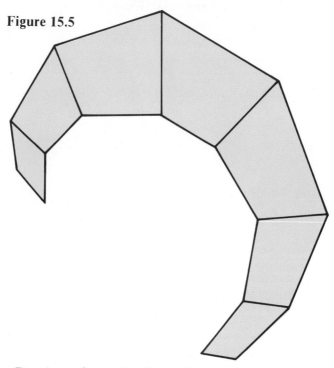

- Develop a floor plan for each scene (see Figure 15.5).
- Create the design for individual set pieces.
- Construct and paint the sets.
- Label and store set pieces after production.

Props Master and Crew
- Make a list of all necessary properties for each scene.
- List any additional properties that may give an added flavor to the play but are not absolutely necessary.
- Find or construct the props.
- Look after the props during production to be sure that they are well cared for and that they are ready for each scene when needed.
- Return any borrowed props after production.
- Label and store any constructed props for future use.
- Handle any of the live cues during performance.

Electrician and Crew
- Work out the cue sheet with the director (see Figure 15.6).

Figure 15.6

Sample Cue Sheet

Instrument Number	Stage Area	Instrument (see Figure 15.5)	Dimmer	Color	Notes
4	1	6" Fresnel	1	light blue	
6	1	6" Fresnel	1	salmon	
5	2	6" Fresnel	2	light blue	
8	2	6" Fresnel	2	salmon	
7	3	6" Fresnel	3	light blue	
9	3	6" Fresnel	3	salmon	
10	4	6" Fresnel	4	light blue	
12	4	6" Fresnel	4	salmon	
22	4	Mini-ellipsoidal	4	salmon	wide angle
11	5	6" Fresnel	5	light blue	
14	5	6" Fresnel	5	salmon	
23	5	Mini-ellipsoidal	5	salmon	wide angle
	6	6" Fresnel	6	light blue	
	6	6" Fresnel	6	salmon	
	6	Mini-ellipsoidal	6	salmon	wide angle
	7	6" Fresnel	7	light blue	
	7	6" Fresnel	7	salmon	
	7	Mini-ellipsoidal		salmon	angle

- Record any sound cues.
- Assign the necessary floor and beam crews to set up equipment and to work the lights, curtains, and sound during performances.

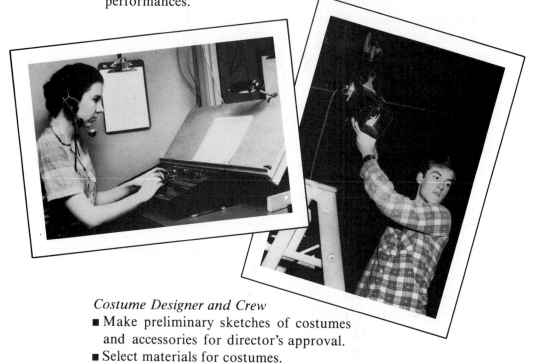

Costume Designer and Crew
- Make preliminary sketches of costumes and accessories for director's approval.
- Select materials for costumes.

- Make or borrow the necessary costumes and accessories.
- Look after the costumes during the performance to make sure that they are well cared for and to repair any loose buttons, snaps, etc.
- Return any borrowed costumes after the performance.
- Label and store the costumes after the performance.

Make-up Artist and Crew
- Prepare make-up sheets for each character (see Figure 15.7).
- Purchase or collect materials needed for make-up, wigs, beards, etc.
- Prepare make-up boxes for crew.
- Assign make-up people to performers.

Figure 15.7

Sample Make-up Sheet

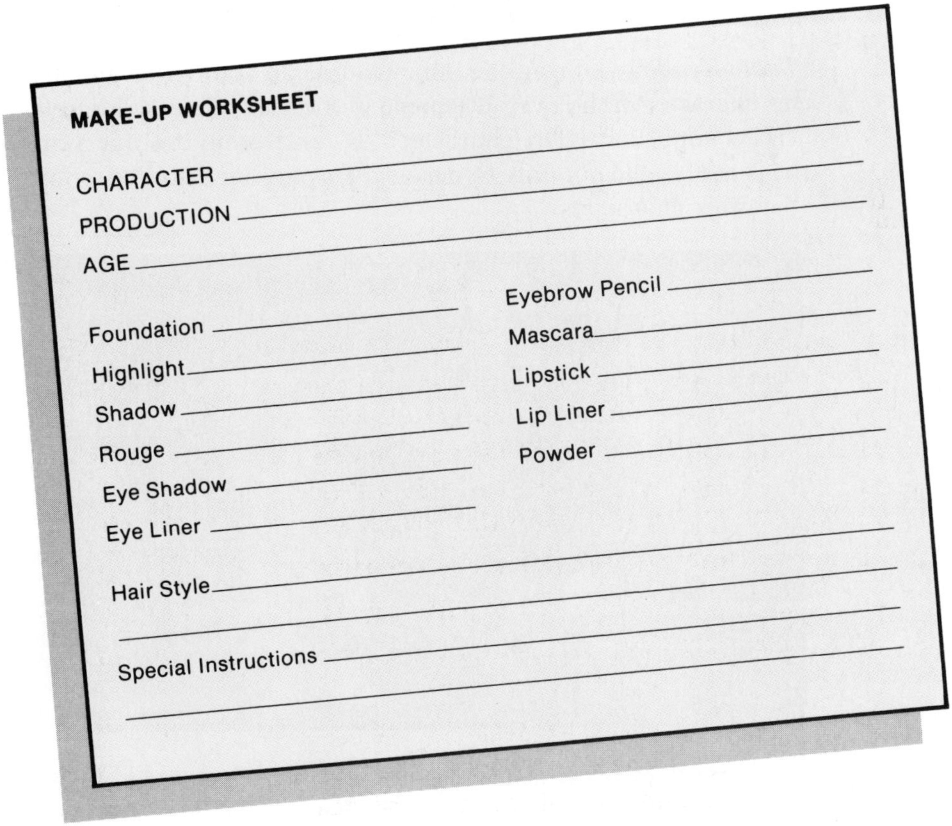

MAKE-UP WORKSHEET

CHARACTER _____

PRODUCTION _____

AGE _____

Foundation _____   Eyebrow Pencil _____

Highlight _____   Mascara _____

Shadow _____   Lipstick _____

Rouge _____   Lip Liner _____

Eye Shadow _____   Powder _____

Eye Liner _____

Hair Style _____

Special Instructions _____

Actors

We have already looked at the step-by-step process of rehearsing from the director's point of view. Now let's look at the process from an actor's point of view.

Table Reading During the table reading an actor tries to place his character in the overall scheme of the play. He asks himself, "How important is my character?" By answering this question, he is better able not only to perform his part but also to support the other characters.

Blocking Rehearsals An actor carefully marks his script, noting all the movements he must make. Before the next rehearsal he practices these movements while saying his lines *aloud*.

Characterization Rehearsals Between the characterization and blocking rehearsals, an actor should construct a character sketch for his character. Figure 15.8 gives a sample sketch. Of course, not all the information listed will necessarily be filled in for every character. However, it is important that an actor fill in as much of the material as possible, for this information is the key to his understanding why his character does what he does. Without this understanding, he cannot create a believable character.

Figure 15.8

Sample Character Sketch

CHARACTER:	Martin Luther
PRODUCTION:	*Till Rome Makes Peace with God*
AGE:	34-38 (over the period of play)
RACE:	Caucasian
SEX:	Male
LEVEL OF EDUCATION:	At this time in Luther's life he had a doctor's degree in theology. He knew both Greek and Hebrew and could thus study the original texts. His study enabled him to discern the discrepancies between Rome's traditions and the Scripture. His knowledge of the ancient languages enabled him eventually to translate the Scripture into the German language.
INTERESTS:	Luther enjoyed singing and playing the lute.
OCCUPATION:	Luther was a university professor. This profession (particularly his teaching of Bible) allowed him to search the Scripture and formulate the ideas which were the fuel that set the Reformation aflame.
ECONOMIC LEVEL:	University professors at that time were not highly paid. They did, however, make enough to live comfortably if they were frugal.

RELIGION:	Catholic. However, he turned from the papacy and Rome's traditions when he found that they conflicted with the Scripture.
PERSONALITY:	Luther was a warm, forthright person. His forthrightness and intelligence made him tenacious in battle. Those who opposed him found him a formidable opponent.
SOCIAL BACKGROUND:	Luther was from an upper-middle-class German background. His father may have been poor when Luther was a small child, but he was quite wealthy by the time Luther was in his teens.
CULTURAL HERITAGE:	Besides the superstitions inherent in sixteenth-century Romanism, Luther inherited all of the pagan superstitions of a backward and pagan sixteenth-century German (witches, wood-gods, etc.). Until his conversion, Luther was controlled by these superstitions.
FAMILY BACKGROUND:	Luther's father was a typical strict German father. He loved his son but was extremely severe with him. Although his mother was a loyal Catholic, she also taught her son the popular pagan superstitions.

Motivation Rehearsals Before these rehearsals an actor should verb his lines. (See Chapter 14 for an example.) He should also work on concentrating not only on what the character says but also on the character's inner monologue. In other words, what is the character thinking when he is not speaking? Often understanding why a character doesn't reveal certain information is as important as understanding what he does say.

Being involved in a production can be instructional not only for your audience but also for you. Producing a play can help you develop self-discipline, individual responsibility, leadership qualities, self-sacrifice, perseverance, and obedience. It can also teach you much about working with others, responding to

pressure, coping with disappointments, and benefiting from success. Your creativity, expressiveness, and reasoning skills will also be sharpened by your study and analysis of the drama. In other words, drama can provide you one more opportunity to glorify God and to benefit others.

Chapter 16

¶ The firste Psalme.

¶ Those that forsake the counsayls and tra=
ditions of the wycked, and wholy geue them sel=
ues to know the lawe of God, and to shew it in
their lyuynge, doeth this Psalme pronounce
blessed, both here and in ye worlde to come: and
the contrary parte in both ye worldes, miserable
and wretched.

Blessed is the
man, that goth
not in the coun
sayll of the vn=
godlye: that a=
bideth not in
(a) the way of
sinners, (b) and
sitteth not in ye
seate of dscor=
nefull.

But delyteth in the lawe of the Lorde,
and exercyseth hym selfe in hys law, both
daye and nyght.

Suche a man is lyke a tree planted by
the watersyde, that bryngeth forth hys
frute in due season.

Hys leaues shall not fall of, and loke
whatsoeuer he doth, it shall prospere.

As for the vngodlye, it is not so wyth
them: but they are lyke the duste, whych the
wynde scattereth away from the ground.

Therfore the vngodly shall not be able
(c) to stand in the iudgemēt, nether the sin
ners in the cōgregacion of the ryghteous.

For the Lorde aloweth the way of the
ryghteous, but the waye of the vngodlye
shall peryshe.

The Notes.

(a) The maners and ordynaunces of sēners
whereon they walke as it were in a waye, are
called the waye of sinners. And in the scrip=
ture is, it is cōmune to take thys way for what
soeuer we do or go aboute, be it good or euell.
So in the last verse of thys psalme.

(b) He sitteth in the seat of the scornefull, that
consyreeth wyth them, and becommeth felowe
of theyr mischefe, as in the psalme. rrb. b.

(c) He standeth in iudgement, that wynneth the
proeesse, and hath sentence pronounced on hys
syde, as he that litterly the proeesse and hath sen
tence pronounced agaynst ryght and trueth, rob
beth iudgement. As in Ga. r. a. So then they
here meaneth no more here, but that the wycked
haue so terrible a sentence geuen vpon them,
that they shall not be able to abide when the
Lorde shall come to the generall iudgement. It
meaneth not that the wycked shall not appeare
in iudgement.

The.ii.Psalme.

¶ They ye know not God are moued agaynste
the kyngdome of Christ wyth wonderful inten
tes, but in baine: yet rūneth their rage thorowe
the whole worlde. The only way to health is
to commit thy selfe to Christ.

Why do the heathen grudge,
why do the people ymagyne
vayne thynges?

The kynges of the earth
stand vp, and the rulers are
come together, agaynste the

The.iii.Psalme.

Lord and agaynste hys anoynted.

＊ Let vs breake theyr bondes asunder
and caste away theyr yocke from vs.

＊ Neuerthelesse he ye dwelleth in hea=
uen, shal laughe them to scorne: yea euen
the Lorde hym selfe shall haue thē in derp=
sion.

Then shall he (a) speake vnto them in
hys wrath, and vere them in hys sore dys=
pleasure.

Yet haue I sette my kyng vpon my ho
ly hyll of Syon.

As for me, I wyl preach the law, wher=
of the Lord hath sayd vnto me: Thou art
my sonne, thys day haue I begotten the.

Desyre of me, ＊ I shal geue the heathē
for thyne inherytaunce: yea the vttermost
partes of the worlde for thy possession.

Thou shalt rule them wyth a (b) rodde
of yron, and breake them in peces lyke an
earthen vessell.

Be wyse now therfore, O ye kynges,
be warned, ye that are iudges of ye earth.

Serue the Lord wyth feare, and reioyse
before hym wyth reuerence.

(c) Kysse the son, lest the Lord be angry,
and so ye perysh from the ryght way.

For hys wrath shalbe kyndled shortly:
blessed are al they ye put theyr trust in him.

The Notes.

(a) God speaketh to men in his wrath, when he
ordeneth and determineth to destroye them, as
Ieremy. rviii. a.

(b) This Irō rodde a sure and vndowable do=
minion, as it is said. Psal. lrrviii. c. v. rliii. b.

(c) This is after the hebrue, and it is a figura=
tiue speach, in whych by the figure is vnderstād
that which is significd therby. For by the kisse
of the kinges hand euen nowe a dayes in many
regions, the subiectes testyfy that they wyll be
in the faith and power of the kynge.
He calleth hym Sonne, because he before brought
in the father, saying: Thou art my Sonne. The
Greke redeth, receyue instruccio or be learned,
meanynge thereby, that they should submit thē
selues vnto the kynge Christe, and receyue hys
instruccion and chastenynge.

The.iii.Psalme.

¶ Dauid speakynge vnto the Lorde, wonde=
reth both at the number and confidence of hys
enemyes, whiche came agaiuste hym, and com=
myteth hym selfe wyth greate fayth vnto hys
helpe, although hys enemyes were at hand rea=
dy to stryke hym, both because no man els can
saue him, and because none can be partakers of
health or saluacion but they that beleue in him,
and truste to him.

A (a) Psalme of Dauid when he fled
from the face of Absalom.

☞ The storie of this dote is in the seconde
of the kinges from the. rv. Chapter vnto
the.ir.

Why are they so many, O Lorde
that trouble me: a great mul=
titude are they ye rise agaynste
me.

Yea many one ther be that saye of my
soule: there is no helpe for hym in God (b)
Selah.

But

The.iiii.Psalm

But thou, O Lorde, arte my
my worshyp, and ye lyfter vp of
I call vpon the Lorde wyth
and he heareth me oute of hys
Selah.

I layed me downe and slept, b
vp agayne, for the Lorde sustayn
I am not afrayed for thousan
people, that compasse me round
Up Lorde, and helpe me O
for thou smytest all myne enem
the cheke bones, and (c) breakes
of the vngodly.

Helpe belongeth vnto the Lo
fore let thy blessynge be vpon th

The Notes.

(a) In the hebrue tong a psalme is a
som, that is a song, or as some wyll
of an harpe.

(b) This word after Rabi Kimchi v
or token of lyftinge vp the voice, an
ception and aduertisment to enforce t
and mynde earnestlye to geue hede t
nynge of the verse, whereunto it is
done, wyll that it sygnyfye perpet
verelye.

(c) The teeth of the vngodlye are by
they: blasphemye is broughte to no
Psalme.lvii.b.

The.iiii.Psalme.

¶ Dauid prayseth the beneuolence
by helpe of God towarde hym in th
cy of Absalon. He reproueth the ma
braders and rulers of Israell that so
agaynste hym, and calleth them ag
nendement: and after glorysed in
dance of goodes, peace, and safer
agaynst vnto hym by the benefyte of

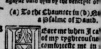

(a) To the Chaunter in (b) N
a Psalme of Dauid.

Eare me when I ca
of my ryghteousn
comfortedst me in
ble: haue mercye
harken vnto my pra

O ye sonnes of men howe lon
blaspheme myne honour, why ha
pleasure in vanyty and seke af
Selah.

Know this, that the Lord bea
uelously wyth hys faynt: and th
vpon the Lorde, he heareth me.

Be angrye, ＊ but sinne not: co
pour own hertes vpon youre bed
remember youre selues.   Selab.

Offer the sacryfyce of ryghteus
put your trust in the Lord.

There be many that say: whe
vs any good? Lord (c) lyfte vp vp
lyght of thy countenaunce.

Thou reioysest myne hart, tha
encrease be greate both in corne
Therfore will I lay me downe
and take my rest: for thou lord o
me in a sure dwellynge.

The Notes.

(a) That wher is here translated, t

A Drama for Analysis

Then to the well-trod stage anon.
—John Milton

TO SERVE
A HIGHER KING

by Donna Hess and Dawn Watkins

CHARACTERS
Central Characters

William Tyndale
(pensive, courageous, guileless)

Richard Tisen
(ingratiating, deceitful)

Thomas Poyntz
(jovial, impetuous, brave)
Henry Monmouth
(wise, patient, generous)

John Phillips
(shrewd, bitter, cynical)
Bishop Tunstall
(self-seeking, ambitious, cautious)

Secondary Characters

Lady Walsh
Lord Walsh
Geoffrey Walsh ✓
Edward Walsh
Father Benedict
First merchant
Second merchant

Friar
German printer ✓
Shopkeeper
Stephen Vaughn
Mistress Poyntz
Jailer
Extras: servants, townspeople

SYNOPSIS OF SCENES

Prologue
Lord Walsh's home, Gloucester, England, 1523.

Act I
Scene 1. Street in London, England, one week later.
Scene 2. Henry Monmouth's home, London, later the same evening.
Scene 3. Bishop Tunstall's residence, London, three days later.
Scene 4. Street in London, two months later.

Act II
Scene 1. Printer's shop, Cologne, Germany, 1525.
Scene 2. Printer's shop, Cologne, 1531.
Scene 3. Printer's shop, Cologne two days later.

Act III
Scene 1. Poyntz's home, Antwerp, 1534.
Scene 2. Jail in Antwerp, 1535.

Epilogue
Henry Monmouth's home, London, England, 1536.

PROLOGUE

Time: 1523. Evening
Place: Gloucester, England
The inside of the Walsh's home. It is a comfortable setting for the times: a large, open room with table, chairs, and benches. A servant is cooking supper over an open fire as Tyndale enters with the Walsh children, Geoffrey and Edward.

Geoffrey: May we go riding again tomorrow, Master Tyndale?

Edward: Yes, do say yes. Every gentleman should know how to ride, shouldn't he?

Tyndale: And every gentleman should know how to read as well.

Enter Lady Walsh.

Lady Walsh: Well, the men have returned, have they? Did my sons perform well today, Master Tyndale?

Tyndale: They performed well, Lady Walsh.

Lady Walsh: Good. Good. Go now, Edward and Geoffrey; your supper is already waiting. We have guests tonight.

Geoffrey and Edward exit.

(To Tyndale) You'll be interested in our guests, being a scholar and a churchman, Master Tyndale.

Tyndale: How is that, my lady?

Lady Walsh: One is a student from Oxford and the other is a learned priest.

Tyndale: Indeed, madam?

Lady Walsh: My husband relishes a good debate, as you know. He thinks the company tonight should be rather lively. What do you think?

Tyndale: I think that debates at table cannot be good for one's digestion.

Lady Walsh: Never seems to affect Lord Walsh's. Eats as much as two men, don't you think? And thanks be—he hunts enough to keep us all well fed. These supper debates are like the hunt to him, I think—only here he provides both the hawk and the game.

Tyndale: Which am I to be tonight—hawk or rabbit?

Lady Walsh: Oh, hawk, surely. My lord is much pleased with your wit. *(Pause)* Tell me, Master Tyndale, will my sons make scholars?

Tyndale: They might if they wished to. At present their interests lie more out-of-doors than in.

Enter Lord Walsh and Richard Tisen. Lord Walsh is carrying his hunting gear.

Lord Walsh: Good even, wife. William, I have brought Master Tisen to supper. This is my wife, Lady Walsh, and our children's tutor, Master William Tyndale. Richard Tisen.

Lady Walsh: Welcome, Master Tisen.

Tyndale: Good even, sir.

Tisen: Good evening.

Lord Walsh: Come, sit down. Let me show you my new bow. *(Hands the bow to Tyndale)* I had it specially made. What do you think of it?

All sit except Tyndale who remains standing to try the bow.

Tisen: A wonderful piece of workmanship.

Tyndale: *(Testing the bow)* It draws smoothly.

Lord Walsh: Do you think my sons could use it?

Tyndale: I think they might, my lord.

A servant enters with Father Benedict.
Tyndale is poised with the bow at full draw. The priest is startled and quickly moves behind the servant as if to protect himself.

Lord Walsh: *(Amused)* Have no fear, friend. It is a new bow— without arrows as yet. Master Tyndale was merely testing it.

Tyndale: Your pardon, sir.

Lord Walsh: Come, meet the company here. This is William Tyndale, of our household, and Richard Tisen. Both scholars out of Oxford. Father Benedict, a monk from Coventry.

Tyndale:	Good even.
Tisen:	I am honored to meet a churchman of your rank, sir. I aspire to service in the church myself.
Benedict:	Is that so, my young friend?
Tisen:	Indeed, sir. My father sent me to Oxford in hopes that I would attach myself to the Holy Mother Church.
Benedict:	To Oxford for that reason?
Tisen:	One must be well learned to be a servant of the Church.
Benedict:	Yes, that is true.

At Lord Walsh's motion the servant begins to serve the meal, and the guests settle down to eat.

Benedict:	And you, Master Tyndale, do you have such aspirations as well?
Tyndale:	I am content with my position here.
Lord Walsh:	Come, William, do not be humble on my account. Surely you would like to be a bishop. Why, a man of your ability might even be a cardinal.
Tyndale:	I prefer a quiet study and a humble life.
Tisen:	By that do you imply, sir, that our Cardinal is not a humble man?
Tyndale:	I mean that the Cardinal is a public man and that I would not like such a life.
Lord Walsh:	But think of the luxury. You will never get fine robes and gold chains from my poor employ.
Benedict:	The Cardinal does not seek these things.
Lord Walsh:	Whether he seeks them or not, he has them, doesn't he?
Benedict:	He has no more than is his due.
Lord Walsh:	Ha! The Cardinal Wolsey has more velvets and satins than any merchant in all of England!
Benedict:	Still the Cardinal is a worthy servant.
Lord Walsh:	But a better politician! He's second only to King Henry. *(Obviously, trying to goad Tyndale into a debate)* What do you say, William, of the noted churchman Wolsey? Is he worthy or not?

Tyndale: *(Cautiously)* If by worthiness you mean godliness, then we must check his behavior by the Scripture. There we are instructed not to lay up treasures for ourselves on earth, where moth and rust corrupt and thieves break through and steal. I would say from what I have heard that the Cardinal would do well to check his wardrobe for moths, his carriage for rust, and his castle for thieves.

Benedict: How dare you speak of your religious superiors in such a manner!

Tisen: He's not the only one. In Germany I heard that a man named Martin Luther brought far bolder accusations against the priests.

Benedict: And mark my words—he'll burn for it!

Lord Walsh: Aye, that is certainly possible, if the arm of the church can reach him there.

Benedict: It shall! It is necessary! For he not only speaks against the clergy but also against the pope himself! And that is not the worst of it; he also seeks to corrupt the Scripture by putting it into the common language.

Tyndale: You say corrupt?

Benedict: Exactly.

Tyndale: But I have heard that Luther did his translating from the ancient languages, carefully studying the texts in order to preserve its meaning with absolute precision. Did I hear wrong?

Benedict: No, but—

Tyndale: *(Calmly interrupting)* Well, then he did not add to the Word of God, did he?

Benedict: No—

Tyndale: *(Again interrupting with quiet persistence)* Nor subtract any part of the Scripture?

Benedict: No—

Tyndale: Well, if he translated precisely, without adding to or subtracting from, I would say that he had preserved God's Word, not corrupted it.

Benedict: *(Greatly agitated)* What I mean to say is that Luther's translation is totally unnecessary.

Tyndale:	Unnecessary? I hardly—
Benedict:	*(Quickly interrupting before Tyndale can argue the point)* The common man does not need the Scripture; the pope will tell him of his duties.
Tyndale:	And who will tell the pope?
Benedict:	He is the vicar of Christ and needs no instruction!
Tyndale:	*(Beginning to lose his temper)* He needs the Word of God as much as any man.
Benedict:	*(Standing, he leans across the table and shakes his finger in Tyndale's face.)* It is clear in church doctrine, Master Tyndale, that what the pope speaks IS the Word of God!
Tyndale:	Where is that in the Scripture?
Benedict:	It is in Church doctrine!
Tyndale:	I defy any doctrine not founded on the Scripture!
Benedict:	*(Threatening)* Take care—I say your words smell of the flame!
Tyndale:	And I say, that if God spares my life, before long every ploughboy in England will know more of the Scripture than you do!

CURTAIN

A Drama for Analysis

ACT I

Scene 1

Time: One week later.
Place: In the streets of London. There are several townspeople on stage; much bustling, talking, buying, and selling. Thomas Poyntz hands a package to a fellow merchant, who quickly moves on. Thomas is then joined by a second merchant and Henry Monmouth.

Merchant 2: Hello, Master Poyntz. How is business with you?

Poyntz: Well enough, my friend. That is, when the dear church keeps her hands off my goods and out of my pockets.

Merchant 2: Peace, good sir. Your words will burn us both.

Monmouth: He has a point, Thomas.

Thomas, Henry, and the merchant move off to the side and converse. Tyndale enters. He is looking for Tunstall's residence. The confusion of the large city seems to confuse him. While he is gazing about, he accidentally bumps into a friar.

Friar: *(Pompously)* Take care who you run against, sir.

As John Phillips saunters up, he overhears the Friar's rudeness.

Tyndale: Your pardon. There are so many to watch out for in this great city.

Phillips: *(Nonchalantly)* Might we rather say, that there are too many in this city who think themselves great?

The friar bristles at this remark, and Tyndale quickly steps between the two men and interrupts in an effort to prevent a confrontation.

Tyndale: Could either of you good men tell me where I might find Bishop Tunstall?

Friar: *(Disdainfully)* And what would you have to do with Bishop Tunstall?

Phillips: *(Again trying to stir up an argument)* Perhaps he seeks some holy man, since he has failed to meet one in the street.

Tyndale: *(Quickly continuing)* I have a letter—a letter of introduction—and a request.

Friar: The Bishop's house is there *(Pointing)*.

The friar turns and leaves without farewell.

Tyndale: *(Calling after the friar)* Thank you, sir. *(Turning to Phillips)* And thank you.

Phillips bows politely. Tyndale moves off toward Tunstall's house. Phillips, who has spied Thomas Poyntz and Henry Monmouth, goes to them.

Phillips: Ah, Thomas, Thomas Poyntz!

Poyntz: Phillips? I thought I left you in Antwerp.

Phillips: So you did, but I am here now and looking for a way back.

Poyntz: *(Shaking his head)* You are a hard man to keep up with. At any rate, before I go to Antwerp I must make my way to Germany.

Phillips: That suits me. I am in no great hurry.

Poyntz: That is good, for I will be here a month or two.

Phillips: *(Moving off)* 'Til later then.

Monmouth: Who is that man?

Poyntz: *(Carelessly)* A mere vagabond, but diverting company.

Monmouth: *(Playfully accusing)* You know, Thomas, I have noted that each time you come to England your stay is shorter.

Poyntz:	That is because each time I come ashore I find things worse than when I left them. I tell you truly, Monmouth, it's so bad that each time before I board my ship I stand upon the dock and make sure that every tariff clerk has fixed his eyes on me—*(Pantomiming his mock defiance)* then I stomp my feet with the greatest vigor!
Monmouth:	*(Jovially)* To show your disapproval of their fees?
Poyntz:	That is only part of it. I also stomp that they might see me clean my boots—lest they turn and charge me for the English dirt I carry off!
Monmouth:	*(Laughing heartily)* Well, before you clean your boots too well, stop by my house this evening for a bit of English venison.
Poyntz:	I would be delighted. But why not come with me now down to the docks?
Monmouth:	Ah no, my friend, I shall stay behind to see the grand procession.
Poyntz:	I forgot that is today—then I'll be gone. If I am fortunate, I may yet have time to miss it.

Poyntz and Monmouth part just as Tyndale is coming out of Tunstall's residence. Poyntz is seen fighting his way through the crowd when a cheer in the street draws everyone's attention. In the background music begins. Someone in the crowd calls out, "The Cardinal is coming!" Poyntz sees that it is now hopeless to escape, and he sits down on a stoop muttering to himself. Monmouth watches, laughs to himself, and then leans against the wall to wait. Tyndale approaches him.

Tyndale:	Sir, what is this ado? Is the Cardinal indeed coming?
Monmouth:	*(Scornful but cautious)* A greater occasion than that, good sir. The Cardinal's hat is coming.
Tyndale:	His hat?
Monmouth:	Indeed, his very hat. Wolsey's wool. The merchant's fleece.

The procession comes into view. There are nobles and clergyman of all ranks. In the center of the procession can be seen Wolsey's hat carried on a litter. As the relic passes, those in the crowd genuflect and then follow the procession off stage. Poyntz is seen in the background. After a reluctant show of reverence, he stomps off in the opposite direction toward the docks. Monmouth and Tyndale are the only two left on stage.

Tyndale:	But why all this for just a hat?
Monmouth:	Why? Because, stranger, we took the relic too lightly when it came before. We have another chance to show our due respect.
Tyndale:	To his hat? *(Pause)* This is strange.
Monmouth:	Yes. But tell me, where are you from that you should know so little of London's marvelous processions?
Tyndale:	I come from Gloucester. To see the Bishop Tunstall on an urgent matter.
Monmouth:	Well, you'll not see him today. He must greet the hat.
Tyndale:	But he WILL see me and when he does, he cannot fail to see the urgency of my proposal. You see, I desire to translate the Scriptures into English, but I cannot without the Bishop's sanction.

Monmouth weighs Tyndale's words. He is trying to evaluate the scholar, but is uncertain how to reconcile Tyndale's apparent naiveté and zeal.

Monmouth:	*(Thoughtfully)* Tunstall's sanction.
Tyndale:	I have friends, the Walshes, who gave me a letter of introduction. They hear the Bishop is a good man.
Monmouth:	Perhaps news from London takes on a goodlier tone in its travel to Gloucester.
Tyndale:	We have news from London, but I never thought it would be so large a city as this. There are so many people. And I know none of them.

Monmouth pauses, then turns to Tyndale, and warmly offers him his hand.

Monmouth:	Well, you know me. I am Henry Monmouth.
Tyndale:	I am William Tyndale.
Monmouth:	Then, Mr. Tyndale, should Bishop Tunstall delay your proposal for any time, I am at your service. My house is the large one past the docks. *(Motions with his hand)* Ask anyone to direct you.
Tyndale:	Thank you, thank you very much.

CURTAIN

Scene 2

Time: Later the same evening.

Place: Henry Monmouth's house. The room is sparsely furnished, but the few furnishings visible indicate that Monmouth is a man of means. Monmouth and Poyntz have just finished dinner and are sitting back to relax.

Poyntz: *(Leaning back in his chair)* Ah, Henry, you serve a meal fit for a king.

Monmouth: *(Drily)* Oh no, my friend; should the king come here he would get no more than porridge.

Poyntz: And I say it would be more than he'd deserve.

Monmouth: I agree. *(Pointedly)* But there are many who do not. And it might be well if you kept our opinions somewhat private.

Poyntz: Ah—what I said in the streets this morning. I knew you'd get around to that. *(Good-naturedly)* But, Monmouth, I tell you now I'll only tolerate your scathing if you put some fire into it! I grow so weary of polite English scoldings.

Monmouth: *(Patiently)* Fire is precisely what I had in mind. And if I am to burn, I prefer it be for something I have said, not you.

Poyntz: Come, Henry, not even an English king would burn you for this loud Dutchman's antics.

Monmouth: Maybe not for your antics, but quite possibly for knowing of your illegal cargo.

Poyntz: Luther's books you mean?

Monmouth: Aye.

Poyntz: *(Emphatically)* In truth, I tell you that it does my heart good to bring them here. And I am certain that it did your heart good to read the one I gave you. Luther is a good man—much like you—but not so polite.

Monmouth: That's what worries me. It is the good men who are condemned.

Poyntz: *(Irascibly)* Only in England. And I have come to the conclusion it is because of that strutting peacock Wolsey—Ah! he is a fool!

Monmouth:	(*Amused*) By the way, I saw that you were unable to escape before the Cardinal's herald announced the coming of the hat.
Poyntz:	Bah!
Monmouth:	You should have stayed by me. I met an interesting man.
Poyntz:	A whole man—or just his hat?
Monmouth:	A whole man, I believe.
Poyntz:	(*Growing interested*) What sort of man? A merchant?
Monmouth:	You might say that of him. He wants to trade a most unusual ware.
Poyntz:	Aye? And what is that?
Monmouth:	His English translation of the Scriptures. He has come to London to ask Bishop Tunstall for permission to translate the Bible into English.
Poyntz:	(*Enthusiastically*) You indeed met a whole man today, Henry. But Bishop Tunstall—he'll have none of this man's translation!
Monmouth:	I think as much, Thomas. So I told the man— William Tyndale was his name—that he may come to me if he should find himself in need of aid.

Poyntz:	Splendid! If you stick with me, I shall cure you of your "cautious" English ways.
Monmouth:	Or better, I shall teach you how to be a cautious Dutchman in England.
Poyntz:	We shall compromise! And I guarantee you that we shall see the Master Tyndale before long. For Tunstall is but a button on the Cardinal Wolsey's cap!

Poyntz rises. Getting carried away with himself, he takes the stance of a court jester and proceeds to mimic the Cardinal's herald.

	Come, come, all ye pompous—I mean, pious monks—come view the dainty relic!
Monmouth:	*(Laughing uproariously)* At least they had only to carry the hat about the street and not the Cardinal.
Poyntz:	*(Staggering under Wolsey's hefty weight)* Dear sir, we seek to humble our monks, not kill them.

Tyndale is led in by a Servant. Poyntz, still play-acting, does not see them enter and staggers into Tyndale nearly knocking him over.

Poyntz: My man, I am sorry! I was just—well—

Poyntz looks to Monmouth for help, but Monmouth, having just regained his own composure, leaves Poyntz to get himself out of the situation. It is the first time Poyntz appears at a loss for words. Tyndale graciously intercedes.

Tyndale: No harm done. I've been bumped and jostled all day long. I dare say I'm growing rather used to it.

Tyndale's response puts them all at ease. Poyntz resumes his jovial air.

Poyntz: Then London is the place for you.

Monmouth: Come. Come, Master Tyndale. I'm glad you're here! This is my friend Thomas Poyntz from Antwerp. I had just finished telling him of you, and believe it or not, I think you two have a great deal in common. But first tell me, have you eaten?

Tyndale: Well, to be honest, no.

Monmouth: I like an honest man. *(To his servant who has been clearing the table)* Go and bring in a plate.

Servant exits as the three men sit down to converse.

Poyntz: Well, Master Tyndale, Henry tells me you are here to see the Bishop.

Tyndale: I am indeed. And I have just received a letter granting me an interview.

Poyntz: *(Irritably)* An interview with that—

Monmouth: *(Cutting Thomas off)* That is excellent.

Poyntz: *(Taking Henry's cue, he tries to control himself)* Uh, yes— yes, and what are you proposing to the Bishop?

Tyndale: An English Bible.

Poyntz: *(Forgetting himself again)* I tell you straight out that is—

Monmouth: *(Glaring at Thomas)* Excellent!

Poyntz: *(Sighing)* Yes, most excellent.

A servant enters and places a plate before Tyndale. Monmouth gives Poyntz a final glare. Tyndale is amused but politely ignores the friends' nonverbal repartee.

CURTAIN

Scene 3

Time: Three days later
Place: Tunstall's residence is lavish, almost to the point of flamboyance. When Tyndale enters, he is polite but purposeful. Tunstall's manner is reserved, at times even stiff.

Tyndale: My lord Tunstall.

Tunstall: Master—

Tyndale: Tyndale. William Tyndale.

Tunstall: *(Moves away from Tyndale)* Ah, yes.

Tyndale: As you know, my lord, I have come concerning a most urgent matter—

Tunstall turns. His expression reveals his irritation, for Tyndale has plunged into his speech before the bishop has invited him to do so.

(Politely) I am sorry. But—I assumed a man of your importance would have little time and would want me to come quickly to my point.

Tyndale genuflects, then rises to wait for permission to proceed.

Tunstall: You assumed—*(pause)* correctly. Proceed.

Tyndale: Sir, I feel called by Almighty God into translation work—

Tunstall: If, Master Tyndale, you are called by God, I should think that would suffice. Why do you come to me?

Tyndale: *(Unabashed)* Indeed his call is sufficient. *(Taking a document from his robe)* But there is the matter of this Oxford document. I know that it is only a formality, but it is stated here that I must be in the service of a bishop if I am to translate the Scripture.

Tunstall: The Scripture? *(Going to his desk, he picks up the copy of Isocrates which Tyndale delivered with the letter of introduction.)* But this you sent me is not the Scripture.

Tyndale: Oh, no—that is only to assure you that I am able—

Tunstall: *(Cutting him off)* Master Tyndale, I am a bishop—

Tyndale: And thus concerned for the people.

Tunstall:	*(Ignoring the interruption)* And I am interested in scholarship—
Tyndale:	*(Enthusiastically)* I knew that too. I did not hesitate to come to you. I was certain that you would be reasonable—more reasonable than those silly monks in the surrounding towns who hide themselves in rich men's chapels.
Tunstall:	Silly monks?
Tyndale:	I beg your pardon if that seems harsh, but it is true! There are some, my lord, who wear religious garb but know nothing of the Scripture. And when you present it to them plainly, they rage and call you heretic.
Tunstall:	Indeed?
Tyndale:	Quite so. I even sat at table with one of late who became so overwrought that he declared that the Pope's word was above the Word of God!
Tunstall:	And what did you reply?
Tyndale:	*(Slightly embarrassed)* Though my words were hot, my head was clear. And I assert to you, though in a kindlier tone, what I said to him: the people need the Scripture. That is why I seek position in your house.
Tunstall:	*(Drily)* My house is full.
Tyndale:	*(A bit stunned)* But a bit of bread and a place to work is all that I require, and I would not ask even that if I did not need your permission to begin.
Tunstall:	You have my permission to translate—
Tyndale:	*(Relieved)* Then I ask no more.
Tunstall:	But not the Scripture.
Tyndale:	But—
Tunstall:	*(Raising his hand to silence him)* At least not now. I am certain that a man of your abilities shall have no difficulty finding a post in London. And who knows—there may come a time in the future when the climate is more seasonable for your endeavor.

Tyndale: *(Coldly)* I have never marked the seasons when I have heard the word of God.

Tunstall hands the copy of Isocrates to Tyndale, but Tyndale does not take the book. Instead, he bows stiffly and turns to go.

Tunstall: Master Tyndale—

Tyndale stops.

I am your religious superior, am I not?

Tyndale: *(Stiffly)* You are.

Tunstall: And as you said, I am to care for the people.

Tyndale: I have so said.

Tunstall: Then take some kindly advice from me. Mark the times. Seek to woo rather than war with your superiors. Seek to learn before you propose to teach. And above all, take time to see the value of your pearls before you cast them to the swine. Good day.

Tyndale stands for a moment to look hard at Tunstall. Then, without a word, he exits. Tunstall muses a moment and then speaks to his Servant.

Tunstall: Send me the new man.

Servant: Yes, my lord.

A servant exits. Tunstall paces thoughtfully until the servant re-enters with Richard Tisen. Tisen enters, admiring the plush surroundings.

Tisen: My lord, I have never seen such a fine display of taste—fine yet discreet.

Tunstall: Do not weary me, Tisen. My time is valuable.

Tisen: I am sorry, sir.

Tunstall: You know this scholar William Tyndale.

Tisen: *(Fearfully)* I have met him only once. I am not of his—

Tunstall: You need not squirm. I merely have an errand for you.

Tisen: Anything, my lord, for your grace.

Tunstall: Or for money.

Tisen: Sir, I am always at the service of the Holy Mother Church. If I can assist in apprehending this heretic—

Tunstall: You call Tyndale heretic? That is a bold accusation.

Tisen: He is a bold heretic.

Tunstall: *(Interested)* What proof have you?

Tisen: I have heard his conversation. He has scorned our monks.

Tunstall: *(Disappointed at the lack of evidence)* There are those who deserve scorn.

Tisen: But he has scoffed at the great Cardinal Wolsey.

Tunstall: And so have many others.

Tisen: He has even defied church doctrine.

Tunstall: What know you of church doctrine?

Tisen: *(Tisen retreats a little)* I have studied, sir—

Tunstall: Indeed? Then may I ask why you did not apprehend this heretic yourself? Why did you not take him in hand, bring him before me, and in your bold and learned way refute his arguments!

Tisen:	*(Stepping even farther back)* I—I did not think to do so, my lord.
Tunstall:	*(Seating himself, replies wearily)* No—I would not imagine that you would.
Tisen:	But I am only—
Tunstall:	Put your feeble mind at rest. I have seen the Master Tyndale and I have discovered that he is zealous. A zealous man is never prudent. Inevitably he WILL be ensnared. He is even now headed for the net. But I need more evidence. That is why I sent for you. Follow him. But mark me; do not let him know that he is watched.

CURTAIN

Scene 4

Time: Two months later
Place: In streets of London. Monmouth paces anxiously. Poyntz enters and approaches Monmouth.

Poyntz:	My ship is ready to sail. Where is William?
Monmouth:	I sent my servant for him.
Poyntz:	Have you told him of the danger?
Monmouth:	There was no time. But I have gathered his books and his few belongings. When he arrives, we have only to persuade him to go with you. Where is Phillips? Was he not to meet you here?
Poyntz:	He was. But that is nothing. What he swears to one day he discards the next. I'll not wait for him. It is too important that I get William away from here. And that book I gave you—Henry, where is it?
Monmouth:	*(Reaching in his cloak)* Here.
Poyntz:	Give it to me. It is no longer safe for you to have any such books.
Monmouth:	And it is for you?
Poyntz:	Once I am at sea—Ah, here they come.

Tyndale and the servant enter.

Tyndale:	Henry, what is it? What's happened?
Monmouth:	It is good you have come so quickly.
Poyntz:	We have heard rumors in the streets.
Tyndale:	That is common.
Poyntz:	These rumors pertain to you.
Tyndale:	That too is becoming common. My sermons—
Monmouth:	It is your translation work.
Poyntz:	You are in grave danger. You must sail with me now.
Tyndale:	Gentlemen, gentlemen, this is my home. I write an English Bible—
Poyntz:	But it cannot be done in England.
Monmouth:	William, you are a learned and good man, but many are not as you. Tunstall is—
Tyndale:	Tunstall is politically cautious, but he will eventually yield to his conscience.
Poyntz:	He has no conscience.
Monmouth:	Many clergymen are serpents in religious garb— for in such costume they may cloak their craftiness.
Tyndale:	I have dealt with crafty priests before.
Poyntz:	None with a sting like Tunstall's.
Monmouth:	He is an opportunist, and I assure you he waits to strike when it will serve his purpose.
Tyndale:	Then he may never strike at all.
Monmouth:	He is already coiled.
Poyntz:	The whole of London is a den of vipers. My crew has been threatened. One man has been accosted—

Phillips enters.

	I sail immediately, Phillips.
Monmouth:	*(Urgently)* William, for your life—for the work that is your life—go to Germany.

A crowd is heard in the background. Several voices are crying out, "Burn the books!" "Burn the heretics!"

Poyntz:	*(Alarmed)* What is that?

Phillips:	It is the mob that follows Tunstall. He comes to speak.
Poyntz:	Come. We have no more time.
Monmouth:	*(Handing money to Tyndale)* Take this—for printing expenses.
Tyndale:	This is too generous, Henry.

Tyndale and Monmouth exchange a warm, but brief farewell.

Poyntz:	Henry, I'll be back. Be careful.

Tyndale, Poyntz, and Phillips exit just as Tunstall and his followers appear on stage. They bring with them a cart laden with books. Tunstall steps up on a raised platform to speak. He and several others in the crowd carry torches and books.

Tunstall:	There are certain sons of iniquity in this city who distribute Lutheran books in great number. They are trying to infect the land with heresy.

The bishop's speech is here and throughout punctuated with cries of affirmation of his words and condemnation of the "heretics."

The Catholic faith may perish utterly unless good
men rise up and meet the danger. Luther is a child
of the devil, full of detestable heresies. He
ventures to resist the Pope and overturn the
teachings of the Church! Some of his followers
are even in this city! They preach heresy in the
very pulpits of our churches.

*Monmouth, who has been on the fringes of the crowd, grows outraged as
Tunstall speaks. Despite his cautious nature, he cannot contain himself, and
he moves forward.*

Monmouth: Listen! Take hold of yourselves, good people.

Tunstall: *(Going on, but glaring at Monmouth)* Go forward
then to this holy work; and win for yourself an
immortal name.

*Tunstall throws the book he is holding onto the cart and puts his torch to
the heap of books. The crowd surges forward to follow his example.
Monmouth tries one last time to stem the growing frenzy.*

Monmouth: Wait! How can—

Tunstall: *(Calling to his guards)* Arrest that man!

Two men move forward, seize Monmouth, and drag him off.

Tunstall: *(To the crowd)* I give you license to defend the
faith!

Tisen enters and calls over the crowd to Tunstall.

Tisen: Your grace! Bishop Tunstall!

*Tunstall quickly moves forward. He does not want those in the street to see
Tisen addressing him. He takes him aside.*

Tunstall: *(Angrily)* What do you want?

Tisen: *(Apprehensively)* The scholar—he is gone.

Tunstall: Well?

Tisen: On a ship, your grace. I have lost him.

Tunstall: But I have not.

Tisen: Sir?

Tunstall: You did not think I would leave so great a matter
in your hands only? Fool! Find another ship and
follow him.

Tisen exits. Tunstall turns back to the crowd and smiles.

CURTAIN

ACT II

Scene 1

Time: Autumn, 1525
Place: Cologne, Germany. Tyndale, Poyntz, Phillips, and Printer are in the back room of the printing shop. The room serves as a study for Tyndale. Poyntz is packing copies of Tyndale's New Testament in barrels. Tyndale is reading from the Old Testament manuscript which he is working on. Printer listens attentively while Phillips lounges about; he too is listening— but with a cynic's air.

Tyndale: And when they saw him afar off before he came at them, they took council against him, for to slay him, and said to one another, Behold this dreamer cometh, come now and let us slay him and cast him into some pit, and let us say that some wicked beast hath devoured him, and let us see what his dreams will come to.

Phillips: And you, William, what will your dreams come to? You may want to reconsider—for you as well may be slain and cast into some pit.
(Nonchalantly) I hardly think it worth the price.

Poyntz: *(Angrily to Phillips)* If you do not believe in our work, why do you stay here?

Phillips: *(Scornfully)* You asked me to look after William, did you not? If I did not distract him from time to time, he would never leave the study. You don't want the scholar to starve, do you?

Tyndale: Friends, please—please. More and more you are at each other's throats. Come, I am grateful to you both for making my work easier. *(Good-naturedly)* But now I must finish the Old Testament, and I cannot if you insist on making my study a meeting place for quarrelers.

Poyntz sheepishly leafs through the Testament he holds. Phillips turns away. Poyntz tries to change the course of conversation to a more edifying topic.

Poyntz: This is a splendid translation, William. I am honored to carry it on my ship.

Tyndale: You will sell them as cheaply as you can, will you not?

Poyntz: I will. Although the English people are willing to pay any price. Some have offered me whole wagonloads of goods just to read one of these books for a few hours.

√Printer: But if you sell the books too cheaply, we will not be able to print more.

Poyntz: You cannot put a price on such words as these: *(Reading)* "Ye shall be brought up before rulers and kings for my sake, for a testimonial unto them. And the gospel must first be published among all nations." *(He stops reading)* There are two printing errors here.

Tyndale: There are many such errors, I fear, Thomas.

√Printer: Mein Herr, it could not be helped.

Tyndale: Friend, I meant no blame to you or your men. No one else could have printed so much at night—and every moment expecting King Henry's men to throw open the door with torches to burn you out. In truth I did not think they would follow me across the sea to gain their vengeance.

Phillips: Still, the errors trouble you, do they not?

Tyndale: God deserves the best.

Poyntz: God understands your heart, William. He knows too that your king seeks your life and forces you to flee from city to city. God sees these precious books—and counts it your best.

Tyndale: Perhaps. Yet, I would wish to send flawless copies of God's Word to England.

Poyntz: God's Word will not come back to Him empty—you have so said. Have faith.

Tyndale: Perhaps when these are sold, we can print better copies.

√Printer: Not without more money.

Poyntz: I am the merchant—I will deal with the money.

Tyndale: But, Thomas, please do not take any more money from Monmouth, no matter how he urges it on you. His generosity to me is the only charge Tunstall has been able to bring against him. You have said that alone keeps him in the tower.

Poyntz: True. But how did Tunstall know of our private transactions? *(Glaring at Phillips)* I mean to know. But until I do—you, William, translate; you, *(To printer)* sir, keep the presses inked and—

Tyndale: And we will leave the provision for this work to the Almighty.

Phillips: We may not need to—*(Catching himself)* or rather, the Almighty may have already interceded on your behalf.

Tyndale: How so?

Phillips: It seems King Henry now has a quarrel with Rome.

Tyndale: I have never known a monarch who has not at some time quarreled with Rome—pride breeds contention.

Phillips: Ah, but this quarrel touches upon the male heir to the throne.

Poyntz: What heir?

Phillips: Precisely the point. Since he has no heir, Henry would rid himself of good Queen Catherine by divorce.

Tyndale: Then his quarrel is with a higher power than the potentate of Rome.

Phillips: That may be. Nevertheless, rumor says that he is soon to wed Anne Boleyn.

Tyndale: But this has nothing to do with my work.

Phillips: Ah, but it does, for you see the king proposes to establish his own church. To please the clergy his new church will adhere to the doctrines of Rome. To please dissenters as well, however, he speaks of publishing an English Bible. It is a compromise.

Poyntz: Spoken like a true Englishman!

Tyndale: *(To Phillips)* And you believe this?

Phillips: Kings change, and when they do, laws change also.

Poyntz: And change and change and change.

Phillips: Come Poyntz—admit it. You simply do not want William to return to his home!

Poyntz:	Exactly! I will never trust the life of my friend to the whims of the English court!
Tyndale:	*(Sternly)* Let us back to work, gentlemen, and leave the whisperings of court for a more profitable labor.

CURTAIN

Scene 2

Time: 1531

Place: Back room of printer's shop one week later. Tyndale is seated at his desk when the door of the shop bursts open. Phillips enters, trying to shake an angry shopkeeper from him. Both are raging. Phillips is obviously drunk.

Phillips:	Off! Hands off, I say, you scab!
Shopkeeper:	Not until I have my money!
Tyndale:	Here, here, what is the meaning of this?
Shopkeeper:	This dog burst into my shop, took my vintage, and did not pay!

Phillips throws the drinking mug across the room at the man. It crashes on the wall above his head.

Phillips:	Such vintage is not worth pay!
Tyndale:	*(Grabbing Phillips sternly)* Get hold of yourself, man.

Phillips makes a mock bow and drawing a flask from his cloak, goes off to the corner to drink. Tyndale picks up several coins from his desk and approaches the shopkeeper.

Is that enough?

Shopkeeper: Quite enough, sir. *(Starting to leave, then turning back)* If you don't mind my saying, I'd look for better company.

Shopkeeper exits. Tyndale turns to Phillips.

Tyndale: *(Stern but not condemning)* You are drunk.

Phillips: Drunk? Yes, I believe I am.

Tyndale: John, I do not understand you. When Thomas is away, you are the only friend I have in this strange country. It grieves me to watch you slowly kill yourself with dissolute living.

Phillips: *(Pulling out his dagger)* Would this be more efficient?

Tyndale: *(Taking the knife from him, he guides Phillips to a chair and sits him down.)* I will get you something decent to drink.

Phillips has spent his rage and now sullenly sits waiting for Tyndale to bring him something to drink.

Phillips: Tell me, how do you sit in this hole—this dungeon—day after day and work without reward?

Tyndale: *(Handing him a mug)* I do not work without reward. And what you call a dungeon I call a comfortable study.

Phillips: *(Dryly)* Of course. *(Despondently)* When I look at something it looks sordid, filthy—but you, whatever you cast your gaze upon becomes pleasant.

Tyndale: That is because you see only with this world's eyes, John.

Phillips: There is no other world! *(Scornfully)* Does my bold speech startle you? *(Losing heart again)* You say I am drunk. That is so— but even when I am drunk, I am certain, certain that this about us is all there is. *(Growing desperate)* We are trapped, trapped in this cage of human flesh and there is no escape, William. And though we hang upon the bars and cry until we can cry no longer, there is no man to free us.

Phillips sinks down weary and despairing. Tyndale, much moved by the man, pauses as if searching for the right thing to say. He at last turns to the only source of comfort he is sure of and taking his Testament from his desk, goes to kneel by Phillips.

Tyndale: You pity yourself too much. I too have felt the torments of your prison. So has every man who would be honest with himself. But Christ has freed me and He would free you as well if you but believe the Scripture. *(Opening the Testament)* It is here—here, John. Let One who loves you more than I shed light into your prison.

Phillips instinctively draws back. Though he cannot deny the sincerity and warmth of Tyndale's kindness, he cannot trust it. He is a man who has lived too long among the selfish and the cruel. He rises and tries to resume his habitual air of nonchalance.

Phillips: One day, perhaps—one day. *(Pausing, he remembers the shopkeeper.)* By the way, thank you for the loan.

Tyndale: I want to help you.

Phillips: Yes, I know. *(Hesitantly)* And your generous nature is at times the greatest burden I have to bear.

The printer enters with Stephen Vaughn. Phillips, relieved with the interruption, moves to the corner, picks up his flask, and again begins to drink.

Printer: *(Apprehensively)* Mein Herr—an Englishman—

Tyndale: I am expecting a visitor.

Printer bows and exits.

(To Vaughn) Good day, Sir.

Vaughn: Master Tyndale?

Tyndale: I am he. This is John Phillips.

Phillips gives an indifferent nod from his corner.

Vaughn: Good afternoon. I am Stephen Vaughn, emissary for his majesty King Henry VIII. Thank you for seeing me.

Tyndale: Sit down, Master Vaughn. I confess I had reservations, but as an Englishman, and a loyal one, I could not refuse you.

Vaughn: I come peaceably, sir, I assure you.

Tyndale: What does the king want of me?

Vaughn: His Majesty desires to have you home.

Tyndale: *(Stunned)* Why?

Phillips becomes interested.

Vaughn: He has read what you have to say about the practice of the prelates. Your wit and logic fit you well to be a court scholar.

Phillips: *(Laughing disdainfully)* I cannot see William at court.

Tyndale: Because of my writings you say? But I have done nothing but castigate the king's favorites. I have called Tunstall a horseleech; I said Wolsey was a vile wolf. And the Pope, I declared, was an antichrist. I am invited back to England on these merits?

Vaughn: Oh, he cares nothing for your railings. He cares only for the advantage your wit will lend his new religious controversy.

Tyndale: I see. But Master Vaughn, surely you would agree that even if the king and I had some of the same religious enemies, it would not necessarily mean that we were on the same side.

Vaughn: You should find the king's religion comfortable, Master Tyndale.

Phillips: Only if it is poorly furnished, like this study.

Tyndale: John, your wine speaks where you would not.

Vaughn: *(Ignoring the interruption)* Sir, you could ably defend the king's new church with your keen pen.

Tyndale: I have no time for political games.

Vaughn: It is no game. The king is in earnest.

Tyndale:	Then what says he of my translating? Has he consented to the publication of an English Bible for the people?
Vaughn:	Not at present.
Tyndale:	Then he would change only the head of the church—not the heart. There is no more to say.
Vaughn:	But there is. Be reasonable, man. Writing for the king is profitable. I am empowered to offer you a large sum of money and a fine home.
Phillips:	You waste your time.
Vaughn:	*(To Tyndale)* Surely a man of your intelligence can see the advantages of living under a king's protection. A fugitive's life is no life at all, is it?
Tyndale:	By my translation of the Scriptures I have transgressed his desires even before I enter his protection. Where's the logic, sir?
Vaughn:	Yet but one more reason. I have good evidence that your life is endangered here—
Tyndale:	I thank you for the news.
Phillips:	His life means nothing to him. But threaten his Bibles.
Vaughn:	They are past threats.
Tyndale:	What do you mean?
Vaughn:	All the English New Testaments were burned this fortnight past in front of St. Dunstan's.
Tyndale:	All of them?
Vaughn:	As I understand. Bishop Tunstall ordered it.
Tyndale:	How could Tunstall get all the Bibles?
Phillips:	He must have had knowledgeable help.
Tyndale:	Silence oft preserves a drunken man, Phillips.
Phillips:	It had to be Poyntz. You know I speak the truth. Who but the merchant?
Tyndale:	*(Desperate)* Be still, man!
Vaughn:	It was a merchant, sir, who sold the books.
Tyndale:	It is no matter how it was done. It is done.
Vaughn:	Reconsider my offer. I will be three days in this city. Send word if you will leave with me.
Tyndale:	I cannot as I have said.

Vaughn:	Will nothing move you?
Tyndale:	Not to England.
Vaughn:	As you say. I am done.
Tyndale:	Good day, Master Vaughn.

Scene 3

Time: Two days later. Evening.
Place: Tyndale and Phillips are at the docks waiting Poyntz's return. Both have their belongings with them.

Phillips:	Are you sure Poyntz is on that ship?
Tyndale:	His letter said he would be here tonight.
Phillips:	But the letter made no mention of the burning of the books?
Tyndale:	You know that it did not.
Phillips:	Poyntz is a sly devil.
Tyndale:	You will not accuse him without proof.
Phillips:	But if he is responsible—how can you blindly consent to sail with him to Antwerp until you know?
Tyndale:	When I have given my trust to a man, I do not withdraw it until there can be no doubt he has betrayed me.

Phillips turns from him furiously.

	Call me a fool, John—but I would do the same for you.

Poyntz enters.

Poyntz:	*(Enthusiastically)* William, my good man, I hope you are as well as I.
Tyndale:	I am well.
Poyntz:	Then God be praised.
Tyndale:	*(Eagerly)* What of the books we sent to England?
Poyntz:	They were sold.
Phillips:	*(Mocking)* Did you get the price you wanted?
Poyntz:	I did—*(Glaring at Phillips)* and more.
Phillips:	So we have heard.

Tyndale:	What we have heard, Thomas, is that the Bibles have been burned.
Poyntz:	That is so.
Tyndale:	Then why did you not tell me? What happened? How could all those Bibles be lost?
Poyntz:	*(Decisively)* I sold them to Tunstall's men.
Tyndale:	*(Bewildered)* You what?
Poyntz:	Tunstall's men were everywhere when I arrived. They were determined to confiscate the Bibles and would have killed to get them. It would have been the people who suffered—suffered after they had sold all they had to possess the Scripture.
Phillips:	*(To Tyndale)* You wanted proof?
Tyndale:	*(Becoming increasingly agitated)* Burned the Scripture—burned the Word of God! And you— you, Thomas. I trusted you.
Poyntz:	*(Sternly)* You do me wrong, William. Did you not say we needed money for a better printing? *(Taking out several bags of money, he gives them to Tyndale)* Then I say let Tunstall and his men pay for it!
Tyndale:	*(Beginning to understand)* You mean—this is—
Poyntz:	The money the good bishop Tunstall paid me for the Bibles with the printing errors—take it, William. Take it and print more and better copies of God's Word!
Tyndale:	It is as the Scriptures say—"Even the wrath of men shall praise him." Good friend, I owe you an apology.
Poyntz:	*(Good naturedly)* I should say. *(He begins gathering up Tyndale's belongings.)*
Tyndale:	*(Helping Poyntz gather things)* You are sly as a fox.
Poyntz:	*(Glancing back at Phillips)* Some would say as a serpent.

Poyntz and Tyndale move toward the ship.
Phillips gathers his things and follows reluctantly.

CURTAIN

ACT III

Scene 1

Time: 1534. Early afternoon.
Place: Antwerp. Poyntz's home. Mistress Poyntz is doing needlework.
Poyntz is standing beside her. They are engaged in earnest conversation.

Mistress: Will not the English king soon need William's translation of the Bible? From what the merchants in this house say, the English people clamor for the king to show his church is different from the Pope's.

Poyntz: My good wife, you are too logical and practical to be a king.

Mistress: How so?

Poyntz: Henry Tudor will indeed soon be forced to appease his subjects. But some of those subjects are Catholic—and if he takes Tyndale's Bible, he'll be called a Lutheran. He must, of course, try to please all the people—so the path he chooses will be more indirect.

Mistress: All this for a new wife, Mistress Anne Boleyn. *(Pause)* Perhaps the Bibles could be published without William's name attached to them.

Poyntz: *(Toying with the idea)* There is a sympathetic noble at Henry's court who knows a man named Coverdale. It may be possible to get the Bible printed under his name—

Tyndale enters. Poyntz and his wife drop their conversation.

Mistress: You are back early today.

Tyndale: I came back early to meet John Phillips.

Mistress: I do not mean to pry, William, but you know that Thomas has grown to distrust that man greatly— and I have grown over these many years to trust my husband.

Tyndale: Thomas has shared his opinions with me. But a man like John—well, it is such men who need our help most.

A servant enters with Phillips.

Mistress:	*(Getting up)* You will excuse me then. The day wanes and I am behind it.
Tyndale:	Of course, of course.
Phillips:	*(To Mistress Poyntz)* I am sorry to intrude upon your household, but it seems that this is where my friend is held captive.
Mistress:	This is a merchant's house, not a prison, sir. Any who do not like it here are free to leave.

Mistress Poyntz exits.

Phillips:	*(To Tyndale, laughing)* Poyntz in a gown, wouldn't you say? *(To Poyntz)* I've come to take Master Tyndale to supper.
Poyntz:	*(Pointedly)* Supper is served here. *(Reluctantly)* You are welcome to join us.
Phillips:	You are kind, but the conversation I have with our scholar here is of a rather personal nature.
Tyndale:	It is important to you then?
Phillips:	It is.
Tyndale:	Very well.

Tyndale exits with Phillips. Once outside Phillips seems uneasy.

Phillips:	About the money you lent me. I cannot repay it just now.
Tyndale:	No matter. Is something else troubling you?
Phillips:	No. I—I have many concerns.
Tyndale:	Can I help you?
Phillips:	You have done more than—no—it is nothing. Let's go to dinner.

Phillips steps back and lets Tyndale go before him. As Tyndale moves ahead, Phillips motions to two men who emerge from a darkened passageway and seize Tyndale.

Tyndale:	What! What is this?

Tyndale struggles to free himself. He manages to turn toward Phillips.

Phillips—go to Thomas—

The two men seem to wait for Phillips. He hesitates.

(Pleading) John?

There is a brief moment—a moment in which Tyndale realizes that Phillips has betrayed him and in which we see Phillips struggle with himself as he stands before Tyndale's gaze. Then Phillips turns and quickly motions them away. Alone, Phillips begins to feel the weight of his deed, but when Tisen enters he is nearly frantic.

Phillips: Where have you been, Tisen? Spending my money? I am not a man to be kept waiting!

Tisen: Just a man to be kept.

Phillips: I earn my money. I work for governors and kings—

Tisen: *(Scornfully)* Kings? Petty clergymen, rather.

Phillips: *(Raging)* What I do for Tunstall is none of your affair! You are nothing but a paltry messenger— or have you forgotten that I am the one they choose to enter the houses?—you they hide in alleys. As for the scholar, you had as much to do with that as I.

Tisen: *(Piously)* At least I had religious reasons for wanting him stopped.

Phillips: *(Clasping him by the throat)* You swine. Don't speak to me of religion. You want favor. *(Threatening)* Now give me my money and we'll both have what we want.

Tisen: *(Breaking away from Phillips)* I do not have the money.

Phillips: Where is it?

Tisen: There is no money.

Phillips: What do you mean? What have you done with it?

Tisen: I never had it.

Phillips: *(Slowly moving toward Tisen)* Don't give me riddles, man. What are you saying?

Tisen: Tunstall will not risk the king's disfavor.

Phillips: What?

Tisen: With Henry's religious controversy every bishop fears for his position—even for his life. Tunstall has decided that he wants no connections which the king may one day question.

Lunging at Tisen, Phillips holds his dagger to his throat.

Phillips: You lie! Give it here!

Tisen: *(Struggling)* Kill me as well, Phillips—but there's no profit in it. We are done.

Phillips: *(Throwing Tisen to the ground)* Wolsey! Wolsey will pay!

Tisen gets to his feet and cautiously holds his hand on his sword.

Tisen: No. The Cardinal also languishes in the king's disfavor.

Phillips: *(Sinking against the wall)* I cannot bear this.

Tisen: *(Glancing furtively about)* Get up—someone may pass. There are other kings and governors, are there not?

Phillips is beside himself. He does not even seem to remember Tisen exists. Tisen begins to realize Phillips' condition.

Phillips: *(Desperately)* The only man who was ever kind. Oh God, oh God!

Phillips buries his head in his hands.
Tisen begins to unsheathe his sword as if he would kill Phillips, but then merely looks on him in disgust.

Tisen: I doubt He hears you.

Looking about quickly, Tisen sees no one and flees.

CURTAIN.

Scene 2

Time: 1535. Winter.
Place: Prison in Antwerp. The jailer enters. Tyndale is seated. His health has obviously deteriorated. He is thin and frail because of his confinement. The jailer hands Tyndale a letter.

Jailer: It is from Master Poyntz.

Tyndale opens the letter and begins to read.
   (Hopefully) Your friend—he yet seeks your release?

Tyndale: God be praised!

Jailer: Then you are free?

Tyndale:	Far better, Peter. My manuscripts are already in the printer's hands.
Jailer:	*(Nonplussed)* King Henry consents to publish your Bible?
Tyndale:	He has no notion that it is mine. It is to be published under another's name—a man named Coverdale.
Jailer:	But it is not his!
Tyndale:	But the influence is—Henry favors him at court and Coverdale has convinced the king that his position as head of the English church rests on his willingness to give the Scripture to the people. *(Continuing to read)* And Henry, my dear friend Henry Monmouth, has been freed from the tower!
Jailer:	But what of you? If something is not done soon, you shall be burned at the stake.
Tyndale:	Peter—look at me. If the politicians do not kill me, the coming winter will.
Jailer:	*(Shamed)* Sir, I have tried to provide for your needs. I have sent for warmer clothes—
Tyndale:	Ah, Peter. I did not mean to grieve you, only to assure you I am not loathe to die. There is, however, one small favor I ask of you.
Jailer:	Anything.
Tyndale:	When I have finished the letter I will write—get it to Thomas.
Jailer:	It is done.

Jailer exits. As Tyndale begins to write, the lights go down, and we hear his voice on audio.

Tyndale: *(Voice over)* Dear Friends, I write to you with a lighter heart than I have had for months. The news of the publication of the Scripture was as water to my thirsty soul. As Paul, I believe that "the time of my departure is at hand. I am ready to be offered"—yea willing. "I have fought a good fight, I have finished my course, I have kept the faith and there is laid up for me a crown of righteousness which the Lord, the righteous judge, shall give me in that day. And not to me only. . . ."

The lights come up, but remain dim, on scene at Monmouth's home. Poyntz and Monmouth are in place, silhouetted, ready to begin the Epilogue.

EPILOGUE

Time: 1536
Place: Monmouth's house. Monmouth and Poyntz are reading Tyndale's letter. Poyntz takes up reading where Tyndale's voice has stopped.
Lights up full.

Poyntz: "But to all those who love his appearing." My dearest friends, do not mourn. The wrath of men has brought praise to God.

Thomas sits down as if despairing.

Monmouth: Come, Thomas, if we mourn, it is only for ourselves. The church has claimed another martyr, but heaven has gained a saint. Let us up and be about the work that God has given us. William would have it so.

Music cue begins.

For I do not doubt that he will ask us when we see him again—"Does every plough boy know the Scripture?"

The lights go down on Monmouth's house and come up again on Tyndale at the stake. The curtain comes down slowly as the music finishes.

END

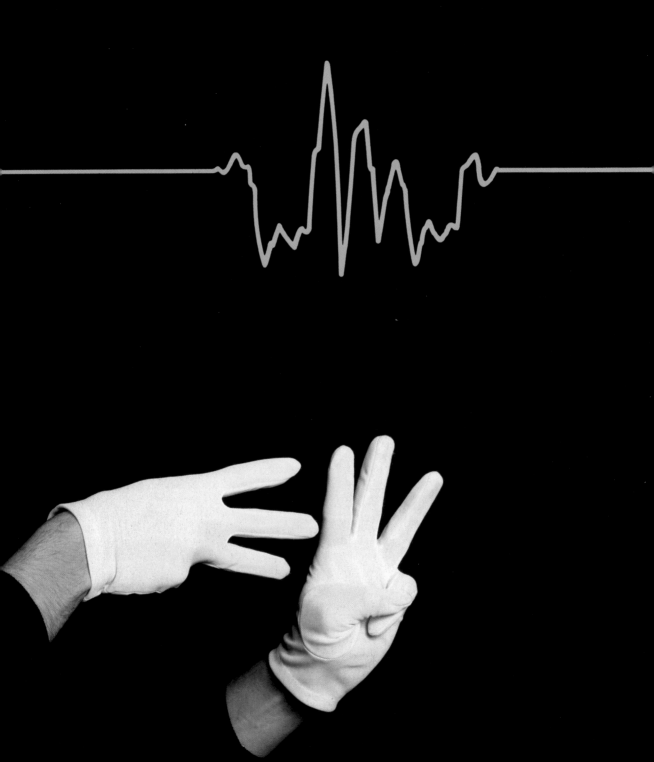

DAN BOONE
Profession: Television producer/director
Professional Experience: all phases of video production
Hobbies: Railroading

kind of influence the program will have. SHOW MY PEOPLE is dedicated to presenting the gospel of Christ through the medium of television. Those who watch the program hear God's Word. We have an opportunity to reach those who would never go to church, and as long as we fulfill our responsibility of keeping our message true to God's Word, our influence will be pleasing to Him.

Interviewer: How do you feel that you have been able to glorify God and edify others?

Dan Boone: In this particular ministry we have the opportunity of taking an idea based on Scripture and weaving together a program that brings glory to the Lord. The type of music and speech we use is God-honoring, and those who perform these selections are dedicated Christians. Our make-up and wardrobe also reflect good Christian standards. And, of course, the message on each program is Christ-centered. We're also able to present Bible principles through discussion of topics in interviews and panels. Every aspect of the program is geared toward lifting Christ up and thus meeting people's needs. We get about fifteen hundred pieces of mail each month from about twenty television stations. When you read what the viewers write, you can get a good idea of the spiritual blessings and results these programs have in the people's lives. Last month we had over two hundred people referred to local churches for spiritual follow-up. So you can see that our television ministry is having as much of a spiritual impact on people as a door-to-door visitation program would. Maybe more.

Interviewer: What specific opportunities exist in this field for Christians?

Dan Boone: A few years ago I would have said very little, but with the advent of cable TV and home video the opportunities are broadening. There are a lot of good churches that have broadcast ministries. Consequently, there are now many

Interviewer: Why did you enter this field?

Dan Boone: Actually I started my studies in radio. But during my senior year of college the SHOW MY PEOPLE television program began, and I volunteered to help. Initially I worked on the make-up and grip crew. At that time we were using an outside production company. In January of 1977, I was hired full-time for the postitions of production manager and cameraman. In the second year SHOW MY PEOPLE bought its own television equipment. I was production manager and editor, and the third year I became director. It's not as if I planned my course. I was simply willing to work in any facet of the ministry where I was needed, and the Lord opened the doors.

Interviewer: What would you say to someone who thinks that there is no ministry in this field for a Christian?

Dan Boone: Television is not inherently evil. It is like radio and film work. It is true that the content of much of what is on TV is evil, but the viewer controls what he will watch. Television can have no evil influence whatever on a person who refuses to watch those programs whose content is sinful. It is the same in television production. Those who produce the programs determine what

more opportunities for service for those trained in media.

Interviewer: Are there any opportunities that do not exist that you would like to see Christians explore?

Dan Boone: There are a couple of areas I think Christians need to be more involved in. One is the production of children's programs. There has been very little done in this area. This may be because there is very little money in it. Christian talk shows are very popular because they get a lot of donations. Other types of religious programs can also rely on audience donations, but children don't have any money. So if you do a children's program, you are doing it as a ministry in the truest sense of the word. There is also a need for good Christian music. People who are musically talented might consider working with a good TV ministry. We need high-quality musicians. Almost everything you hear on television is contemporary gospel-type music played with a bass guitar in the background. The producers of these religious programs do that because they think that is all the audience want to hear. We don't believe that is true. Consequently, there is a great need for musicians with high musical standards to get into the video and radio field.

Interviewer: What one warning would you give someone who wanted to work with the media?

Dan Boone: I would warn him about getting involved in trends. Of course, you want to keep abreast of new ideas and techniques in the field, but you must also be careful about maintaining a basic philosophy. When a trend comes along, examine it and ask yourself, "Is this something we are able to use without sacrificing the message we are trying to convey?" Let me illustrate what I mean. There are some TV directors who visualize their musical numbers as if they were turning the pages of a book. For example, someone may begin singing the first verse of a song in one location; then during the second verse he will totally change locations. Or on one line of a song they may have people grouped one way and on the second line have them grouped totally differently. They may even have the singers in one costume for one verse and another for a second verse. To me, this type of directing removes the audience from reality. There is no logical progression from one location or set to another. I feel that it is an existential approach. The director has drawn peo-

ple from the real world but directed the scene in in such a way that it is beyond reality. In reality, you don't change locations in the middle of your solo. Consequently, I couldn't use this type of approach in my directing. If I have people go from one place to another, I show them walking from one location to the next. I don't simply shoot them in one setting and then cut to another setting. If the audience can see them going from one set to another, it is not confusing; it is logical, real, concrete. If you are trying to illustrate a particular thing in a song, you may want to do something nonreal, nontime. If you do, be sure to fill your audience in on what you are doing. For example, I did a prayer-type song, and on the interludes I wanted to use different choir people who were either praying or in a prayerful mood in a natural outdoor setting. What I did on the interludes was to take that scene and to put a circle around it, a soft white, vignetted circle so that it was more of a dream or a nonreal sequence. I didn't simply "pop" someone out of the choir into a walking-along frame and then back into the choir after the interlude. By doing that, I was saying, "Folks, this is not real. We're illustrating the song here, giving you a mental picture." Never sacrifice your message to a new technique. The message is what's important.

One other trend that is particularly prevalent is the trend to use contemporary music. Many Christian ministries who are very orthodox in their preaching will be "trendy" in their music. The music simply doesn't match the message. A night club or soft rock sound is not Christ-honoring. It is worldly. Why try to preach Christ with the world's music? You can have fresh, moving, well-recorded, technically competent music that will support your message rather than pull against it. You should not settle for anything less. Never lose sight of your goal—to honor Christ. Keeping Him before you will help you avoid pitfalls not only in the type of programming you produce but also in the way you produce it.

Chapter 17

Understanding the Media

"Radio and television are the most powerful forces in the world today for affecting the minds and emotions of humankind."

—Robert Hilliard, Writing for Television and Radio

The decade of the 1980s has been called "The Age of Information." Computer technology, satellite distribution, and other space-age developments are rapidly reshaping the way we conduct business, collect data, and receive information. At the heart of the media culture are radio and television industries.

HISTORY

Radio

Few Americans were initially aware of the developments in radio transmission in the early 1900s. In the 1920s, however, KDKA (Pittsburgh, Pennsylvania) set up the first official radio

station in the country. The novelty of listening to "free" music, news, and entertainment programs at home stirred public interest. Soon a number of independently-owned and operated radio stations signed on the air. Several radio networks were formed in the late 1920s to improve the quality and reduce the costs of live programming, producing a variety of original radio drama and family entertainment programs. Though in 1921 there were only five AM radio stations in operation (FM was not added until later), by the 1930s there were 618 stations on the air.

In the 1950s television emerged and began to dominate programming and advertising. By the late 1950s radio stations were struggling to survive. Radio manufacturers stepped up the productions of transistor radios and car radios. In the 1960s the American public discovered take-anywhere, play-anytime radio. Advertising revenues jumped from thirty-five million dollars in 1960 to eight billion dollars by the end of the decade.

To hold their audiences, radio stations developed new programming in the 1970s. Some stations took on "all talk" formats which gave news and information. Other stations devoted their schedules to religious programs or educational material, while others played various types of music most of the broadcasting day. Unfortunately, many radio stations also began to adopt rock formats to attract younger audiences.

In the 1980s came the "Era of Deregulation." The Federal Communications Commission relaxed the rules of the radio industry, giving the broadcasters more freedom in operating their stations. For example, the 18-minute-per-hour limit on commercial spot announcements was lifted. Also, the operator licensing system was modified to allow virtually any American citizen over fourteen years of age to qualify to operate a broadcast station.

Although many of the formal rules and regulations are changing, the Federal Communications Commission still stands firmly behind its original philosophy: the airwaves belong to the *public,* not to radio station owners or to the broadcasters themselves, and the needs and interest of the public must be served. But *how* those needs and interests are served is being increasingly left to the broadcasters to decide.

Television

In 1928 the RCA company received the first experimental TV license, and later that same year the General Electric Company used its own station (WGX) to broadcast the first live drama. Despite these advances, however, the development of television was slow at first. Few people could afford to buy televisions, and the programming was far inferior to that on the radio. However, at the 1939 World's Fair, President Franklin Delano Roosevelt made a special TV appearance. National interest in television revived.

Since the 1930s, television has made remarkable advances.

The commercial TV industry was given official approval on July 1, 1941 by the National Television System Committee and the Federal Communications Committee. Much of the early programming was adapted directly from network radio programs like "The Lone Ranger." By the late 1940s television was growing rapidly. Color television was first aired in 1954, and in 1956 videotape improved the quality of program production, reduced the cost of programming, and virtually eliminated all live performances. TV westerns, situation comedies, dramas, crime and detective shows, variety programs, news and sports broadcasts began to develop. By 1960 TV had become a billion dollar industry.

During the 1960s individuals and organizations began to analyze the effects of television. Critical observers noted that TV, more than just a pastime, also had the power *to inform and to persuade.* In the 1970s when TV began to deal with current social issues such as drug abuse, nuclear disaster, and the disintegration of the family, government and private critics alike became convinced that television could alter the thinking and lifestyle of its viewers.

Knowing the intent of television programming, what is our Christian responsibility? We must first realize that unstructured, unregulated TV viewing can be destructive. In other words, television should not be our *primary* pastime. Nor should we fail to evaluate those programs we do select. We should judge a drama, comedy, or variety show as we would any story or play we read. What is its moral tone? Are the heroes and heroines noble? Does the action encourage us to desire virtue and reject vice? Is good rewarded and evil punished? Is wisdom honored and foolishness scorned? Does the theme of the show conflict with Scriptural principles? Evil is evil and good is good—whether it is in a book or on the TV.

We also need to evaluate those programs geared to inform or to persuade. Documentaries and special features such as National Geographic specials are informative programs. Commercials and editorials are persuasive. News broadcasts can fall into either category; although presented as informative, they often employ persuasive techniques. Remember our formula for ethical persuasion?

ARGUMENTATION + MOTIVATION = PERSUASION

Not all programs persuade ethically. Some use propaganda devices. To help you recognize when you are being led unethically to a conclusion, study the following information.

PROPAGANDA DEVICES

1. **Name Calling:** This device uses negative words or phrases to get you to condemn a person or idea on the basis of the word used rather than on evidence. For example, to call someone a *fanatic* without specific facts to support the charge would be name calling.

2. **Transfer:** This device is the opposite of name calling. It tries to transfer, or carry-over, the respect we have for a person or idea to the subject being presented. For example, politicians often stand in front of the flag while giving a speech, hoping that this symbol will help the audience accept them as patriotic.

3. **Testimonial:** This device uses recommendations from famous people to promote a person, product, or idea. Commercials especially use this device. For example, sports heroes promote soft drinks although they are no more qualified to judge the "superiority" of the product than any viewer.

4. **Plain Folks:** This device plays on a person's sense of community. People who use this device are trying to show that they are just common people. For example, Jimmy Carter campaigned as a "hometown boy."

5. **Band Wagon:** This device plays on the listener's desire to be accepted. Phrases like "Don't be left out" or "Everyone's going to Danvey's restaurant" make the listener feel that he will be an "outsider" if he doesn't comply.

6. **Card Stacking:** This device uses all forms of deception— lies, distorted evidence, and misrepresentation. For example, a pollster might say, "Well over half of the people surveyed bought Brand X," when, in fact, the exact figure was 51%.

PERFORMANCE

Many of the skills of public speaking also serve in effective radio and television speaking. A radio announcer must have good breath support, clear diction, and the ability to "ad lib" on many subjects. A TV announcer must be able to control his facial expression, use good eye contact, and gesture smoothly. However, the presence of a microphone or a camera between the announcer and his audience requires a few additional skills.

Radio performance

- Keep your voice at a moderate level. The proper distance to work from a radio microphone is three to six inches.
- Use a calm, conversational tone as you speak.
- Maintain a one-to-one relationship with each listener.
- Avoid making strong plosive sounds, especially the consonants *k* and *p* , into the microphone. Instead of popping these sounds directly into the microphone, direct their force across the front of the microphone.
- When reading from a radio script, avoid tilting your head down toward the table or counter. Hold your script to one side so that you can look up and and speak directly into the microphone.
- Regulate your rate or speed of delivery. Timing in both radio and television is very important and you must pace yourself to each speaking assignment.

Television Performance

- Unless you are performing before a studio audience, think of the camera lens as the person to whom you're speaking. When you're talking before a studio audience, the camera serves more as an "eavesdropper" to the conversation.

- Be careful not to stare at the camera lens.
- Avoid dramatic facial expressions.
- Make all hand movement purposeful, smooth, and a little slower than in real life.
- When sitting down for the performance, keep your spine straight and lean slightly forward in your chair. This technique helps you appear alert and poised.
- Block and rehearse any major movement to be used during performance.
- When working with props or small objects, make sure the camera can get a clear view of them. Hold the object steady and when possible rest it against your body or on a solid surface.
- When using cue cards, concentrate on moving your eyes *down* the script rather than from left to right.

Work Out

• Keep in mind these radio and television principles, and try performing the following spots.

SFX:	1 FOUR CHIMES FROM
	2 GRANDFATHER'S CLOCK
SFX:	3 AN INTERIOR DOOR OPENS
	4 (SLIGHTLY OFF MIC)
JAMES:	5 (ENGLISH BUTLER—OFF MIC)
	6 Madam, tea is served.
LADY I:	7 (BRITISH ARISTOCRAT) Oh, thank
	8 you James. Please serve in here.
LADY II:	9 Lady Shrewsbury, I envy you. A good
	10 butler is so hard to come by.
LADY I:	11 Indeed, Lady Hatfield. James is a
	12 jewel.
JAMES:	13 (FADE ON) Your tea, madam.
SFX:	14 TRAY OF TEA SET DOWN
Ladies I & II:	15 (GASP HORRIFIED)

LADY I:	16 (SHOCKED) James, what is that?
JAMES:	17 Why madam, it is Plipton's Instant
	18 Iced Tea.
LADY II:	19 (AGHAST) It most likely comes from
	20 those dreadful Colonies!
LADY I:	21 James, what is the meaning of this?
	22 We always have English hot tea!
JAMES:	23 Madam, it is time for a change!
LADY I:	24 A change?
JAMES:	25 Yes, m'lady. Plipton's Instant Iced Tea
	26 is extremely quick and easy to make.
	27 All one has to do is add sugar to taste.
LADY I:	28 Really?
JAMES:	29 And do you know, Lady Hatfield, that
	30 Plipton's Instant Iced Tea has a dash
	31 of real lemon flavor?
LADY II:	32 Why, no.
JAMES:	33 Then try it. You will be convinced
	34 after one taste!
LADY I:	35 (TENTATIVELY) Well...(PAUSE TO
	36 TASTE)...Why, it is
	37 delicious...absolutely marvelous! Try
	38 it, Lady Hatfield.
LADY II:	39 (TASTING) Hmmm...Yes, superb!
	40 James, you have done it again!
JAMES:	41 Plipton's Instant Iced Tea deserves
	42 your praise.
LADY I:	43 And it comes from the Colonies?
JAMES:	44 Yes, madam.
LADY I:	45 Extraordinary!

SFX:	1 WIND BLOWING SOFTLY
ANNCR:	2 Once upon a time, not so long ago, a
	3 dusty, parched desert town was held
	4 prisoner by a dastardly group of
	5 villains called—the Thirsties!

SFX:	6	WICKED LAUGHTER (UP AND
	7	UNDER)
ANNCR:	8	Then one day a stranger came to town.
SFX:	9	FADE ON SLOW DELIBERATE
	10	FOOTSTEPS (CONTINUE
	11	THROUGH LINE 12)
ANNCR:	12	The stranger had come to town armed
	13	to kill the Thirsties. His holsters were
	14	bulging with the weapon that had
	15	caused the Thirsties for miles around
	16	to fear for their lives—Sprazzle Soda!
SFX:	17	WICKED THIRSTIES GASP IN
	18	TERROR
SFX:	19	CAN POPPING OPEN
STRANGER:	20	Take that, you wretched Thirsty!
SFX:	21	SCREAM & DIE AWAY
SFX:	22	ANOTHER CAN POPS OPEN
STRANGER:	23	And that!
SFX:	24	ANOTHER SCREAM & DIE AWAY
SFX:	25	ANOTHER CAN POPS OPEN
STRANGER:	26	And that! Sprazzle will get you!
SFX:	27	SEVERAL CANS POP OPEN IN
	28	SUCCESSION
SFX:	29	FADING CHORUS OF SCREAMS
ANNCR:	30	And that was the end of the Thirsties,
	31	my friends. No Thirsty can survive
	32	where Sprazzle Soda is.
MUSIC:	33	SHORT FAST TAG

VIDEO	1	AUDIO
MUSIC/SFX:	2	GENERAL CAFE NOISES (BG
	3	MOOD MUSIC, PEOPLE,
	4	TALKING, CLATTER OF DISHES
	5	& UTENSILS)

	6	(BILL IS EATING A SANDWICH &
	7	SOME SOUP AS HE LOOKS OVER
	8	SOME REPORTS. HIS ATTACHE
	9	CASE IS OPEN ON THE TABLE
	10	WITH A CAN OF TKS IN IT. HE
ANNCR:	11	SPILLS SOUP ON HIS TIE.) Oh
	12	no!—not again! . . .(WIPES TIE
	13	WITH NAPKIN) It never fails . . . just
	14	the time you need to look your best—
	15	soup on the tie. What to do? No sweat
	16	. . . (TAKE CAN OF TKS OUT OF
	17	ATTACHE CASE 7 HOLD IT
	18	TOWARD CAMERA) just whip out
	19	the old TKS Spray Spot Lifter. I never
	20	go anywhere without it. It's as simple
	21	as this. (DEMONSTRATE AS COPY
	22	SUGGESTS) Take off the top . . .
	23	spray a little on the spot . . . let it sit
	24	for a few minutes so that the powerful
	25	cleaning ingredients in TKS begin
	26	lifting the dirt from the material to the
	27	surface. . . . Oh, by the way, my
	28	name's Bill Davis. I'm a corporation
	29	product exhibitor—that means
	30	meeting with all the top advertising
	31	execs in all the big cities. You can see
	32	why I can't afford dirty spots. TKS
	33	should have done its work by now. . . .
	34	(DEMONSTRATE AS COPY
	35	INDICATES) Just brush off the white
	36	residue . . . there! As you see, TKS
	37	really works, and no fuss, no bother. .
	38	. . (LOOKS AT WATCH) And there's
	39	still time to finish lunch before my
	40	next appointment. When you get a
	41	dirty spot . . . use TKS . . . it really
	42	works!

Chapter 18

Inside
the Station

The listeners' imagination is the stage of radio.
—Edgar E. Willis, Writing Television and
Radio Programs

The following is a radio station tour written in radio script form. Our special thanks to WMUU of Greenville, South Carolina, for providing the information for the script and the personnel for the photographs.

(Remember that no two radio stations are run exactly alike; this station's procedures will, however, help you understand some of the terms and activities of a radio station.)

SFX:	1	FADE IN SOUNDS OF CLASS
	2	EXCHANGE—SHUFFLING
	3	FOOTSTEPS, LAUGHING,
	4	TALKING.
	5	CLASS BELL RINGS; NOISE
	6	UNDER.
TEACHER:	7	O.K. Let's have it quiet. We've got a
	8	lot to cover today.
SFX:	9	NOISE GRADUALLY DWINDLES
	10	OUT.
TEACHER:	11	Now, first—how many of you out
	12	there have cars? Why? Well, because
	13	I'd like to take you to the radio station
	14	on the edge of town today for class.
	15	O.K. hands up— one, two—what?
	16	Uh—no, Edgar, I didn't think about
	17	extra gas money.
SFX:	18	MURMURING UP AND UNDER.
TEACHER:	19	You say you have a better idea?
	20	What's that?
SFX:	21	MURMURING STOPS.
TEACHER:	22	Use imagination?
SFX:	23	GENERAL AGREEMENT UP AND
	24	OUT.
TEACHER:	25	Well, I agree imagining yourself on a
	26	radio tour conserves energy and saves
	27	gas money but it's just not like being
	28	there so—forget it, Edgar. Now, let's
	29	go.
SFX:	30	LIGHT TRANSITIONAL MUSIC
	31	UP AND UNDER.
	32	STATION MANAGER'S VOICE
	33	FADES IN. MUSIC OUT.
STATION MANAGER:	34	Welcome—welcome to your favorite
	35	radio station YNOT—where all news
	36	is good news and the sounds you hear
	37	are actually music. Come right this
	38	way. There are many people I want
	39	you to meet—

SFX: ___ _ _ _	40 DOOR OPENS. SHUFFLING OF
	41 FEET UP AND UNDER AS DOOR
	42 CLOSES. GENERAL OFFICE
	43 SOUNDS FADE IN. ANOTHER
	44 DOOR OPENS. OFFICE SOUNDS
	45 FADE AS THIS DOOR CLOSES.
	46 SHUFFLING DIES OUT.
STATION	47 Ah, here we are the in **music library,**
MANAGER:	48 and this is our musicologist.

49 Her primary duty is to produce—**sweeps**
50 (QUICKLY CONTINUING) I know, I
51 know, you want to know what a sweep
52 is, right? In radio lingo a sweep is a
53 quarter hour segment of music.
54 Actually, it is eleven to thirteen
55 minutes in length—that leaves us a
56 little time for announcements,

57 advertisements, and other such things.
58 Each sweep might be thought of as a
59 little program in itself. The principle of
60 production we use is called the
61 **matched flow technique.** Operating on
62 this concept, a musicologist matches
63 each song with the song that comes
64 before it and the song that comes after
65 it. He tries to produce a wave or flow
66 from high to low and back up again
67 throughout the sweep. Oh yes, one
68 other job of our musicologist is
69 **formatting** each day's program. You
70 see, a radio day must be divided into
71 different sections. For example, our
72 morning music needs to be up tempo.
73 I'm sure you'd agree that "Seventy-Six
74 Trombones" gets you out of bed and
75 to your alarm faster than "Clair de
76 Lune" would. Excuse me, miss?
77 Everybody but Edgar, you say? Who's
78 Edgar? The fellow leaning on the door
79 jamb? Yes, well. Back to our music.
80 Later in the day we let you relax a
81 little, and then we close the day with
82 more up tempo music— but not as up
83 tempo as what we got you out of bed
84 with. I suppose you could say that the
85 day's program is formatted into a wave
86 pattern, just like the smaller sweeps.
87 After sweeping and formatting, our
88 musicologist **researches** information
89 used in biographical sketches and
90 historical backdrops for the pieces
91 used on the air—particularly for the
92 major works like the operas and
93 symphonies. AND when that is
94 finished he works on **cataloguing** the
95 materials kept in the music library.
96 AND when that is done he plans the

	97	station's program guide. Which means,
	98	by the way, that daily programming
	99	must be formatted a couple of months
	100	in advance and though—pardon?
	101	You've made up your mind not to be a
	102	musicologist? Really, Edgar, the job is
	103	very interesting and with computers
	104	some of the tasks have been simplified.
	105	(SLIGHT NERVOUS LAUGH)
	106	However, maybe we'd better move on
	107	before you get the wrong impression.
	108	This way please.
SFX:	109	DOOR OPENS. SHUFFLING OF
	110	FEET UP AND UNDER AS DOOR
	111	CLOSES. GENERAL OFFICE
	112	SOUNDS FADE IN. ANOTHER
	113	DOOR OPENS. OFFICE SOUNDS
	114	FADE AS THIS DOOR CLOSES.
	115	SHUFFLING DIES OUT.
STATION	116	This is the room we use for **on-the-air**
MANAGER:	117	**call-in or interview programs.** Here
	118	our **announcers** have to be at their
	119	best.
	120	Their research ability, general
	121	knowledge, communication skills, and
	122	ability to think quickly and logically
	123	are all put to the test. What? You don't
	124	think you want be an announcer
	125	either? But, Edgar, we just got here.
	126	Let me tell you a bit more. When you
	127	see how exciting it can be, you may
	128	change your mind. Now, how well a
	129	program of this sort flows and how
	130	much excitement it generates depend
	131	almost entirely on the announcer. I
	132	will confess that at times it can be a bit
	133	complicated, but most people like a
	134	challenge. What? How much of a
	135	challenge? Well, for example, an
	136	announcer may have to coordinate a

137 conversation between himself, two
138 people being interviewed, and someone
139 calling in on the phone. The challenge
140 is carrying on a conversation with
141 someone on the phone and someone in
142 the room and making it all sound
143 natural and conversational. Pardon?
144 (AGHAST) No, Edgar, we have never
145 had an announcer rip the phone off
146 the wall during an interview! You must
147 remember that training helps. Besides,
148 these programs have two safeguards.
149 The first is a **dump button;** all call-in
150 shows have a dump button. If the
151 caller's remarks are inappropriate, the
152 announcer can push this button and
153 cut off—dump— the intruder.
154 Stations—pardon? That's happened to
155 you before. Uh, that's unfortunate,
156 yes. Mmm-hm. Well, as I was saying,
157 stations can also use a **delay**

	158	**mechanism.** This device plays the
	159	program at a slower-than-life pace.
	160	This is not discernible by the listening
	161	audience; it may only be a five or ten
	162	second delay. Then when a caller is
	163	dumped, the tape automatically
	164	catches up to the live broadcast—again
	165	the listener can't discern the change—
	166	and the announcer makes an
	167	appropriate comment about why the
	168	caller was sent to "never-never land"
	169	and the program goes on. Meanwhile,
	170	the delay device begins to stretch out
	171	the program again. So, you see things
	172	aren't as uncontrollable as they first
	173	appeared. (PAUSE) You still haven't
	174	changed your mind? Ah, well—let's go
	175	next door to the studio with the
	176	operating board.
SFX: _ _ _	177	DOOR OPENS. SHUFFLING OF
	178	FEET UP AND UNDER AS DOOR
	179	CLOSES. GENERAL OFFICE
	180	SOUNDS FADE IN. ANOTHER
	181	DOOR OPENS. OFFICE SOUNDS
	182	FADE AS THIS DOOR CLOSES.
	183	SHUFFLING DIES OUT.
STATION MANAGER:	184	Maybe you'll find something to
	185	interest you here. Our **operating board**
	186	is used to make **master tapes** of the
	187	music stored in the music library.
	188	These tapes are an hour long and are
	189	for use here or for syndication to other
	190	stations. You could say that this is the
	191	room where the programs are
	192	mechanically produced. But let me say
	193	one quick word about **soundproofing**
	194	before we look at the operating board
	195	and its special effects. Notice the heavy
	196	drapes, the hard surfaces, and the slant
	197	of the double-paned windows. All of

198 these things help keep out sounds that
199 might disrupt the taping sessions.

200 Now, back to the operating board.
201 This board has a variety of special
202 features. One of these wonderful
203 mechanical marvels is the **stereo**
204 **synthesizer.** When our operator wants
205 to make a mono record sound like
206 stereo on the tape, he uses this device
207 to perform his magic. **Impulse noise**
208 **reduction** is another special feature of
209 this operating board. Using this device,
210 the operator can mask the clicks, pops,
211 and scratches found on the record so
212 that they can't be heard on the tape.
213 After all, there's nothing more
214 enjoyable than listening to music with
215 the mellow sound of click, click, click
216 in the background, don't you agree?
217 Finally, if you'll turn around for a
218 moment, we have this little machine
219 here—the record cleaner. Removing
220 the dust and static electricity from the

221 records to be taped keeps this machine
222 off the unemployed list. All right,
223 group. If you'll follow me around the
224 corner here, we'll take a look at the
225 production control room—where we
226 make all the spots for the programs.
227 Oh, on your way you might want to
228 take a quick look at the **AP teletype**
229 machine in the closet—there to your
230 right. Yes, that's this hand here.
231 Anyway, from this machine we get any
232 special news bulletins that would need
233 to be read live on the air—say, a late
234 breaking story of some kind. Now let's
235 move on.

SFX: _ _ _ _ 236 DOOR OPENS. SHUFFLING OF
237 FEET UP AND UNDER AS DOOR
238 CLOSES. GENERAL OFFICE
239 SOUNDS FADE IN. ANOTHER
240 DOOR OPENS. OFFICE SOUNDS
241 FADE AS THIS DOOR CLOSES.
242 SHUFFLING DIES OUT.

STATION MANAGER:

243   Here we are. It's in this room that you
244   would find the key tool of the radio
245   industry—the **endless loop cartridge.**
246   Excuse me? No, Edgar it's not like the
247   latest ride at Six Flags. It's merely a
248   tape cartridge that you don't have to
249   rewind. It plays for a certain amount
250   of time—thirty seconds to ten or
251   fifteen minutes—and then it's back at
252   the beginning, ready to be played
253   again. Matching the cartridge to the
254   length of the spot or special program
255   becomes important. If the spot is to
256   last thirty seconds, you would tape the
257   program on a forty-second cartridge.
258   Then when the spot is over, it's ready
259   to be broadcast over again—
260   automatically. By the way, in radio
261   lingo **spots** are all those special
262   programs like advertisements, public
263   service announcements, or the
264   Scripture verse for the day. Some
265   might even label as a spot those short
266   programs—5 to 15 minutes—that
267   occur throughout the radio day. These
268   spots usually originate from outside
269   the station and are sent in on certain
270   days, probably a week's worth at a
271   time. They come into the station in a
272   variety of forms—records, reel-to-reel
273   tapes, cassettes, and so on. Question?
274   Yes, some of them are done by our
275   people live—so to speak. Either way,
276   everything must be put on these
277   cartridges. Yes? When do we tape
278   these spots? Good question, Edgar. I'm
279   surprised—I mean impressed. Anyway,
280   these spots are made during our
281   infamous night owl shift—11 p.m. to 7
282   a.m. Usually, the announcer completes

283 15 to 20 spots on a given night. Now,
284 perhaps the most important device on
285 this **mixing console** is the **equalizer**
286 which is used to tone down or mellow
287 the noises on a tape—to improve its
288 quality in other words. You can
289 imagine the differences in the quality
290 of the spots and programs we receive
291 here at the station. The equalizer
292 makes them all ready for broadcasting.
293 Let's go see the operating board in the
294 that next room—the one you can see
295 through the window there.

SFX: 296 DOOR OPENS. SHUFFLING OF
297 FEET UP AND UNDER AS DOOR
298 CLOSES. GENERAL OFFICE
299 SOUNDS FADE IN. ANOTHER
300 DOOR OPENS. OFFICE SOUNDS
301 FADE AS THIS DOOR CLOSES.
302 SHUFFLING DIES OUT.

STATION 303 This is the **on-air operating board,** and
MANAGER: 304 this lady is our announcer for this time
305 slot. Can you hear both stations
306 playing at once—our AM and FM
307 broadcasts? The AM broadcast is live
308 and the FM station is on **automation.**

309 As well as being the announcer for the
310 AM station, the person operating this
311 board has a variety of other
312 responsibilities. Periodically, she will
313 check the **transmitter** sites, the towers
314 located on nearby mountains that send
315 out the programs. It's hooked up to
316 the transmitters on the mountains. So,
317 by simply checking these she can tell
318 how the transmitter is doing. She must
319 also keep in touch by telephone with
320 the weather bureau and the stock
321 market for updates. She must make
322 sure that the meeting at the top of the
323 hour between the local station and the
324 network news goes smoothly. Now one
325 of the most important combinations in
326 the on-the-air studio is that fantastic
327 duo **the slow speed logger** and the
328 **silent sensor.** When the computer
329 malfunctions or the cartridges or tapes
330 fail and that deadly menace of silence
331 invades the studio—the silent sensor
332 knows. How does it react? It lets out a
333 loud whistle telling everyone within
334 hearing distance that something was
335 missed that should have been
336 broadcast. The computer then waits
337 for ten seconds and goes on to the next
338 scheduled program and keeps on going
339 until it finds something that will play.
340 The whistle also tells the announcer
341 that something has been missed. Of
342 course, if the announcer is in the
343 studio, she would notice the pause.
344 But, if she is out of the studio—say
345 changing a tape or making a spot in
346 the next studio—how will she know
347 what was missed? Ah, yes. The
348 incredible slow-speed logger to the

349 rescue. What does it do? What it's
350 supposed to do is record both stations
351 at slow speed. Thus, if there's a
352 problem, and the operator is out of the
353 room, she can just rewind the slow
354 speed logger a little way, play it back,
355 and see what was missed, using the
356 program log as a reference. Yes? Why
357 do we need to know what was missed?
358 Economics. We're a commercial
359 station, which means that most of
360 what we broadcast someone has paid
361 for. Consequently, if something is
362 missed, we have to find a way to get it
363 on the air before the day is over.
364 Anything else would be dishonest. An
365 unbeatable combination, the silent

366 sensor and the slow speed logger often
367 save the day—not to mention the
368 integrity of the station. Okay, let's
369 review. Do you remember what the

370 responsibilities of the announcer are?
371 Monitoring the FM broadcast. Right.
372 Serving as the announcer on the AM
373 station. Good. Making spots. That's
374 right, especially the the announcer on
375 the night-owl shift. Finding what was
376 missed using the slow speed logger.
377 Yes, and then putting the program or
378 spot back into the schedule as well.
379 Don't forget that. Anything else?
380 Updating the weather and and stock
381 market reports. Good. Checking the
382 transmitters. Uh-huh. Making sure the
383 meeting with the network for the news
384 is on time. Excellent. Just think, she
385 does all this while listening to two
386 radio stations at the same time. I
387 wonder what she does with all her
388 spare time? Pardon? Makes a lot of
389 static? Sure. Hmmm. Looks as if we
390 finally found a job for you,
391 Edgar.Okay let's move around back
392 here and I'll introduce you to **Otto** and

393 our engineer. The **engineer** is one of
394 those key, behind-the-scene
395 contributors to any radio station. His
396 role on our team is vital since he
397 makes sure that all the equipment is
398 working properly and efficiently. He
399 tests and repairs equipment both at the
400 station and at the transmitter sites. In
401 addition, he designs and builds any
402 new equipment the station has a need
403 for. His biggest responsibility is Otto—
404 the automation system that runs the
405 FM station. If something goes wrong
406 with this computer, things could really
407 go haywire. Perhaps the best way to
408 show you the many mechanical things
409 that could go wrong and require
410 maintenance would be to tell you some
411 of the devices found on Otto. First,
412 there are five tape decks—five reels—
413 of music. The computer operates these
414 reels and also switches from one tape
415 to the other depending on what type of
416 music is supposed to be on the air. If
417 Otto fails to activate a tape or
418 activates the wrong tape—confusion
419 reigns. Otto also has a **dead roll load** .
420 This tape contains pretimed musical
421 selections. These are used at times to
422 insure a proper meeting between the
423 station and the network news. For
424 example, if there are two minutes until
425 the news, then the announcer just
426 plays a one-minute-and-forty-five
427 second selection of music from the
428 dead roll, announces the news, and
429 makes the meeting with the network
430 right on time. If the dead roll load
431 fails, the announcer may find himself
432 humming two minutes of "Old

433 MacDonald Had a Farm." Of course,
434 there are also the **carousels** that hold
435 the endless loop cartridges and their
436 programs and ads—all of which must
437 be activated by Otto at precisely the
438 right time. Then there are tapes that
439 have certain announcers' voices on
440 them telling the time of day and other
441 such buffers. Certain announcers are
442 identified with certain times of day and
443 their voices are recorded giving the
444 time of day, et cetera, during those
445 time slots. Consequently, the
446 announcer you hear on the FM station
447 may not even be there. These tapes are
448 also run by the computer. Tapes that
449 record the news and other things that
450 come into the station from the outside
451 are also run by the computer, Otto. An
452 example? Well, the network news is
453 sent from Washington to our city via
454 satellite and then on to the station by
455 telephone. The computer, based on a
456 tone it hears, knows what type of
457 program is being called in and records

458 it automatically on the proper tape.
459 This is particularly important for the
460 news because we usually play the first
461 two and a half minutes of the hourly
462 news at the half-hour mark. Otto is
463 obviously a complex piece of
464 equipment. The tremendous
465 responsibility to keep it running
466 belongs to the engineer—and this is
467 just one piece of equipment.
468 Okay, let's go up to the main office
469 and then we'll be finished for the day.

SFX: 470 DOOR OPENS. SHUFFLING OF
471 FEET UP AND UNDER AS DOOR
472 CLOSES. GENERAL OFFICE
473 SOUNDS FADE IN. ANOTHER
474 DOOR OPENS. OFFICE SOUNDS
475 FADE AS THIS DOOR CLOSES.
476 SHUFFLING DIES OUT.

STATION 477 This computer used by my secretary
MANAGER: 478 prints the daily program logs, handles
479 correspondence and business needs—a
480 lot of things. Everywhere you turn in
481 the radio industry you find technology
482 evident. Yes? What are my

483 responsibilities? Well, as **station**
484 **manager** you could sum up my
485 responsibilities in one phrase: I'm
486 ultimately responsible for everything. I
487 hire and fire personnel, serve as a
488 public relations man at times, work
489 with advertisers, make programming
490 decisions, even design and record
491 programs and music myself.

492 Sometimes, you may even find me
493 conducting a tour of the radio station
494 to explain to students how a typical
495 station works. You never know. Well,
496 thanks again for coming, and I hope
497 the tour has been interesting,
498 informative and—yes, Edgar? You say
499 you found a place you think might be
500 for you? (PLEASED) Well, I'm glad.
501 Uh, where is that? The room in the
502 back? You mean the one with the
503 coffee pot and the soft blue sofa?
504 (DESPERATE) But, Edgar, that's the
505 lounge! (DESPONDENT) Well, yes, I
506 suppose there is a place in this station
507 for everyone.

Work Out

- Follow the format of the example above, and write a short radio commercial of your own.

Chapter 19

On the Set

Few educators, churchmen, or politicians possess the moral influence of a TV writer.
—Robert Hilliard
Writing for Radio and Television

Production Elements

Camera Shots

The cameraman selects what the viewer will see. He orients you to the setting with a *master shot.* He controls how many people you will see with a *one-shot* (one person), a *two-shot* (two people), a *three-shot* (three people), or a *group shot.* And he provides the perspective by varying the distance of the camera from the subject or setting. He may use a *long shot* (LS), *medium shot* (MS), *close up* (CU), or some variation on these. The chart below will help you see these shots in relationship to the human figure.

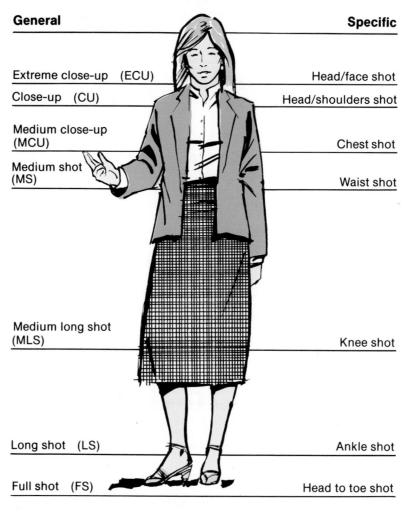

General		Specific
Extreme close-up (ECU)		Head/face shot
Close-up (CU)		Head/shoulders shot
Medium close-up (MCU)		Chest shot
Medium shot (MS)		Waist shot
Medium long shot (MLS)		Knee shot
Long shot (LS)		Ankle shot
Full shot (FS)		Head to toe shot

Camera Angles

Two basic camera angles establish point of view for the audience: *subjective* and *objective*. Subjective camera angle shows the action from the camera's (or audience's) point of view. For example, if you were viewing a roller coaster ride, a subjective angle would allow you to view it as a person in the roller coaster would. An objective angle keeps the audience "out of the scene." In this case you would be watching others ride the roller coaster.

Other angles are *high, low,* and *reverse.* In a high angle the camera looks down on its subject; in a low angle the camera looks up at the subject. In the reverse angle the camera shifts from one point of view to another. For example, if you were viewing a conversation between a man and a woman, you might first be looking over the woman's shoulder to the man. A reverse angle would cut to a view over the man's shoulder to the woman.

Camera Movements

Basic camera shots are often modified by the following specific camera movements:

- A *pan* is a smooth horizontal movement of the camera.
- A *tilt* is a smooth vertical movement of the camera.
- A *zoom,* by use of a special lens, moves toward or away from the subject.

Transitional Devices

Transitional devices replace one shot with another, thereby getting us from one action to another or from one scene to another. The following are the basic transitional devices:

- A *cut* is an immediate change from one action or scene to another.
- A *dissolve* is a momentary blending of two pictures giving a more gradual change from one action or scene to the next. This gradual change can help establish a passage of time or a close relationship between two scenes.
- A *fade* is the gradual appearance or disappearance of a picture.

Production Script

The rest of the chapter will show you how a script for a thirty-minute sacred musical program goes into production. Along the way you will find some general terms defined and will see some of the crew doing their jobs. Keep in mind that this discussion covers a specific program with a specific production company. Some techniques and terms will vary from company to company, but you can get an idea of how much it takes to put one show on the air.
(Our special thanks to the "Show My People" crew for this production script and the look behind the scenes.)

PAGE 1

1 FEATURE SPEAKER (:20)

2 TEASER FOR PANEL

3   DISSOLVE TO:

4 OPENING (1:00)

5 "I KNOW WHOM

6 I HAVE BELIEVED"

7   DISSOLVE TO:

8 MUSIC (4:15) ORCHESTRA

9 "I AM HIS AND HE IS MINE"

10 INTRODUCTION

11 Loved with everlasting love,

12 Led by grace that love to know;

13 Spirit, breathing from above,

14 Thou has taught me it is so!

15 Oh, this full and perfect peace!

16 Oh, this transport all divine!

17 In a love which cannot cease,

18 I am His, and He is mine.

19 In a love which cannot cease,

20 I am His, and He is mine.

21 Heav'n above is softer blue,

22 Earth around is sweeter green!

23 Something lives in every hue

24 Christless eyes have never seen:

25 Birds with gladder songs o'erflow

26 Flow'rs with deeper beauties shine,

27 Since I know, as now I know,

28 I am His, and He is mine.

1

2

4

8

CLOSE-UP

BACK OFF

BACK OFF

On the Set

1 Since I know, as now I know,

2 I am His and He is mine.

3 INTERLUDE

4 His forever, only His;

5 Who the Lord and me shall part?

6 Ah, with what a rest of bliss

7 Christ can fill the loving heart!

8 Heav'n and earth may fade and flee,

9 First-born light in gloom decline;

10 But while God and I shall be,

11 I am His, and He is mine.

12 But while God and I shall be,

13 I am His, and He is mine.

14   DISSOLVE TO:

15 FEATURE SPEAKER (7:30)

16 PANEL - PART I

17   DISSOLVE TO:

ANNCR (1:10)   18 Day after day, week after week, year

19 after year, running a house and raising

20 a family can seem so tedious and hard.

21 But you can break through the

22 drudgery by seeing the sunshine

23 sparkling on the soapsuds. In this well-

24 known series by Beneth Peters Jones,

25 wife of Dr. Bob Jones III, and one of

BACK OFF

15   16

ZOOM IN

18

PAGE 3

1 today's panelists, you'll see how God
2 can shine through the experiences of the
3 home. Smile, weep, rejoice with Mrs.
4 Jones as you together learn heart and
5 soul lessons that enrich and mature your
6 life. *More Sunshine On the Soapsuds*
7 can be yours free of charge. Simply write
8 for offer #91 to BJU, Box TV, Gville,
9 SC. Your eyes will be opened to God's
10 sunshine all around you, even on life's
11 darkest days. Write for *More Sunshine*
12 *on the Soapsuds.* Our address again is
13 BJU, Box TV, Gville, SC, 29614. Now
14 let's return to today's discussion.
15   DISSOLVE TO:
16 FEATURE SPEAKER (9:00)
17 PANEL - PART II
18 MENTION   GIFT   OFFER   AND
19 AUTHOR
20 INTRO. MALE QUARTET
21   DISSOLVE TO:
22 MUSIC (1:30)
23 "HOW CAN IT BE"
24 (MALE QUARTET)
25 O Savior as my eyes behold
26 The wonders of Thy might untold
27 The heavens in glorious light arrayed
28 The vast creation Thou hast made

  8  13

 17

  **ZOOM IN**

  18  22

1 And yet to think Thou lovest me

2 My heart cries out "How can it be?"

3 How can it be?

4 How can it be?

5 That God should love a soul like me

6 How can it be?

7 As at the cross I humbly bow

8 And gaze upon Thy thorn crowned

9 brow

10 And view the precious bleeding form

11 By cruel nails so bruised and torn

12 Knowing Thy suffering was for me

13 In grief I cry "How can it be?"

14 How can it be?

15 How can it be?

16 That God should love a soul like me

17 How can it be?

18   DISSOLVE TO:

ANNCR (:35) 19 If you'd like to study today's

20 discussion on the biblical role of

21 women or perhaps would like to share

22 it with a friend, copies are available

23 free of charge. Our address again is

24 BJU, Box TV, Gville, SC. 29614. We

25 leave you with Proverbs 31:30; "Favor

26 is deceitful, and beauty is vain: but a

ZOOM IN

BACK OFF   BACK OFF

19   24   ZOOM IN

PAGE 5

1 woman that feareth the Lord, she shall
2 be praised." This is David Yearick
3 saying goodbye from SMP.
4   DISSOLVE TO:
5 CLOSING (:30)
6 THEME AND CREDITS
7 GO TO BLACK
8 END

5

7

Production Personnel

Director

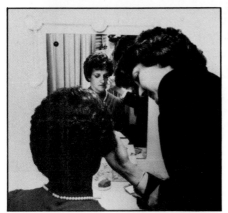

Production Coordinator

Music Director

Production Manager

Cameraman

Production Assistant

Audio/Video Technician

Work Out

• Use the radio commercial you wrote, and adapt it for television, using the format above as an example.

Appendix A

Germany's Claims

A speech delivered by Adolf Hitler February 20, 1938

Despite the really exemplary discipline, strength and restraint which National Socialists preserved in their revolution, we have seen that a certain portion of the foreign press inundated the new Reich with a virtual flood of lies and calumnies. It was a remarkable mixture of arrogance and deplorable ignorance which led them to act as the judges of people who should be presented as models to these democratic apostles.

The best proof for showing up these lies is success. For if we had acted during these five years like the democratic world citizens of Soviet Russia, that is, like those of the Jewish race, we would not have succeeded in making out of a Germany, which was in the deepest material collapse, a country of material order. For this very reason we claim the right to surround our work with that protection which renders it impossible for criminal elements or for the insane to disturb it.

Whoever disturbs this mission is the enemy of the people, whether he pursues his aim as a bolshevist democrat, a revolutionary terrorist or a reactionary dreamer. In such a time of necessity those who act in the name of God are not those who, citing Bible quotations, wander idly about the country and spend the day partly doing nothing and partly criticizing the work of others; but those whose prayers take the highest form of uniting man with his God, that is the form of work.

I had a right to turn against everyone who, instead of helping, thought his mission was to criticize our work. Foreign nations contributed nothing apart from this spirit, for their rejection was tinged by hate or a spirit of knowing better than we know.

It was the A B C of our creed to find help in our own strength. The standard of living of the nation is the outcome of its total production; in other words, the value of every wage and salary corresponds to the volume of goods produced as a result of the work performed. This is a very unpopular doctrine in a time resounding with cries such as "higher wages and less work."

Next to the United States, Germany today has become the greatest steel country in the world. I could give many more examples. They are documentary proof of the work such as our people never before achieved. To these successes will be added in a few years the gigantic results of the Four-Year Plan. Is it not a joke of history when those very countries which themselves have only crises think they can criticize us and give us advice?

We have given the German nation that weapon of steel which presents a wall at our frontiers against the intentions of the malicious international press campaign.

At the conclusion of the next decade the German people will bear in mind the success of their efficiency and will be filled with a supreme pride. One of these achievements is the construction of a national leadership which is far removed from parliamentary democracy as it is from military dictatorship.

If ever international agitation or poisoning of opinion should attempt to rupture the peace of the Reich, then steel and iron would take the German people and German homesteads under their protection. The world would then see, as quick as lightning, to what extent this Reich, people, party and these armed forces are fanatically inspired with one spirit, one will.

If Great Britain should suddenly dissolve today and England become dependent solely on her own territory, then the people there would, perhaps, have more understanding of the seriousness of the economic tasks which confront us. If a nation which commands no gold reserves, no foreign exchange—not because National Socialism reigns but because a parliamentary, democratic State was exploited for fifteen years by a world hungry after loot; in other words, if a nation which must feed 140 people to the square kilometer and has no colonies, if a nation which lacks numerous raw materials and is not willing to live an illusory life through credits, reduces the number of its unemployed in five years to nil and improves its standard of living, then all those should remain silent who, despite great economic advantages, scarcely succeed in solving their own unemployment problems.

The claim for German colonial possessions, therefore, will be voiced from year to year with increasing vigor. These possessions, which Germany did not take away from other countries and which today are practically of no value to these powers, are indispensable for our own people.

I should like to refute here the hope that such claims can be averted by granting credits. Above all, we do not wish for naive assurances that we shall be permitted to buy what we need. We reject such statements once and for all.

You will not expect me to discuss in detail the individual international plans which appear to arouse the varied interests of the various governments. They are too uncertain and they lack the clarity necessary for me to be able to express myself on these questions. Above all, however, take note of my deep-seated distrust of all so-called conferences which may provide interesting hours of conversation for those taking part in them, but generally lead to the disappointment of hopeful mankind.

I cannot allow our natural claims to be coupled with political business. Recently rumors have been cropping up, rumors that Germany was about to revise her opinion concerning her return to the League of Nations. I should like again to declare that in 1919 the peace treaty was forced upon some countries. This treaty brought in its train far-reaching inroads upon the lives of the peoples involved. The rape of national and economic destinies and of the communal lives of the nations took place under a cloud of moralizing phrases which, perhaps, tended to salve the uneasy conscience of those who instituted the affair.

After the revision of the map of the world and of territorial and racial spheres, which was as thorough as it was fundamental, had been effected by means of force, a League of Nations was founded whose task it was to crystallize these crazy, unreasonable proceedings and to coordinate its results into an everlasting and unalterable basis of life.

I notice very often that English politicians would be glad to give back to us our colonies if they were not so disturbed by the thought of the wrong and violence which would thus be done to the native inhabitants.

All those colonial empires have not come into being through plebiscites. They are today naturally integral parts of the States in question and form, as such, part of that world order which always has been designated to us, especially by democratic policies, as the "world order of right."

That right the League of Nations now has been ordered to protect. I cannot understand why a nation which itself has been robbed by force should join such illustrious company and I cannot permit the conclusion to be drawn that we should not be prepared to fight for the principles of justice just because we are not in the League of Nations. On the contrary, we do not belong to the League of Nations because we believe that it is not an institution of justice but an institution for defending the interests of Versailles.

A number of material considerations must, however, be added.

First, we left the League of Nations because—loyal to its origin and obligations—it refused us the right to equal armament and just as equal security.

Second, we will never re-enter it because we do not intend to allow ourselves to be used anywhere in the world by a majority vote of the League of Nations for the defense of an injustice.

Third, we believe we will please all those nations who are misled by misfortune to rely on and trust the League of Nations as a factor of genuine help. We should have regarded it as more correct, for instance, in the case of the Ethiopian war, for the League to have shown more understanding for vital Italian needs and less disposition to help the Ethiopians with promises. This would, perhaps, have enabled a more simple and reasonable solution for the whole problem.

Fourth, on no account will we allow the German nation to become entangled in conflicts in which the nation itself is not interested. We are not willing to stand up for the territorial or economic interests of others without the slightest benefits to Germans being visible. Moreover, we ourselves do not expect such support from others. Germany is determined to impose upon herself wise moderation in her interests and demands. But if German interests should be seriously at stake we shall not expect to receive support from the League of Nations but we shall assume the right from the beginning to shoulder our task ourselves.

Fifth, we do not intend to allow our attitude to be determined in the future by any international institution which, while excluding official recognition of indisputable facts, resembles less the acts of a man of considered judgment than the habits of a certain type of large bird [evidently the ostrich]. The interests of nations in so far as their existence or non-existence are ultimately concerned are stronger than formalistic considerations. For in the year 2038 it is possible that new States may have arisen or others disappeared without this new state of affairs having been registered at Geneva.

Germany will not take part in such unreasonable proceedings by being a member of the League of Nations.

With one country alone have we scorned to enter into relations. That State is Soviet Russia. We see in bolshevism more now than before the incarnation of human destructive forces. We do not blame the Russian people as such for this gruesome ideology of destruction. We know it is a small Jewish intellectual group which led a great nation into this position of madness. If this doctrine would confine itself territorially to Russia maybe one could put up with it. Alas, Jewish international bolshevism attempts to hollow out the nations of the world from its Soviet center.

As I have more than once stated Germany has in Europe no more territorial demands to make of France. With the return of the Saar we trust the period of Franco-German territorial differences is finally closed.

Germany also has no quarrel with England apart from her colonial wishes. However, there is no cause for any conceivable conflict. The only thing that has poisoned and thus injured the common life of these two countries is the utterly unendurable press campaign which in these two countries has existed under the motto "freedom of personal opinion."

The British Government desires the limitation of armaments or the prohibition of bombing. I myself proposed this some time ago. However, I also suggested at the time that the most important thing was to prevent the poisoning of the world's public opinion by infamous press articles. That which strengthened our sympathy with Italy, if this were possible, is the fact that in the country State policy and press policy tread the same road.

There are more than 10,000,000 Germans in States adjoining Germany which before 1866 were joined to the bulk of the German nation by a national link. Until 1918 they fought in the great war shoulder to shoulder with the German soldiers of the Reich. Against their own free will they were prevented by peace treaties from uniting with the Reich.

This was painful enough, but there must be no doubt about one thing: Political separation from the Reich may not lead to deprivation of rights, that is the general rights of racial self-determination which were solemnly promised to us in Wilson's fourteen points as a condition for the armistice. We cannot disregard it just because this is a case concerning Germans.

In the long run it is unbearable for a world power, conscious of herself, to know there are citizens at her side who are constantly being inflicted with severest sufferings for their sympathy or unity with the total nation, its faith and philosophy.

We well know there can scarcely be a frontier line in Europe which satisfies all. It should be all the more important to avoid the torture of national minorities in order not to add to the suffering of political separation, the suffering of persecution on account of their belonging to a certain people.

That it is possible to find ways leading to the lessening of tension has been proved. But he who tries to prevent by force such lessening of tension through creating an equilibrium in Europe will some day inevitably conjure up force among the nations themselves. It cannot be denied that Germany herself, as long as she was powerless and defenseless, was compelled to tolerate many of these continual persecutions of the German people on our frontier.

But just as England stands up for her interests all over the globe, present-day Germany will know how to guard its more restricted interests. To these interests of the German Reich belong also the protection of those German peoples who are not in a position to secure along our frontiers their political and philosophical freedom by their own efforts.

I may say that since the League of Nations has abandoned its continuous attempts at disturbance in Danzig and since the advent of the new commissioner this most dangerous place for European peace has entirely lost its menace.

Poland respects the national conditions in the Free City of Danzig and Germany respects Polish rights.

Now I turn to Austria. It is not only the same people but above all a long communal history and culture which bind together the Reich and Austria.

Difficulties which emerged in the carrying out of the agreement of July 11, 1936, made essential an attempt to remove misunderstandings and obstacles to final reconciliation. It is clear that whether we wished it or not an intolerable position might have developed that would have contained the seeds of catastrophe. It does not lie in the power of man to stop the rolling stone of fate which through neglect or lack of wisdom has been set moving.

I am happy to say that these ideas correspond with the viewpoint of the Austrian Chancellor, whom I invited to visit me. The underlying intention was to bring about a detente in our relations which would guarantee to National Socialist sympathizers in Austria within the limits of the law the same rights enjoyed by other citizens.

In connection with it there was to be an act of conciliation in the form of a general amnesty and better understanding between the two States through closer and friendlier relations in the various spheres of cultural, political and economic cooperation. All this is a development within the framework of the treaty of July 11.

I wish to pay tribute to the Austrian Chancellor for his efforts to find together with me a way which is just as much in the interests of both countries as in that of the entire German people whose sons we all are regardless of where we came from. I believe we have thus made a contribution to European peace.

Our satisfactory relations with other countries are known to all. Above all it is to be mentioned our cooperation with those two great powers which, like Germany, have recognized bolshevism as a world danger and are therefore determined to resist the Comintern with a common defense. It is my earnest wish to see this cooperation with Italy and Japan more and more extended.

The German people is no warlike nation. It is a soldierly one which means it does not want a war but does not fear it. It loves peace but it also loves its honor and freedom.

The new Reich shall belong to no class, no profession but to the German people. It shall help the people find an easier road in this world. It shall help them in making their lot a happier one. Party, State, armed forces, economics are institutions and functions which can only be estimated as a means toward an end. They will be judged by history according to the services they render toward this goal. Their purpose, however, is to serve the people.

I now pray to God that He will bless in the years to come our work, our deeds, our foresight, our resolve; that the Almighty may protect us from both arrogance and cowardly servility, that He may help us find the right way which He has laid down for the German people and that He may always give us courage to do the right thing and never to falter or weaken before any power or any danger.

Long live Germany and the German people.

Dunkirk

A speech delivered by Winston Churchill June 4, 1940

From the moment when the defenses at Sedan on the Meuse were broken at the end of the second week in May only a rapid retreat to Amiens and the south could have saved the British-French armies who had entered Belgium at the appeal of the Belgian King.

This strategic fact was not immediately realized. The French High Command hoped it would be able to close the gap. The armies of the north were under their orders. Moreover, a retirement of that kind would have involved almost certainly the destruction of a fine Belgian Army of twenty divisions and abandonment of the Whole of Belgium.

Therefore, when the force and scope of the German penetration was realized and when the new French Generalissimo, General [Maxime] Weygand, assumed command in place of General Gamelin, an effort was made by the French and British Armies in Belgium to keep holding the right hand of the Belgians and give their own right hand to the newly created French Army which was to advance across the Somme in great strength.

However, the German eruption swept like a sharp scythe south of Amiens to the rear of the armies in the north—eight or nine armored divisions, each with about 400 armored vehicles of different kinds divisible into small self-contained units.

This force cut off all communications between us and the main French Army. It severed our communications for food and ammunition. It ran first through Amiens, afterward through Abbeville, and it shore its way up the coast to Boulogne and Calais, almost to Dunkirk.

Behind this armored and mechanized onslaught came a number of German divisions in lorries, and behind them, again, plodded comparatively slowly the dull, brute mass of the ordinary German Army and German people, always ready to be led to the trampling down in other lands of liberties and comforts they never have known in their own.

I said this armored scythe stroke almost reached Dunkirk—almost but not quite. Boulogne and Calais were scenes of desperate fighting. The guards defended Boulogne for a while and were then withdrawn by orders from this country.

The rifle brigade of the Sixtieth Rifles (Queen Victoria's Rifles), with a battalion of British tanks and 1,000 Frenchmen, in all about 4,000 strong, defended Calais to the last. The British brigadier was given an hour to surrender. He spurned the offer. Four days of intense street fighting passed before the silence reigned in Calais which marked the end of a memorable resistance.

Only thirty unwounded survivors were brought off by the navy, and we do not know the fate of their comrades. Their sacrifice was not, however, in vain. At least two armored divisions which otherwise would have been turned against the

B.E.F. had to be sent to overcome them. They have added another page to the glories of the light division.

The time gained enabled the Gravelines water line to be flooded and held by French troops. Thus the port of Dunkirk was held open. When it was found impossible for the armies of the north to reopen their communications through Amiens with the main French armies, only one choice remained. It seemed, indeed, a forlorn hope. The Belgian and French armies were almost surrounded. Their sole line of retreat was to a single port and its neighboring beaches. They were pressed on every side by heavy attacks and were far outnumbered in the air.

When a week ago today I asked the House to fix this afternoon for the occasion of a statement, I feared it would be my hard lot to announce from this box the greatest military disaster of our long history.

I thought, and there were good judges who agreed with me, that perhaps 20,000 or 30,000 men might be re-embarked, but it certainly seemed that the whole French First Army and the whole B.E.F., north of the Amiens-Abbeville gap would be broken up in open field or else have to capitulate for lack of food and ammunition.

These were the hard and heavy tidings I called on the House and nation to prepare themselves for.

The whole root and core and brain of the British Army, around which and upon which we were building and are able to build the great British armies of later years, seemed due to perish upon the field. That was the prospect a week ago, but another blow which might have proved final was still to fall upon us.

The King of the Belgians called upon us to come to his aid. Had not this ruler and his government severed themselves from the Allies who rescued their country from extinction in the late war, and had they not sought refuge in what has been proved to be fatal neutrality, then the French and British armies at the outset might well have saved not only Belgium but perhaps even Holland.

At the last moment, when Belgium was already invaded, King Leopold called upon us to come to his aid, and even at the last moment we came. He and his brave and efficient army of nearly half a million strong guarded our eastern flank; this kept open our only retreat to the sea.

Suddenly, without any prior consultation and with the least

possible notice, without the advice of his ministers and on his own personal act, he sent a plenipotentiary to the German Command surrendering his army and exposing our flank and the means of retreat.

I asked the House a week ago to suspend its judgment because the facts were not clear. I do not think there is now any reason why we should not form our own opinions upon this pitiful episode. The surrender of the Belgian Army compelled the British Army at the shortest notice to cover a flank to the sea of more than thirty miles' length which otherwise would have been cut off.

In doing this and closing this flank, contact was lost inevitably between the British and two of three corps forming the First French Army who were then further from the coast than we were. It seemed impossible that large numbers of Allied troops could reach the coast. The enemy attacked on all sides in great strength and fierceness, and their main power, air force, was thrown into the battle.

The enemy began to fire cannon along the beaches by which alone shipping could approach or depart. They sowed magnetic mines in the channels and seas and sent repeated waves of hostile aircraft, sometimes more than 100 strong, to cast bombs on a single pier that remained and on the sand dunes.

Their U-boats, one of which was sunk, and motor launches took their toll of the vast traffic which now began. For four or five days the intense struggle raged. All armored divisions, or what was left of them, together with great masses of German infantry and artillery, hurled themselves on the ever narrowing and contracting appendix within which the British and French armies fought.

Meanwhile the Royal Navy, with the willing help of countless merchant seamen and a host of volunteers, strained every nerve and every effort and every craft to embark the British and Allied troops.

Over 220 light warships and more than 650 other vessels were engaged. They had to approach this difficult coast, often in adverse weather, under an almost ceaseless hail of bombs and increasing concentration of artillery fire. Nor were the seas themselves free from mines and torpedoes.

It was in conditions such as these that our men carried on with little or no rest for days and nights, moving troops across dangerous waters and bringing with them always the men whom they had rescued. The numbers they brought back are the measure of their devotion and their courage.

Hospital ships, which were plainly marked, were the special target for Nazi bombs, but the men and women aboard them never faltered in their duty.

Meanwhile the R. A. F., who already had been intervening in the battle so far as its range would allow it to go from home bases, now used a part of its main metropolitan fighter strength to strike at German bombers.

The struggle was protracted and fierce. Suddenly the scene has cleared. The crash and thunder has momentarily, but only for the moment, died away. The miracle of deliverance achieved by the valor and perseverance, perfect discipline, faultless service, skill and unconquerable vitality is a manifesto to us all.

The enemy was hurled back by the British and French troops. He was so roughly handled that he dare not molest their departure seriously. The air force decisively defeated the main strength of the German Air Force and inflicted on them a loss of at least four to one.

The navy, using nearly 1,000 ships of all kinds, carried over 335,000 men, French and British, from the jaws of death back to their native land and to the tasks which lie immediately before them.

We must be very careful not to assign to this deliverance attributes of a victory. Wars are not won by evacuations, but there was a victory inside this deliverance which must be noted.

Many of our soldiers coming back have not seen the air force at work. They only saw the bombers which escaped their protective attack. This was a great trial of strength between the British and German Air Forces.

Can you conceive of a greater objective for the power of Germany in the air than to make all evacuations from these beaches impossible and to sink all of the ships, numbering almost 1,000? Could there have been an incentive of greater military importance and significance to the whole purpose of the war?

They tried hard and were beaten back. They were frustrated in their task; we have got the armies away and they have paid fourfold for any losses sustained. Very large formations of German airplanes were turned on several occasions from the attack by a quarter their number of R. A. F. planes and dispersed in different directions. Twelve airplanes have been hunted by two. One airplane was driven into the water and cast away by the charge of a British airplane which had no more ammunition.

All of our types and our pilots have been vindicated. The

Hurricane, Spitfires and Defiance have been vindicated. When I consider how much greater would be our advantage in defending the air above this island against overseas attacks, I find in these facts a sure basis on which practical and reassuring thoughts may rest, and I will pay my tribute to these young airmen.

May it not be that the cause of civilization itself will be defended by the skill and devotion of a few thousand airmen? There never has been, I suppose, in all the history of the world such opportunity for youth.

The Knights of the Round Table and the Crusaders have fallen back into distant days, not only distant but prosaic; but these young men are going forth every morning, going forth holding in their hands an instrument of colossal shattering power, of whom it may be said that every morn brought forth a noble chance and every chance brought forth a noble deed. These young men deserve our gratitude, as all brave men who in so many ways and so many occasions are ready and will continue to be ready to give their life and their all to their native land.

I return to the army. In a long series of very fierce battles, now on this front, now on that, fighting on three fronts at once, battles fought by two or three divisions against an equal or sometimes larger number of the enemy, and fought very fiercely on old ground so many of us knew so well, our losses in men exceed 30,000 in killed, wounded and missing. I take this occasion for expressing the sympathy of the House with those who have suffered bereavement or are still anxious.

The President of the Board of Trade (Sir Andrew Duncan) is not here today. His son has been killed, and many here have felt private affliction of the sharpest form, but I would say about the missing—we have had a large number of wounded come home safely to this country—there may be very many reported missing who will come back home some day.

In the confusion of departure it is inevitable that many should be cut off. Against this loss of over 30,000 men we may set the far heavier loss certainly inflicted on the enemy, but our losses in material are enormous. We have perhaps lost one-third of the men we lost in the opening days of the battle on March 21, 1918, but we have lost nearly as many guns—nearly 1,000—and all our transport and all the armored vehicles that were with the army of the north.

These losses will impose further delay on the expansion of our military strength. That expansion has not been proceeding as fast as we had hoped. The best of all we had to give has been given to the B. E. F., and although they had not the number of tanks and some articles of equipment which were desirable they were a very well and finely equipped army. They had the first fruits of all our industry had to give. That has gone and now here is further delay.

How long it will be, how long it will last depends upon the exertions which we make on this island. An effort, the like of which has never been seen in our records, is now being made. Work is proceeding night and day, Sundays and week days. Capital and labor have cast aside their interests, rights and customs and put everything into the common stock. Already the flow of munitions has leaped forward. There is no reason why we should not in a few months overtake the sudden and serious loss that has come upon us without retarding the development of our general program.

Nevertheless, our thankfulness at the escape of our army with so many men, and the thankfulness of their loved ones, who passed through an agonizing week, must not blind us to the fact that what happened in France and Belgium is a colossal military disaster.

The French Army has been weakened, the Belgian Army has been lost and a large part of those fortified lines upon which so much faith was reposed has gone, and many valuable mining districts and factories have passed into the enemy's possession.

The whole of the channel ports are in his hands, with all the strategic consequences that follow from that, and we must expect another blow to be struck almost immediately at us or at France.

We were told that Hitler has plans for invading the British Isles. This has often been thought of before. When Napoleon lay at Boulogne for a year with his flat-bottomed boats and his Grand Army, some one told him there were bitter weeds in England. There certainly were and a good many more of them have since been returned. The whole question of defense against invasion is powerfully affected by the fact that we have for the time being in this island incomparably more military forces than we had in the last war. But this will not continue. We shall not be content with a defensive war. We have our duty to our Allies.

We have to reconstitute and build up the B. E. F. once again under its gallant Commander in Chief, Lord Gort. All this is en train. But now I feel we must put our defense in this island into such a high state of organization that the fewest possible numbers will be required to give effectual security and that the largest possible potential offensive effort may be released.

On this we are engaged. It would be very convenient to enter upon this subject in secret sessions. The government would not necessarily be able to reveal any great military secrets, but we should like to have our discussions free and without the restraint imposed by the fact that they would be read the next day by the enemy.

The government would benefit by the views expressed by the House. I understand that some request is to be made on this subject, which will be readily acceded to by the government. We have found it necessary to take measures of increasing stringency, not only against enemy aliens and suspicious characters of other nationalities but also against British subjects who may become a danger or a nuisance should the war be transported to the United Kingdom.

I know there are a great many people affected by the orders which we have made who are passionate enemies of Nazi Germany. I am very sorry for them, but we cannot, under the present circumstances, draw all the distinctions we should like to do. If parachute landings were attempted and fierce fights followed, those unfortunate people would be far better out of the way for their own sake as well as ours.

There is, however, another class for which I feel not the slightest sympathy. Parliament has given us powers to put down fifth column activities with the strongest hand, and we shall use those powers subject to the supervision and correction of the House without hesitation until we are satisfied and more than satisfied that this malignancy in our midst has been effectually stamped out.

Turning once again to the question of invasion, there has, I will observe, never been a period in all those long centuries of which we boast when an absolute guarantee against invasion, still less against serious raids, could have been given to our people. In the days of Napoleon the same wind which might have carried his transports across the Channel might have driven away a blockading fleet. There is always the chance, and it is that chance which has excited and befooled the imaginations of many continental tyrants.

We are assured that novel methods will be adopted, and when we see the originality, malice and ingenuity of aggression which our enemy displays we may certainly prepare ourselves for every kind of novel stratagem and every kind of brutal and treacherous manoeuvre. I think no idea is so outlandish that it should not be considered and viewed with a watchful, but at the same time steady, eye.

We must never forget the solid assurances of sea power and those which belong to air power if they can be locally exercised. I have myself full confidence that if all do their duty and if the best arrangements are made, as they are being made, we shall prove ourselves once again able to defend our island home, ride out the storms of war and outlive the menace of tyranny, if necessary, for years, alone.

At any rate, that is what we are going to try to do. That is the resolve of His Majesty's Government, every man of them. That is the will of Parliament and the nation. The British Empire and the French Republic, linked together in their cause and their need, will defend to the death their native soils, aiding each other like good comrades to the utmost of their strength, even though a large tract of Europe and many old and famous States have fallen or may fall into the grip of the Gestapo and all the odious apparatus of Nazi rule.

We shall not flag nor fail. We shall go on to the end. We shall fight in France and on the seas and oceans; we shall fight with growing confidence and growing strength in the air.

We shall defend our island whatever the cost may be; we shall fight on beaches, landing grounds, in fields, in streets and on the hills. We shall never surrender and even if, which I do not for the moment believe, this island or a large part of it were subjugated and starving, then our empire beyond the seas, armed and guarded by the British Fleet, will carry on the struggle until in God's good time the New World, with all its power and might, sets forth to the liberation and rescue of the Old.

Appendix B

The purpose of the following exercises is to help you improve and maintain your speech skills. These exercises in breathing and relaxation, in articulation and pronunciation, and in posture and poise are foundational and should be performed regularly. However, as is true of all exercise programs, unless you use the exercises correctly they will be of no use to you. The following governing rules will help you establish profitable practice sessions:

1. Do not attempt too much at first or your program will collapse. Set realistic goals and work toward them.
2. Start slowly to avoid muscle fatigue and soreness.
3. Keep your exercise period short at first. Begin by practicing at least ten minutes a day.
4. Vary your drills and exercises. Escape boredom through variety.
5. Find a pleasant place, a convenient time, and a comfortable outfit in which to work. Establish a routine and follow it.
6. Use your voice and articulation drill sessions as lead-in or warm-up drills before practicing class projects.

Breathing and Relaxation Exercises

1. Feel the action of your diaphragm by placing your left hand directly below your sternum and your right hand on top of your left shoulder. As you inhale, you should feel your diaphragm pull down, thereby pushing out certain internal organs and abdominal muscles against your left hand. Be sure that your shoulders do not rise during inhalation. Next, place your hands on your waist, thumbs toward the front, to feel the expansion of your ribs, sides, and back during inhalation. Once again, concentrate on eliminating excessive upper-chest movements.
2. Imagine a tape measure around your lower ribs. With each breath the tape measure should register a large expansion of the lower ribs. While you are speaking, the tape measure should register an increase proportional to the length of the phrase.
3. Take a deep breath. As you exhale, slowly count aloud as follows:

   Inhale, Exhale—1, 2, 3, 4, 5
   Inhale, Exhale—1, 2, 3, 4, 5, 6

Inhale, Exhale—1, 2, 3, 4, 5, 6, 7
Inhale, Exhale—1, 2, 3, 4, 5, 6, 7, 8

4. Repeat the counting exercise, except this time substitute short rhyming words like the following for the numbers:

Inhale, Exhale—fun, sun, run
Inhale, Exhale—fun, sun, run, shun
Inhale, Exhale—fun, sun, run, shun, gun
Inhale, Exhale—fun, sun, run, shun, gun, stun

5. Practice the following selection aloud. Be careful to notice the punctuation in the poem. While reading, you should use your abdominal muscles and diaphragm for tone support. Slowly inhale before each phrase. Elongate important words and sustain important phrases. Imagine that each word is floating on a strong column of air.

A Hymn to God the Father
Wilt Thou forgive that sin where I begun,
Which is my sin, though it were done before?
Wilt thou forgive those sins through which I run,
And do run still, though still I do deplore?
When Thou hast done, Thou hast not done,
For I have more.

Wilt Thou forgive that sin by which I've won
Others to sin? and made my sin their door?
Wilt Thou forgive that sin which I did shun
A year or two, but wallowed in a score?
When Thou hast done, Thou hast not done,
For I have more.

I have a sin of fear, that when I've spun
My last thread, I shall perish on the shore;
Swear by Thyself, that at my death Thy Son
Shall shine as He shines now, and heretofore;
And, having done that, Thou hast done,
I fear no more.

John Donne

6. Lie on the floor, flat on your back. Place a book below your sternum. Practice slow, controlled inhaling and exhaling. Watch the book rise and fall with each breath. Work to centralize and control the movement of the diaphragm.

7. Rag doll or limp old sock drill.
Sit in a wooden, straight-backed chair. Close your eyes and

concentrate on locating any tension in your body. Relax the muscles in your feet, legs, hips, abdomen, hands, arms, shoulders, neck, and jaw—in that order. Begin a pattern of slow, even breathing. Do not allow your shoulders to tense and rise during each inhalation. Imagine that you are a rag doll or an old limp sock. While drooping forward from the waist, gently swing your arms back and forth. Once you feel completely relaxed, immediately proceed to the next drill.

8. Reach for the sky drill.
Stand up and move away from your chair. Lift your arms energetically above your head, and then bring them out to the sides, stretching even to your finger tips. Concentrate to feel the stretching sensation across your rib cage. Imagine moving all your physical tensions out through your finger tips. Slowly lower your arms parallel with the floor; then suddenly drop them limply to your sides. Immediately inhale and repeat the first drill. Complete both drills at least twice.

9. When you have finished the first two drills, stand with good relaxed posture. Slowly rotate your head in a circular motion, allowing the neck muscles to relax fully. Next, gently bob your head in each direction seven times.

Articulation and Pronunciation Exercises

Vowels

e

initial—each, even, erase, ear
medial—beam, fever, receive, feel
final—agree, decree, tea, flee
He had three degrees of fever.
I believe they will flee the erosion of the sea.

i

initial—impart, index, illiterate
medial—dip, mitten, sister
final—funny, many, needy
He was an illiterate, needy kinsman.
It is a forbidden industry.

e

initial—edge, effort, else
medial—belt, lend, bent
"Forever . . . thy word is settled in heaven." (Ps. 119:89)
It meant the effort of everyone.

a

initial—advance, at, and
medial—draft, pass, grasp
He had a chance to amass a fortune.
Your aunt is a terrible task master.

a

initial—age, ape, aid
medial—may, late, rate
He was late bringing the hay to the scales.
Don't berate your mate for something you hate.

Consonants

Plosives

p—pear, apple, hope, peer, appeal, lip, pen, happen, nap
He hoped his appeal would catch the prosecution napping.
Put the purple pears onto Pete's plate.

b—black, able, mob, book, robber, drab, brain, obey, rub
He bent his back for the brief exertion.
The mob robbed the barber shop.

t—time, battle, quiet, tell, matter, nut, talk, detect, meet
Ten tots need ten teachers to keep track of them.
Tie the teddy bears to the tinsel tree.

d—dinner, leader, add, dust, produce, end, descend, despondent, load
The division of leadership produced disaster.
Do your duty without doubting.

k—cost, declare, pink, clipper, racket, joke, coal, decline, take
The cost of coal was declared high.
Keep the costly cutlery clean.

g—game, degree, bag, girl, rugged, dog, grain, luggage, hug
The girl dropped her luggage to hug her dog.
Give the gardenias to the girl in green.

Nasals

m—mall, humor, film, meat, temper, poem, money, famous, cream
Money was made by the men and women at the mall.
Make the most of your time.

n—nap, lint, raisin, new, ninety, vine, night, pencil, clean
His earnings never kept up with his spending.

ng—eating, king, farming, long, longing, getting, spring, springing
The youngster was riding on the wrong road.

nk—hunk, think, rank, mink, trunk, sinking, crank, banker
What does the banker think of the "sinking fund"?

Glides

w—wave, quart, twine, web, conquest, twang, wife, squander, unwind
The wife unwound the spool of twine.

l—lily, allow, fuel, leave, elbow, lull, least, quilt, vocal
The little lilies lived a long while.

r—right, arrest, roar, real, kernel, here, road, learn, year
Did you travel on the wrong road?

y—yam, junior, young, yellow, million, genius, yawn, onion, civilian
The youngster used the yellow yarn.

Fricatives

f—fall, helpful, cuff, fear, profane, laugh, fig, trifle, rough
The defense was offended by the refutation.

v—voice, shovel, crave, very, flavor, give, vow, liver, have
The advice was valuable and varied.

th (unvoiced)—theater, panther, growth, theory, ruthless, mirth, thirst, bathtub, path
Wealth and authority are thought to be worthwhile.

th (voiced)—then, heather, clothe, than, mother, tithe, there, neither, bathe
Would you rather gather this clothing together?

s—sight, cross, summer, frisky, pass, supper, husky, twice
Assist the grocer in sorting the stock.

z—lizard, nose, zinc, hazel, please, zone, wisdom, quiz
His hazel eyes were pleasing.

sh—shine, ashen, plush, ship, issue, wish, sure, ration, brush
Surely the issue of rationing will come in this session.

zh—casual, treasure, massage, decision, vision, explosion, measure, rouge
They envisioned a measure of leisure.

h—hard, behind, human, hear, inhabit, high, hat, perhaps, unharmed
Perhaps the hat will enhance her charm.

Consonant Combinations

ch—cheer, feature, march, chime, future, preach, chip, natural, rich
Naturally the choice was for the charming picture.

j—jam, dejected, grudge, job, rejoice, range, jury, subject, ridge

The open range beyond the ridge ended in a deep gorge.

wh—while, white, meanwhile, whim, whisker, nowhere, wheat, whistle, which

"Was that the white whale called Moby Dick?" they whispered.

Posture and Poise

Stand with your back against the wall. Attempt to make your heels, the center of your back, and your shoulders touch the wall. When you are relaxed in this position, slowly move from the wall and walk across the room. Be sure to maintain good posture while moving.

Sit in a straight-backed chair. Hold your upper body erect, place your hands in your lap, and put one foot slightly forward. Slowly rise from the chair. Be sure to maintain good posture. Do not bend at the waist or lead with the chin. Also try to rise without pushing yourself up by your hands; let your legs do the work.

Appendix C

Categorical syllogism is based on the idea of sets or categories. The major premise sets forth a characteristic of a category. The minor premise identifies a member of that category; then the conclusion applies the characteristic to the particular member. The "Socratic" syllogism is one example of this type, and now let's look at another example:

major premise: All sinners must die. (Rom. 6:23)
(characteristic of category)
minor premise: All men are sinners. (Rom. 3:23)
(membership in category)
conclusion: Therefore, all men must die. (Rom. 5:12)
(characteristic applied to member)

This type of syllogism is invalid when you assume that two things with a common characteristic must belong to the same category:

major premise: All men are sinners.
minor premise: All women are sinners.
conclusion: Therefore, all men and women are sinners.

This fallacy is called the *shared characteristic,* or *undistributed middle.*

Hypothetical syllogism has an "if-then" statement in the major premise. For the conclusion to be valid, the minor premise must either affirm the "if" part or deny the "then" part:

major premise: If there is no resurrection of the dead, then Christ did not rise. (I Cor. 15:16)
minor premise: There is no resurrection of the dead.
conclusion: Therefore, Christ did not rise.

minor premise: Christ did rise. (I Cor. 15:20)
conclusion: Therefore, there is a resurrection. (I Cor. 15:21ff)

In the first example the minor premise is false and so is the conclusion. The form is valid, but the conclusion is not true. The second example is both valid and true.

This type of syllogism is invalid if you deny the "if" part or affirm the "then" part:

major premise: If Jane loves me, she will marry me.
minor premise: Jane does not love me.
conclusion: Therefore, she will not marry me.

minor premise: Jane will marry me.
conclusion: Therefore, she loves me.

What's wrong with these syllogisms? Even if the major premise is true, the conclusions could be wrong. Jane might marry you because you have money or because her father says she has to. In short, the conclusions are probably false because the form of the syllogism is invalid.

Disjunctive syllogism contains a major premise with an "either-or" statement. You use it validly when you deny one or the other of the alternatives:

> major premise: Either my teaching is from God, or I speak of myself. (John 7:17)
> minor premise: I do not speak of myself. (John 7:18)
> conclusion: Therefore, my teaching is from God.

There are three ways this form can be invalid. You might give alternatives that are not really separate:

> major premise: I like either steak or beef.
> minor premise: I do not like beef.
> conclusion: Therefore, I like steak.

The problem here is that steak is a type of beef; the alternatives are not distinct. If you dislike beef, you cannot possibly like steak.

The second fallacy comes when you fail to list all of the possible alternatives:

> major premise: Pets are either cats or dogs.
> minor premise: Our parrot is not a cat.
> conclusion: Therefore, our parrot is a dog.

The obvious problem here is that the major premise does not list all the possibilities.

The final fallacy is assuming that if one possibility happens, then the other cannot. Remember, the major premise says only that at least one of the two must happen; it does not say that both must happen:

> major premise: Writers are either bad-tempered or flaky.
> minor premise: Dan, a writer, is flaky.
> conclusion: Therefore, Dan is not bad-tempered.

As you can see, the conclusion assumes that Dan cannot be *both* bad-tempered and flaky, both of which he might well be.

APPENDIX D

Dr. Heidegger's Experiment

Nathaniel Hawthorne

That very singular man, old Dr. Heidegger, once invited four venerable friends to meet him in his study. There were three white-bearded gentlemen, Mr. Medbourne, Colonel Killigrew, and Mr. Gascoigne, and a withered gentlewoman, whose name was the Widow Wycherly. They were all melancholy old creatures, who had been unfortunate in life, and whose greatest misfortune it was that they were not long ago in their graves. Mr. Medbourne, in the vigor of his age, had been a prosperous merchant, but had lost his all by a frantic speculation, and was now little better than a mendicant. Colonel Killigrew had wasted his best years, and his health and substance, in the pursuit of sinful pleasures, which had given birth to a brood of pains, such as the gout, and divers other torments of soul and body. Mr. Gascoigne was a ruined politician, a man of evil fame, or at least had been so till time had buried him from the knowledge of the present generation, and made him obscure instead of infamous. As for the Widow Wycherly, tradition tells us that she was a great beauty in her day; but, for a long while past, she had lived in deep seclusion, on account of certain scandalous stories which had prejudiced the gentry of the town against her. It is a circumstance worth mentioning that each of these three old gentlemen, Mr. Medbourne, Colonel Killigrew, and Mr. Gascoigne, were early lovers of the Widow Wycherly, and had once been on the point of cutting each other's throats for her sake. And, before proceeding further, I will merely hint that Dr. Heidegger and all his four guests were sometimes thought to be a little beside themselves—as is not unfrequently the case with old people, when worried either by present troubles or woeful recollections.

"My dear old friends," said Dr. Heidegger, motioning them to be seated, "I am desirous of your assistance in one of those little experiments with which I amuse myself here in my study."

If all stories were true, Dr. Heidegger's study must have been a very curious place. It was a dim, old-fashioned chamber, festooned with cobwebs, and besprinkled with antique dust. Around the walls stood several oaken bookcases, the lower shelves of which were filled with rows of gigantic folios and black-letter quartos, and the upper with little parchment-covered duodecimos. Over the central bookcase was a bronze bust of Hippocrates, with which, according to some authorities, Dr. Heidegger was accustomed to hold consultations in all difficult cases of his practice. In the obscurest corner of the room stood a tall and narrow oaken closet, with its door ajar, within which doubtfully appeared a skeleton. Between two of the bookcases hung a looking glass, presenting its high and dusty plate within a tarnished gilt frame. Among many wonderful stories related of this mirror, it was fabled that the spirit of all the doctor's deceased patients dwelt within its verge, and would stare him in the face whenever he looked thitherward. The opposite side of the chamber was ornamented with the full-length portrait of a young lady, arrayed in the faded magnificence of silk, satin, and brocade, and with a visage as faded as her dress. Above half a century ago, Dr. Heidegger had been on the point of marriage with this young lady; but being affected with some slight disorder, she had swallowed one of her lover's prescriptions, and died on the bridal evening. The greatest curiosity of the study remains to be mentioned; it was a ponderous folio volume, bound in black leather, with massive silver clasps. There were no letters on the back, and nobody could tell the title of the book. But it was well known to be a book of magic; and once, when a chambermaid had lifted it, merely to brush away the dust, the skeleton had rattled in its closet, the picture of the young lady had stepped one foot upon the floor, and several ghastly faces had peeped forth from the mirror; while the brazen head of Hippocrates frowned and said, "Forbear!"

Such was Dr. Heidegger's study. On the summer afternoon of our tale, a small round table, as black as ebony, stood in the center of the room, sustaining a cut-glass vase of beautiful form and elaborate workmanship. The sunshine came through the window, between the heavy festoons of two faded damask curtains, and fell directly across this vase; so that a mild splendor was reflected from it on the ashen visages of the five old people who sat around.

"My dear old friends," repeated Dr. Heidegger, "may I reckon on your aid in performing an exceedingly curious experiment?"

Now Dr. Heidegger was a very strange old gentleman, whose eccentricity had become the nucleus for a thousand fantastic stories. Some of these fables, to my shame be it spoken, might possibly be traced back to my own veracious self; and if any passages of the present tale should startle the reader's faith, I must be content to bear the stigma of a fictionmonger.

When the doctor's four guests heard him talk of his proposed experiment, they anticipated nothing more wonderful than the murder of a mouse in an air pump, or the examination of a cobweb by the microscope, or some similar nonsense, with which he was constantly in the habit of pestering his intimates. But, without waiting for a reply, Dr. Heidegger hobbled across the chamber and returned with the same ponderous folio, bound in black leather, which common report affirmed to be a book of magic. Undoing the silver clasps, he opened the volume and took from among its black-letter pages a rose, or what was once a rose, though now the green leaves and crimson petals had assumed one brownish hue, and the ancient flower seemed ready to crumble to dust in the doctor's hands.

"This rose," said Dr. Heidegger, with a sigh, "this same withered and crumbling flower, blossomed five and fifty years ago. It was given me by Sylvia Ward, whose portrait hangs yonder; and I meant to wear it in my bosom at our wedding. Five and fifty years it has been treasured between the leaves of this old volume. Now, would you deem it possible that this rose of half a century could ever bloom again?"

"Nonsense!" said the Widow Wycherly, with a peevish toss of her head. "You might as well ask whether an old woman's wrinkled face could ever bloom again."

"See!" answered Dr. Heidegger.

He uncovered the vase and threw the faded rose into the water which it contained. At first, it lay lightly on the surface of the fluid, appearing to imbibe none of its moisture. Soon, however, a singular change began to be visible. The crushed and dried petals stirred and assumed a deepening tinge of crimson, as if the flower were reviving from a deathlike slumber; the slender stalk and twigs of foliage became green; and there was the rose of half a century, looking as fresh as when Sylvia Ward had first given it to her lover. It was scarcely full blown; for some of its delicate red leaves curled modestly around its moist bosom, within which two or three dewdrops were sparkling.

"That is certainly a very pretty deception," said the doctor's friends; carelessly, however, for they had witnessed greater miracles at a conjurer's show; "pray how was it effected?"

"Did you never hear of the 'Fountain of Youth'?" asked Dr. Heidegger, "which Ponce de Leon, the Spanish adventurer, went in search of two or three centuries ago?"

"But did Ponce de Leon ever find it?" said the Widow Wycherly.

"No," answered Dr. Heidegger, "for he never sought it in the right place. The famous Fountain of Youth, if I am rightly informed, is situated in the southern part of the Floridian peninsula, not far from Lake Macaco. Its source is overshadowed by several gigantic magnolias, which, though numberless centuries old, have been kept as fresh as violets by the virtues of this wonderful water. An acquaintance of mine, knowing my curiosity in such matters, has sent me what you see in the vase."

"Ahem!" said Colonel Killigrew, who believed not a word of the doctor's story; "and what may be the effect of this fluid on the human frame?"

"You shall judge for yourself, my dear colonel," replied Dr. Heidegger; "and all of you, my respected friends, are welcome to so much of this admirable fluid as may restore to you the bloom of youth. For my own part, having had much trouble in growing old, I am in no hurry to grow young again. With your permission, therefore, I will merely watch the progress of the experiment."

While he spoke, Dr. Heidegger had been filling four glasses with the water of the Fountain of Youth. It was apparently impregnated with an effervescent gas, for little bubbles were continually ascending from the depths of the glasses, and bursting in silvery spray at the surface. As the liquor diffused a pleasant perfume, the old people doubted not that it possessed cordial and comfortable properties; and though utter skeptics as to its rejuvenescent power, they were inclined to swallow it at once. But Dr. Heidegger besought them to stay a moment.

"Before you drink, my respectable old friends," said he, "it would be well that, with the experience of a lifetime to direct you, you should draw up a few general rules for your guidance, in passing a second time through the perils of youth. Think what a sin and shame it would be, if, with your peculiar advantages, you should not become patterns of virtue and wisdom to all the young people of the age!"

The doctor's four venerable friends made him no answer, except by a feeble and tremulous laugh; so very ridiculous was the idea that, knowing how closely repentance treads behind the steps of error, they should ever go astray again.

"Drink, then," said the doctor, bowing. "I rejoice that I have so well selected the subjects of my experiment."

With palsied hands, they raised the glasses to their lips. The liquor, if it really possessed such virtues as Dr. Heidegger imputed to it, could not have been bestowed on four human beings who needed it more woefully. They looked as if they had never known what youth or pleasure was, but had been the offspring of Nature's dotage, and always the gray, decrepit, sapless, miserable creatures who now sat stooping round the doctor's table, without life enough in their souls or bodies to be animated even by the prospect of growing young again. They drank off the water, and replaced their glasses on the table.

Assuredly there was an almost immediate improvement in the aspect of the party, not unlike what might have been produced by a glass of generous wine, together with a sudden glow of cheerful sunshine brightening over all their visages at once. There was a healthful suffusion on their cheeks, instead of the ashen hue that had made them look so corpselike. They gazed at one another and fancied that some magic power had really begun to smooth away the deep and sad inscriptions which Father Time had been so long engraving on their brows. The Widow Wycherly adjusted her cap, for she felt almost like a woman again.

"Give us more of this wondrous water!" cried they, eagerly. "We are younger—but we are still too old! Quick—give us more!"

"Patience, patience!" quoth Dr. Heidegger, who sat watching the experiment with philosophic coolness. "You have been a long time growing old. Surely, you might be content to grow young in half an hour! But the water is at your service."

Again he filled their glasses with the liquor of youth, enough of which still remained in the vase to turn half of the old people in the city to the age of their own grandchildren. While the bubbles were yet sparkling on the brim, the doctor's four guests snatched their glasses from the table, and swallowed the contents at a single gulp. Was it delusion? Even while the draught was passing down their throats, it seemed to have wrought a change on their whole systems. Their eyes grew clear and bright; a dark shade deepened among their silvery locks, they sat around the table, three gentlemen of middle age, and a woman, hardly beyond her buxom prime.

"My dear widow, you are charming!" cried Colonel

Killigrew, whose eyes had been fixed upon her face, while the shadows of age were flitting from it like darkness from the crimson daybreak.

The fair widow knew, of old, that Colonel Killigrew's compliments were not always measured by sober truth; so she started up and ran to the mirror, still dreading that the ugly visage of an old woman would meet her gaze. Meanwhile, the three gentlemen behaved in such a manner as proved that the water of the Fountain of Youth possessed some intoxicating qualities; unless, indeed, their exhilaration of spirits were merely a lightsome dizziness caused by the sudden removal of the weight of years. Mr. Gascoigne's mind seemed to run on political topics, but whether relating to the past, present, or future could not easily be determined, since the same ideas and phrases have been in vogue these fifty years. Now he rattled forth full-throated sentences about patriotism, national glory, and the people's right; now he muttered some perilous stuff or other, in a sly and doubtful whisper, so cautiously that even his own conscience could scarcely catch the secret; and now, again, he spoke in measured accents, and a deeply deferential tone, as if a royal ear were listening to his well-turned periods. Colonel Killigrew all this time had been trolling forth a jolly bottle song, and ringing his glass in symphony with the chorus, while his eyes wandered toward the buxom figure of the Widow Wycherly. On the other side of the table, Mr. Medbourne was involved in a calculation of dollars and cents, with which was strangely intermingled a project for supplying the East Indies with ice, by harnessing a team of whales to the polar icebergs.

As for the Widow Wycherly, she stood before the mirror curtsying and simpering to her own image, and greeting it as the friend whom she loved better than all the world beside. She thrust her face close to the glass, to see whether some long-remembered wrinkle or crow's foot had indeed vanished. She examined whether the snow had so entirely melted from her hair that the venerable cap could be safely thrown aside. At last, turning briskly away, she came with a sort of dancing step to the table.

"My dear old doctor," cried she, "pray favor me with another glass!"

"Certainly, my dear madam, certainly!" replied the complaisant doctor; "See! I have already filled the glasses."

There, in fact, stood the four glasses, brimful of this wonderful water, the delicate spray of which, as it effervesced from the surface, resembled the tremulous glitter of diamonds. It was now so nearly sunset that the chamber had grown duskier than ever; but a mild and moonlike splendor gleamed from within the vase, and rested alike on the four guests and on the doctor's venerable figure. He sat in a high-backed, elaborately carved oaken armchair, with a gray dignity of aspect that might have well befitted that very Father Time, whose power had never been disputed, save by this fortunate company. Even while quaffing the third draught of the Fountain of Youth, they were almost awed by the expression of his mysterious visage.

But, the next moment, the exhilarating gush of young life shot through their veins. They were now in the happy prime of youth. Age, with its miserable train of cares and sorrows and diseases, was remembered only as the trouble of a dream, from which they had joyously awaked. The fresh gloss of the soul, so early lost, and without which the world's successive scenes had been but a gallery of faded pictures, again threw its enchantment over all their prospects. They felt like new-created beings in a new-created universe.

"We are young! We are young!" they cried exultingly.

Youth, like the extremity of age, had effaced the strongly marked characteristics of middle life, and mutually assimilated them all. They were a group of merry youngsters, almost maddened with the exuberant frolicsomeness of their years. The most singular effect of their gaiety was an impulse to mock the infirmity and decrepitude of which they had so lately been the victims. They laughed loudly at their old-fashioned attire, the wide-skirted coats and flapped waistcoats of the young men, and the ancient cap and gown of the blooming girl. One limped across the floor like a gouty grandfather; one set a pair of spectacles astride of his nose, and pretended to pore over the black-letter pages of the book of magic; a third seated himself in an armchair, and strove to imitate the venerable dignity of Dr. Heidegger. Then all shouted mirthfully, and leaped about the room. The Widow Wycherly—if so fresh a damsel could be called a widow—tripped up the doctor's chair, with a mischievous merriment in her rosy face.

"Doctor, you dear old soul," cried she, "get up and dance with me!" And then the four young people laughed louder than ever, to think what a queer figure the poor old doctor would cut.

"Pray excuse me," answered the doctor quietly. "I am old and rheumatic, and my dancing days were over long ago. But either of these gay young gentlemen will be glad of so pretty a partner."

"Dance with me, Clara!" cried Colonel Killigrew.

"No, no, I will be her partner!" shouted Mr. Gascoigne.

"She promised me her hand, fifty years ago!" exclaimed Mr. Medbourne.

They all gathered round her. One caught both her hands in his passionate grasp—another threw his arm about her waist—the third buried his hand among the glossy curls that clustered beneath the widow's cap. Blushing, panting, struggling, chiding, laughing, her warm breath fanning each of their faces by turns, she strove to disengage herself, yet still remained in their triple embrace. Never was there a livelier picture of youthful rivalship, with bewitching beauty for the prize. Yet, by a strange deception, owing to the duskiness of the chamber, and the antique dresses which they still wore, the tall mirror is said to have reflected the figures of the three old, gray, withered grandsires ridiculously contending for the skinny ugliness of a shriveled grandam.

But they were young: their burning passions proved them so. Inflamed to madness by the coquetry of the girl-widow, who neither granted nor quite withheld her favors, the three rivals began to interchange threatening glances. Still keeping hold of the fair prize, they grappled fiercely at one another's throats. As they struggled to and fro, the table was overturned, and the vase dashed into a thousand fragments. The precious Water of Youth flowed in a bright stream across the floor, moistening the wings of a butterfly, which, grown old in the decline of summer, had alighted there to die. The insect fluttered lightly through the chamber, and settled on the snowy head of Dr. Heidegger.

"Come, come, gentlemen!—come, Madam Wycherly," exclaimed the doctor, "I really must protest against this riot."

They stood still and shivered; for it seemed as if gray Time were calling them back from their sunny youth, far down into the chill and darksome vale of years. They looked at old Dr. Heidegger, who sat in his carved armchair, holding the rose of half a century, which he had rescued from among the fragments of the shattered vase. At the motion of the hand, the four rioters resumed their seats; the more readily, because their violent exertions had wearied them, youthful though they were.

"My poor Sylvia's rose!" ejaculated Dr. Heidegger, holding it in the light of the sunset clouds; "it appears to be fading again."

And so it was. Even while the party were looking at it, the flower continued to shrivel up, till it became as dry and fragile as when the doctor had first thrown it into the vase. He shook off the few drops of moisture which clung to its petals.

"I love it as well thus as in its dewy freshness," observed he, pressing the withered rose to his withered lips. While he spoke, the butterfly fluttered down from the doctor's snowy head, and fell upon the floor.

His guests shivered again. A strange chillness, whether of the body or spirit they could not tell, was creeping gradually over them all. They gazed at one another, and fancied that each fleeting moment snatched away a charm, and left a deepening furrow where none had been before. Was it an illusion? Had the changes of a lifetime been crowded into so brief a space, and were they now four aged people, sitting with their old friend Dr. Heidegger?

"Are we grown old again, so soon?" cried they, dolefully.

In truth they had. The Water of Youth possessed merely a virtue more transient than that of wine. The delirium which it created had effervesced away. Yes! they were old again. With a shuddering impulse, that showed her a woman still, the widow clasped her skinny hands before her face, and wished that the coffin lid were over it, since it could be no longer beautiful.

"Yes, friends, ye are old again," said Dr. Heidegger, "and lo! the Water of Youth is all lavished on the ground. Well— I bemoan it not; for if the fountain gushed at my very doorstep, I would not stoop to bathe my lips in it—no, though its delirium were for years instead of moments. Such is the lesson ye have taught me!"

But the doctor's four friends had taught no such lesson to themselves. They resolved forthwith to make a pilgrimage to Florida, and quaff at morning, noon, and night, from the Fountain of Youth.

The Bit of String

Guy De Maupassant

Along all the roads leading to Goderville the peasants and their wives were going toward the town, for it was market-day. The men walked at an easy pace, the whole body thrown ahead at each movement of the long, crooked legs, men deformed by rude labor, by guiding the plow, which at once forces the right shoulder upward and twists the waist; by reaping, which spreads the knees, for solid footing; by all the patient and painful toil of the country. Their blue blouses, glossy with starch, as though varnished, ornamented at the neck and wrists by a simple pattern in white, swelled out round their bony chests, like captive balloons from which heads, arms, and legs were protruding.

Some were leading by a cord a cow or calf, and their wives behind the animals were hastening their pace by the strokes of branches stripped of their leaves. The women carried on their arms great baskets, out of which hung, here and there, heads of chickens or ducks. They walked with shorter steps than their husbands, and at a more rapid pace, spare, erect and wrapped in scant shawls pinned across their flat chests, their heads enveloped in white linen drawn closely over the hair and surmounted by a bonnet.

Now a pleasure wagon passed at a jerky pony trot, shaking fantastically two men seated side by side, and a woman at the back of the vehicle, holding on to its sides to soften the hard jolts.

In the square of Goderville was a crowd—a jam of mingled human beings and beasts. The horns of cattle, the high hats of the rich farmers and the head-dresses of the women, emerged from the surface of the assembly; and discordant voices, clamorous, bawling, kept up a continuous and savage babel, overtopped now and then by a shout from the robust lungs of a merry countryman, or the lowing of a cow attached to the wall of a house. All this mass was redolent of the stable and soilure, of milk, of hay, of sweat, and diffused that rank, penetrating odor, human and bestial, peculiar to people of the fields.

Master Hauchecorne of Bréauté had just arrived at Goderville, and was going toward the square when he saw on the ground a bit of string. Master Hauchecorne, economist, like every true Norman, thought that anything might be of use worth picking up, and he bent down painfully, for he suffered from rheumatism. He took up the piece of string, and was winding it carefully, when he noticed Malandin, the harness-maker, watching him from his doorway. The two men had long ago had a quarrel about a halter, and both being vindictive, had remained unfriendly. Hauchecorne was seized with a kind of shame, at thus being seen by his enemy picking a bit of twine out of the mud. He quickly hid his prize under his blouse, then in his breeches pocket; then he pretended to search the ground again for something which he did not find, and he went off toward the market, his head in advance, bent double by his infirmities.

He was forthwith lost in the noisy, shuffling crowd everywhere in motion from innumerable buyings and sellings. The peasants examined the cows, went away, came back, hesitated, always fearful of being outwitted, never daring to decide, peering into the face of the vender, endlessly searching to discover the ruse in the man and the fault in the beast.

The women, putting their great baskets down at their feet, had drawn out their fowls, which were lying on the ground, legs bound, eyes wild, combs scarlet. They listened to offers, held to their prices unmoved, their faces inscrutable; or suddenly deciding to accept an offer, cried out to the would-be purchaser slowly moving away:

"Agreed, Master Hutine; I will give it at your price."

Then little by little the square emptied, and the Angelus sounding noon, those who lived too far to go home dispersed in the various public houses.

At Jourdain's the great dining-room was full of feasters, as the vast court was full of vehicles of every pedigree—carts, gigs, tilburies, pleasure vans, carioles innumerable, yellow with mud, mended, out of order, lifting to heaven their shafts, like two arms, or nosing the ground, rear in the air.

Opposite the tables of diners the great chimney-piece, full of bright flame, threw a lively warmth on the backs of the row at the right. Three spits were turning, weighted with chickens, pigeons, and legs of mutton, and a delectable odor of roast flesh and of juice streaming over its golden brown skin, escaped from the hearth, put every one in gay humor, and made mouths water. All the aristocracy of the plow dined there with Master Jourdain, innkeeper and horse-dealer, a shrewd fellow, who had his dollars.

The platters were passed and emptied as were the tankards of yellow cider. Each one talked of his affairs, his purchases, his sales. The harvest was discussed. The weather was good for grass, but a little sharp for grain.

All at once the drum sounded in the court before the house. All save a few indifferent fellows were quickly on their feet, and running to the door or the windows, their mouths full, their napkins in their hands.

When he had finished his roulade the public crier held forth in a jerky voice, cutting his phrases at the wrong place:

"It is made known to the inhabitants of Goderville and in general to all—the people present at market, that there was lost this morning, on the Benzeville road between—nine and ten o'clock, a wallet containing five hundred francs and important papers. You are asked to return—it to the town hall, without delay, or to the house of Master Fortuné Houlèbreque, of Manneville. There will be twenty francs reward."

Then the crier went on. One heard once more far off the muffled beating of his drum, and his voice enfeebled by the distance. Then they all began to talk of the event, estimating Master Houlebreque's chances of finding or not finding his wallet.

And the meal went on.

They were finishing the coffee when the chief of police appeared at the door.

"Where is Master Hauchecorne of Bréauté?" he asked.

Hauchecorne, seated at the farther end of the table, replied:

"I'm here."

The chief proceeded:

"Master Hauchecorne, will you have the kindness to accompany me to the town hall? The mayor wishes to speak with you."

The countryman, surprised and disquieted, emptied at a draft his little glass of rum, arose, and, still more bent than in the morning, for the first movement after each relaxation was particularly difficult, he set out, repeating:

"I'm here, I'm here."

And he followed the chief.

The mayor was waiting for him, seated in his fauteuil. He was the notary of the vicinity, a big, solemn man, of pompous phrases.

"Master Hauchecorn," said he, "you were seen to pick up, on the Benzeville road, this morning, the wallet lost by Master Houlèbreque, of Manneville."

The peasant, astonished, looked at the mayor, frightened already, without knowing why, by this suspicion which had fallen on him.

"What! what! I picked up the wallet?"

"Yes; you yourself."

"Word of honor, I didn't even know of it."

"You were seen."

"Seen? What? Who saw me?"

"Monsieur Malandin, the harness-maker."

Then the old man remembered, understood, reddened with anger.

"He saw meh, th' lout? He saw meh pick up that string! See here, m'sieu major," and feeling in his pocket, he drew out the bit of cord.

But the mayor, incredulous, shook his head.

"You won't make me believe, Master Hauchecorne, that Malandin, who is a man worthy of credence, took that thread for a wallet."

The peasant, furious, raised his hand, spit, to attest his innocence, and declared:

"Yet it's the truth of God, the sacred truth, m'sieu mayor. On my soul and my salvation, I repeat it."

The mayor continued:

"After picking up the object you went on searching in the mud a long time to see if some piece of money mightn't have escaped you."

The old man gasped with indignation and fear.

"May one tell—may one tell lies like that to injure an honest man? May one say—"

His protest was vain. He was not believed. He was confronted with Monsieur Malandin, who repeated and sustained his former affirmation. For an hour the two men hurled insults at each other. Hauchecorne was searched, at his demand, and nothing was found on him. Finally the mayor, greatly perplexed, sent him away, warning him that he should inform the council and await orders.

The news spread. When he came out of the town hall the old man was surrounded and questioned with a curiosity serious or mocking, but with no ill-will in it.

He began to recount the story of the string, but no one believed him—they only laughed.

He went on, stopped by everybody, stopping his acquaintances, beginning anew his tale and his protestations, turning his pockets inside out to prove that he had nothing.

"Move on, old quibbler," they said to him.

And he became angry, exasperated, feverish, sick at heart, at not being believed. He did not know what to do, but told his story over and over.

Night came. It was time to go home. He set out with three of his neighbors, to whom he pointed out the place where he had picked up the bit of cord, and all the way home he talked of his adventure. In the evening he made a circuit of the village of Bréauté to tell it to everybody. He met only incredulity. He was ill all night from his trouble.

The next day, toward one o'clock in the afternoon, Marius Paumelle, a farm hand, of Ymanville, returned the wallet and its contents to Monsieur Houlèbreque, of Manneville. The man stated, in effect, that he had found the wallet in the road, but not knowing how to read, had taken it home to his employer.

The news spread all about. Master Hauchecorne was told of it. He at once set out again on his travels, and began to narrate his story, completed by the denouement. He was triumphant.

"It's not the thing 'at grieved me most, you understand," he said, "but it's the lie. Nothing harms you like being charged with a lie."

All day long he talked of his adventure. He told it on the streets to men passing, in the taverns to men drinking, after church next Sunday. He stopped strangers to tell it to them. Now he was tranquil, yet something half disturbed him, without his knowing exactly what. People had an amused air as they listened to him. They did not appear convinced. He thought he detected whispers behind his back.

Tuesday of the following week he betook himself to the market of Goderville, driven there by the need of exploiting his case. Malandin, standing in his doorway, began to laugh when he saw him passing. Why? He accosted a farmer of Criquetot, who did not let him finish, but giving him a blow in the pit of the stomach, cried in his face:

"Go your way, humbug!"

Master Hauchecorne was dumfounded, and more and more ill at ease. Why had he been called a humbug?

When he was seated at table in Jourdain's inn he again began to explain the affair. A jockey of Montivilliers cried to him:

"Come, come, old croaker, I know about your string!"

Hauchecorne stammered:

"But since it is found—the wallet?"

The other answered:

"Hold your tongue, father. One finds, another returns. I know nothing about it, but I implicate you."

The peasant was left choking. He understood at last. He was accused of having returned the wallet through an accomplice. He tried to protest. The whole table began to laugh. He could not finish his dinner, and went out in the midst of mockeries.

He returned home, ashamed and disgraced, strangling with rage and confusion, so much the more overwhelmed, in that he was capable, with his Norman duplicity, of doing the very thing of which he was accused, and even boasting of it as a good stroke. Confusedly he saw his innocence impossible to prove, his chicanery being well known, and he felt himself cut to the heart by the injustice of the suspicion.

Then he commenced again to recount his adventure, lengthening each day his story, adding each time new reasonings, more energetic protestations, more solemn oaths, which he invented and arranged in his hours of solitude, his mind occupied solely with the story of the string. He was believed the less in proportion to the complication of his defense and the subtlety of his argument.

"That's the reasoning of a liar," they said behind his back.

He felt it, spent himself, wore his life out in useless efforts. He wasted away visibly. Wags now made him tell "the string" for their amusement, as one makes a soldier who has fought recount his battle. His mind, harassed and unsettled, grew feeble.

Toward the end of December he took to his bed. He died early in January, and in the delirium of his agony he attested his innocence, repeating:

"A little string . . . a little string . . . wait, here it is m'sieu mayor!"

The Last Leaf

O. Henry

In a little district west of Washington Square the streets have run crazy and broken themselves into small strips called "places." These "places" make strange angles and curves. One street crosses itself a time or two. An artist once discovered a valuable possibility in this street. Suppose a collector with a bill for paints, paper and canvas should, in traversing this route, suddenly meet himself coming back, without a cent having been paid on account!

So, to quaint old Greenwich Village the art people soon came prowling, hunting for north windows and eighteenth-century gables and Dutch attics and low rents. Then they imported some pewter mugs and a chafing dish or two from Sixth Avenue, and became a "colony."

At the top of a squatty, three-story brick Sue and Johnsy had their studio. "Johnsy" was familiar for Joanna. One was from Maine; the other from California. They had met at the *table d'hote* of an Eighth Street "Delmonico's," and found their tastes in art, chicory salad and bishop sleeves so congenial that the joint studio resulted.

That was in May. In November a cold, unseen stranger, whom the doctors called Pneumonia, stalked about the colony, touching one here and there with his icy fingers. Over on the east side this ravager strode boldly, smiting his victims by scores, but his feet trod slowly through the maze of the narrow and moss-grown "places."

Mr. Pneumonia was not what you would call a chivalric old gentleman. A mite of a little woman with blood thinned by California zephyrs was hardly fair game for the red-fisted, short-breathed old duffer. But Johnsy he smote; and she lay, scarcely moving, on her painted iron bedstead, looking through the small Dutch window-panes at the blank side of the next brick house.

One morning the busy doctor, with a shaggy, gray eyebrow, invited Sue into the hallway.

"She has one chance in—let us say, ten," he said, as he shook down the mercury in his clinical thermometer. "And that chance is for her to want to live. This way people have of lining-up on the side of the undertaker makes the entire pharmacopoeia look silly. Your little lady has made up her mind that she's not going to get well. Has she anything on her mind?"

"She—she wanted to paint the Bay of Naples some day," said Sue.

"Paint?—bosh! Has she anything on her mind worth thinking about twice—a man, for instance?"

"A man?" said Sue, with a jew's-harp twang in her voice. "Is a man worth—but, no, doctor; there is nothing of the kind."

"Well, it is the weakness, then," said the doctor. "I will do all that science, so far as it may filter through my efforts, can accomplish. But whenever my patient begins to count the carriages in her funeral procession I subtract 50 per cent from the curative power of medicines. If you will get her to ask one question about the new winter styles in cloak sleeves I will promise you a one-in-five chance for her, instead of one in ten."

After the doctor had gone Sue went into the workroom and cried a Japanese napkin to a pulp. The she swaggered into Johnsy's room with her drawing board, whistling ragtime.

Johnsy, lay, scarcely making a ripple under the bedclothes, with her face toward the window. Sue stopped whistling, thinking she was asleep.

She arranged her board and began a pen-and-ink drawing to illustrate a magazine story. Young artists must pave their way to Art by drawing pictures for magazine stories that young authors write to pave their way to Literature.

As Sue was sketching a pair of elegant horseshow riding trousers and a monocle on the figure of the hero, an Idaho cowboy, she heard a low sound, several times repeated. She went quickly to the bedside.

Johnsy's eyes were open wide. She was looking out the window and counting—counting backward.

"Twelve," she said, and a little later "eleven"; and then "ten," and "nine"; and then "eight" and "seven," almost together.

Sue looked solicitously out of the window. What was there to count? There was only a bare, dreary yard to be seen, and the blank side of the brick house twenty feet away. An old, old ivy vine, gnarled and decayed at the roots, climbed half way up the brick wall. The cold breath of autumn had stricken its leaves from the vine until its skeleton branches clung, almost bare, to the crumbling bricks.

"What is it, dear?" asked Sue.

"Six," said Johnsy, in almost a whisper. "They're falling faster now. Three days ago there were almost a hundred. It made my head ache to count them. But now it's easy. There goes another one. There are only five left now."

"Five what, dear? Tell your Sudie."

"Leaves. On the ivy vine. When the last one falls I must go, too. I've known that for three days. Didn't the doctor tell you?"

"Oh, I never heard of such nonsense," complained Sue, with magnificent scorn. "What have old ivy leaves to do with your getting well? And you used to love that vine, so, you naughty girl. Don't be a goosey. Why, the doctor told me this morning that your chances for getting well real soon were—let's see exactly what he said—he said the chances were ten to one! Why, that's almost as good a chance as we have in New York when we ride on the street cars or walk past a new building. Try to take some broth now, and let Sudie go back to her drawing, so she can sell the editor man with it, and buy port wine for her sick child, and pork chops for her greedy self."

"You needn't get any more wine," said Johnsy, keeping her eyes fixed out the window. "There goes another. No, I don't want any broth. That leaves just four. I want to see the last one fall before it gets dark. Then I'll go, too."

"Johnsy, dear," said Sue, bending over her, "will you promise me to keep your eyes closed, and not look out the window until I am done working? I must hand those drawings in by to-morrow. I need the light, or I would draw the shade down."

"Couldn't you draw in the other room?" asked Johnsy, coldly.

"I'd rather be here by you," said Sue. "Besides, I don't want you to keep looking at those silly ivy leaves."

"Tell me as soon as you have finished," said Johnsy, closing her eyes, and lying white and still as a fallen statue, "because I want to see the last one fall. I'm tired of waiting. I'm tired of thinking. I want to turn loose my hold on everything, and go sailing down, down, just like one of those poor, tired leaves."

"Try to sleep," said Sue. "I must call Behrman up to be my model for the old hermit miner. I'll not be gone a minute. Don't try to move 'til I come back."

Old Behrman was a painter who lived on the ground floor beneath them. He was past sixty and had a Michael Angelo's Moses beard curling down from the head of a satyr along the body of an imp. Behrman was a failure in art. Forty years he had wielded the brush without getting near enough to touch the hem of his Mistress's robe. He had been always about to paint a masterpiece, but had never yet begun it. For several years he had painted nothing except now and then a daub in the line of commerce or advertising. He earned a little by serving as a model to those young artists in the colony who could not pay the price of a professional. He drank gin to excess, and still talked of his coming masterpiece. For the rest he was a fierce little old man, who scoffed terribly at softness in any one, and who regarded himself as especial mastiff-in-waiting to protect the two young artists in the studio above.

Sue found Behrman smelling strongly of juniper berries in his dimly lighted den below. In one corner was a blank canvas on an easel that had been waiting there for twenty-five years to receive the first line of the masterpiece. She told him of Johnsy's fancy, and how she feared she would, indeed, light and fragile as a leaf herself, float away, when her slight hold upon the world grew weaker.

Old Behrman, with his red eyes plainly streaming, shouted his contempt and derision for such idiotic imaginings.

"Vass!" he cried. "Is dere people in de world mit der foolishness to die because leafs dey drop off from a confounded vine? I haf not heard of such a thing. No, I will not bose as a model for your fool hermit-dunder-head. Vy do you allow dot silly pusiness to come in der brain of her? Ach, dot poor leetle Miss Yohnsy."

"She is very ill and weak," said Sue, "and the fever has left her mind morbid and full of strange fancies. Very well, Mr. Behrman, if you do not care to pose for me, you needn't. But I think you are a horrid old—old flibbertigibbet."

"You are just like a woman!" yelled Behrman. "Who said I will not bose? Go on. I come mit you. For half an hour I haf peen trying to say dot I am ready to bose. Dis is not any blace in which one so goot as Miss Yohnsy shall lie sick. Some day I vill baint a masterpiece, and ve shall all go away."

Johnsy was sleeping when they went upstairs. Sue pulled the shade down to the window-sill, and motioned Behrman into the other room. In there they peered out the window fearfully at the ivy vine. Then they looked at each other for a moment without speaking. A persistent, cold rain was falling, mingled with snow. Behrman, in his old blue shirt, took his seat as the hermit miner on an upturned kettle for a rock.

When Sue awoke from an hour's sleep the next morning

she found Johnsy with dull, wide-open eyes staring at the drawn green shade.

"Pull it up; I want to see," she ordered, in a whisper.

Wearily Sue obeyed.

But, lo! after the beating rain and fierce gusts of wind that had endured through the livelong night, there yet stood out against the brick wall one ivy leaf. It was the last on the vine. Still dark green near its stem, but with its serrated edges tinted with the yellow of dissolution and decay, it hung bravely from a branch some twenty feet above the ground.

"It is the last one," said Johnsy. "I thought it would surely fall during the night. I heard the wind. It will fall to-day, and I shall die at the same time."

"Dear, dear!" said Sue, leaning her worn face down to the pillow, "think of me, if you won't think of yourself. What would I do?"

But Johnsy did not answer. The lonesomest thing in all the world is a soul when it is making ready to go on its mysterious, far journey. The fancy seemed to possess her more strongly as one by one the ties that bound her to friendship and to earth were loosed.

The day wore away, and even through the twilight they could see the lone ivy leaf clinging to its stem against the wall. And then, with the coming of the night the north wind was again loosed, while the rain still beat against the windows and pattered down from the low Dutch eaves.

When it was light enough Johnsy, the merciless, commanded that the shade be raised.

The ivy leaf was still there.

Johnsy lay for a long time looking at it. And then she called to Sue, who was stirring her chicken broth over the gas stove.

"I've been a bad girl, Sudie," said Johnsy. "Something has made that last leaf stay there to show me how wicked I was. It is a sin to want to die. You may bring me a little broth now, and some milk with a little port in it, and—no; bring me a hand-mirror first, and then pack some pillows about me, and I will sit up and watch you cook."

An hour later she said:

"Sudie, some day I hope to paint the Bay of Naples."

The doctor came in the afternoon, and Sue had an excuse to go into the hallway as he left.

"Even chances," said the doctor, taking Sue's thin, shaking hand in his. "With good nursing you'll win. And now I must see another case I have downstairs. Behrman, his name is— some kind of an artist, I believe. Pneumonia, too. He is an old, weak man, and the attack is acute. There is no hope for him; but he goes to the hospital to-day to be made more comfortable."

The next day the doctor said to Sue: "She's out of danger. You've won. Nutrition and care now—that's all."

And that afternoon Sue came to the bed where Johnsy lay, contentedly knitting a very blue and very useless woollen shoulder scarf, and put one arm around her, pillows and all.

"I have something to tell you, white mouse," she said. "Mr. Behrman died of pneumonia to-day in the hospital. He was ill only two days. The janitor found him on the morning of the first day in his room downstairs helpless with pain. His shoes and clothing were wet through and icy cold. They couldn't imagine where he had been on such a dreadful night. And then they found a lantern, still lighted, and a ladder that had been dragged from its place, and some scattered brushes, and a palette with green and yellow colors mixed on it, and—look out the window, dear, the last ivy leaf on the wall. Didn't you wonder why it never fluttered or moved when the wind blew? Ah, darling, it's Behrman's masterpiece—he painted it there the night that the last leaf fell."

Rip Van Winkle

Washington Irving

Whoever has made a voyage up the Hudson must remember the Kaatskill Mountains. They are a dismembered branch of the great Appalachian family, and are seen away to the west of the river, swelling up to a noble height, and lording it over the surrounding country. Every change of season, every change of weather, indeed every hour of the day, produces some change in the magical hues and shapes of these mountains; and they are regarded by all the good wives, far and near, as perfect barometers. When the weather is fair and settled, they are clothed in blue and purple, and print their bold outlines on the clear evening sky; but sometimes, when the rest of the landscape is cloudless, they will gather a hood of gray vapors about their summits, which, in the last rays of the setting sun, will glow and light up like a crown of glory.

At the foot of these fairy mountains, the voyager may have descried the light smoke curling up from a village whose shingle roofs gleam among the trees, just where the blue tints of the upland melt away into the fresh green of the nearer landscape. It is a little village of great antiquity, having been founded by some of the Dutch colonists, in the early times of the province, just about the beginning of the government of the good Peter Stuyvesant (may he rest in peace!), and there were some of the houses of the original settlers standing within a few years, built of small yellow bricks brought from Holland, having latticed windows and gable fronts, surmounted with weathercocks.

In that same village, and in one of these very houses (which, to tell the precise truth, was sadly time-worn and weather-beaten), there lived many years since, while the country was yet a province of Great Britain, a simple, good-natured fellow, of the name of Rip Van Winkle. He was a descendant of the Van Winkles who figured so gallantly in the chivalrous days of Peter Stuyvesant, and accompanied him to the siege of Fort Christina. He inherited, however, but little of the martial character of his ancestors. I have observed that he was a simple, good-natured man; he was moreover a kind neighbor, and an obedient henpecked husband. Indeed, to the latter circumstance might be owing that meekness of spirit which gained him such universal popularity; for those men are most apt to be obsequious and conciliating abroad who are under the discipline of shrews at home. Their tempers, doubtless, are rendered pliant and malleable in the fiery furnace of domestic tribulation, and a curtain lecture is worth all the sermons in the world for teaching the virtues of patience and long-suffering. A termagant wife may, therefore, in some respects, be considered a tolerable blessing; and if so, Rip Van Winkle was thrice blessed.

Certain it is that he was a great favorite among all the good wives of the village, who, as usual with the amiable sex, took his part in all family squabbles, and never failed, whenever they talked those matters over in their evening gossipings, to lay all the blame on Dame Van Winkle. The children of the village, too, would shout with joy whenever he approached. He assisted at their sports, made their playthings, taught them to fly kites and shoot marbles, and told them long stories of ghosts, witches, and Indians. Whenever he went dodging about the village, he was surrounded by a troop of them hanging on his skirts, clambering on his back, and playing a thousand tricks on him with impunity; and not a dog would bark at him throughout the neighborhood.

The great error in Rip's composition was an insuperable aversion to all kinds of profitable labor. It could not be from the want of assiduity or perseverance; for he would sit on a wet rock, with a rod as long and heavy as a Tartar's lance, and fish all day without a murmur, even though he should not be encouraged by a single nibble. He would carry a fowling-piece on his shoulder, for hours together, trudging through woods and swamps, and up hill and down dale, to shoot a few squirrels or wild pigeons. He would never refuse to assist a neighbor even in the roughest toil, and was a foremost man at all country frolics for husking Indian corn, or building stone fences. The women of the village, too, used to employ him to run their errands, and to do such little odd jobs as their less obliging husbands would not do for them; in a word, Rip was ready to attend to anybody's business but his own; but as to doing family duty, and keeping his farm in order, he found it impossible.

In fact, he declared it was of no use to work on his farm; it was the most pestilent little piece of ground in the whole country; everything about it went wrong, and would go wrong in spite of him. His fences were continually falling to pieces;

his cow would either go astray, or get among the cabbages; weeds were sure to grow quicker in his fields than anywhere else; the rain always made a point of setting in just as he had some outdoor work to do; so that though his patrimonial estate had dwindled away under his management, acre by acre, until there was little more left than a mere patch of Indian corn and potatoes, yet it was the worst conditioned farm in the neighborhood.

Rip's sole domestic adherent was his dog Wolf, who was as much henpecked as his master; for Dame Van Winkle regarded them as companions in idleness, and even looked upon Wolf with an evil eye, as the cause of his master's going so often astray. True it is, in all points of spirit befitting an honorable dog, he was as courageous an animal as ever scoured the woods—but what courage can withstand the ever-during and all-besetting terrors of a woman's tongue? The moment Wolf entered the house, his crest fell, his tail drooped to the ground, or curled between his legs, he sneaked about with a gallows air, casting many a sidelong glance at Dame Van Winkle, and at the least flourish of a broomstick or ladle, he would fly to the door with yelping precipitation.

Times grew worse and worse with Rip Van Winkle, as years of matrimony rolled on: a tart temper never mellows with age, and a sharp tongue is the only edge tool that grows keener with constant use. For a long while he used to console himself, when driven from home, by frequenting a kind of perpetual club of the sages, philosophers, and other idle personages of the village, which held its sessions on a bench before a small inn, designated by a rubicund portrait of his Majesty George the Third. Here they used to sit in the shade, of a long lazy summer's day, talking listlessly over village gossip, or telling endless sleepy stories about nothing. But it would have been worth any statesman's money to have heard the profound discussions which sometimes took place, when by chance an old newspaper fell into their hands, from some passing traveler. How solemnly they would listen to the contents, as drawled out by Derrick Van Bummel, the schoolmaster, a dapper learned little man, who was not to be daunted by the most gigantic word in the dictionary; and how sagely they would deliberate upon public events some months after they had taken place.

The opinions of this junto were completely controlled by Nicholas Vedder, a patriarch of the village, and landlord of the inn, at the door of which he took his seat from morning till night, just moving sufficiently to avoid the sun, and keep in the shade of a large tree; so that the neighbors could tell the hour by his movements as accurately as by a sun-dial.

From even this stronghold the unlucky Rip was at length routed by his termagant wife, who would suddenly break in upon the tranquillity of the assemblage, and call the members all to naught; nor was that august personage, Nicholas Vedder himself, sacred from the daring tongue of this terrible virago, who charged him outright with encouraging her husband in habits of idleness.

Poor Rip was at last reduced almost to despair, and his only alternative to escape from the labor of the farm and the clamor of his wife was to take gun in hand, and stroll away into the woods. Here he would sometimes seat himself at the foot of a tree, and share the contents of his wallet with Wolf, with whom he sympathized as a fellow-sufferer in persecution. "Poor Wolf," he would say, "thy mistress leads thee a dog's life of it; but never mind, my lad, while I live thou shalt never want a friend to stand by thee!" Wolf would wag his tail, look wistfully in his master's face, and if dogs can feel pity, I verily believe he reciprocated the sentiment with all his heart.

In a long ramble of the kind, on a fine autumnal day, Rip had unconsciously scrambled to one of the highest parts of the Kaatskill Mountains. He was after his favorite sport of squirrel-shooting, and the still solitudes had echoed and re-echoed with the reports of his gun. Panting and fatigued, he threw himself, late in the afternoon, on a green knoll covered with mountain herbage, that crowned the brow of a precipice. From an opening between the trees, he could overlook all the lower country for many a mile of rich woodland. He saw at a distance the lordly Hudson, far, far below him, moving on its silent but majestic course, with the reflection of a purple cloud, or the sail of a lagging bark, here and there sleeping on its glassy bosom, and at last losing itself in the blue highlands.

On the other side he looked down into a deep mountain glen, wild, lonely, and shagged, the bottom filled with fragments from the impending cliffs, and scarcely lighted by the reflected rays of the setting sun. For some time Rip lay musing on this scene; evening was gradually advancing; the mountains began to throw their long blue shadows over the valleys; he saw that it would be dark long before he could reach the village; and he heaved a heavy sigh when he thought of encountering the terrors of Dame Van Winkle.

As he was about to descend he heard a voice from a distance hallooing, "Rip Van Winkle! Rip Van Winkle!" He looked around, but could see nothing but a crow winging its solitary flight across the mountain. He thought his fancy must have deceived him, and turned again to descend, when he heard the same cry ring through the still evening air, "Rip Van Winkle! Rip Van Winkle!"—at the same time Wolf bristled up his back, and giving a low growl, skulked to his master's side, looking fearfully down into the glen. Rip now felt a vague apprehension stealing over him: he looked anxiously in the same direction, and perceived a strange figure slowly toiling up the rocks and bending under the weight of something he carried on his back. He was surprised to see any human being in this lonely and unfrequented place, but supposing it to be some one of the neighborhood in need of his assistance, he hastened down to yield it.

On nearer approach, he was still more surprised at the singularity of the stranger's appearance. He was a short square-built old fellow, with thick bushy hair, and a grizzled beard. His dress was of the antique Dutch fashion—a cloth jerkin strapped round the waist—several pairs of breeches, the outer one of ample volume, decorated with rows of buttons down the sides, and bunches at the knees. He bore on his shoulders a stout keg, that seemed full of liquor, and made signs for Rip to approach and assist him with the load. Though rather shy and distrustful of this new acquaintance, Rip complied with his usual alacrity, and mutually relieving each other, they clambered up a narrow gully, apparently the dry bed of a mountain torrent. As they ascended, Rip every now and then heard long rolling peals, like distant thunder, that seemed to issue out of a deep ravine or rather cleft between lofty rocks, toward which their rugged path conducted. He paused for an instant, but supposing it to be the muttering of one of those transient thundershowers which often take place in mountain heights, he proceeded. Passing through the ravine, they came to a hollow, like a small amphitheatre, surrounded by perpendicular precipices, over the brinks of which impending trees shot their branches, so that you only caught glimpses of the azure sky, and the bright evening cloud. During the whole time, Rip and his companion had labored on in silence; for though the former marveled greatly what could be the object of carrying a keg of liquor up this wild mountain, yet there was something strange and incomprehensible about the unknown, that inspired awe and checked familiarity.

On entering the amphitheatre new objects of wonder presented themselves. On a level spot in the centre was a company of odd-looking personages playing at nine-pins. They were dressed in a quaint outlandish fashion: some wore short doublets, others jerkins, with long knives in their belts, and most of them had enormous breeches, of similar style with that of the guide's. Their visages, too, were peculiar: one had a large head, broad face, and small piggish eyes; the face of another seemed to consist entirely of nose, and was surmounted by a white sugar-loaf hat, set off with a little red cock's tail. They all had beards, of various shapes and colors. There was one who seemed to be the commander. He was a stout old gentleman, with a weather-beaten countenance; he wore a laced doublet, broad belt and hanger, high-crowned hat and feather, red stockings, and high-heeled shoes, with roses in them. The whole group reminded Rip of the figures in an old Flemish painting, in the parlor of Dominie Van Schaick, the village parson, and which had been brought over from Holland at the time of the settlement.

What seemed particularly odd to Rip was, that though these folks were evidently amusing themselves, yet they maintained the gravest faces, the most mysterious silence, and were, withal, the most melancholy party of pleasure he had ever witnessed. Nothing interrupted the stillness of the scene but the noise of the balls, which, whenever they were rolled, echoed along the mountains like rumbling peals of thunder.

As Rip and his companion approached them, they suddenly desisted from their play, and stared at him with such a fixed statue-like gaze, and such strange, uncouth, lack-lustre countenances, that his heart turned within him, and his knees smote together. His companion now emptied the contents of the keg into large flagons, and made signs to him to wait upon the company. He obeyed with fear and trembling; they quaffed the liquor in profound silence, and then returned to their game.

By degrees, Rip's awe and apprehension subsided. He even ventured, when no eye was fixed upon him, to taste the beverage, which he found had much of the flavor of excellent Hollands. He was naturally a thirsty soul, and was soon tempted to repeat the draught. One taste provoked another, and he reiterated his visits to the flagon so often that at length his senses were overpowered, his eyes swam in his head, his head gradually declined, and he fell into a deep sleep.

On waking, he found himself on the green knoll from whence he had first seen the old man of the glen. He rubbed his eyes—it was a bright sunny morning. The birds were hopping and twittering among the bushes, and the eagle was wheeling aloft, and breasting the pure mountain breeze. "Surely," thought Rip, "I have not slept here all night." He recalled the occurrences before he fell asleep. The strange man with the keg of liquor—the mountain ravine—the wild retreat among the rocks—the woebegone party at nine-pins—the flagon—"Oh, that wicked flagon!" thought Rip—"what excuse shall I make to Dame Van Winkle?"

He looked round for his gun, but in place of the clean well-oiled fowling piece, he found an old firelock lying by him, the barrel incrusted with rust, the lock falling off, and the stock worm-eaten. He now suspected that the grave roisterers of the mountain had put a trick upon him, and having dosed him with liquor, had robbed him of his gun. Wolf, too, had disappeared, but he might have strayed away after a squirrel or partridge. He whistled after him, and shouted his name, but all in vain; the echoes repeated his whistle and shout, but no dog was to be seen.

He determined to revisit the scene of the last evening's gambol, and if he met with any of the party, to demand his dog and gun. As he rose to walk, he found himself stiff in the joints and wanting in his usual activity. "These mountain beds do not agree with me," thought Rip, "and if this frolic should lay me up with a fit of rheumatism, I shall have a blessed time with Dame Van Winkle." With some difficulty he got down into the glen; he found the gully up which he and his companion had ascended the preceding evening; but to his astonishment a mountain stream was foaming down it, leaping from rock to rock, and filling the glen with babbling murmurs. He, however, made shift to scramble up its sides, working his toilsome way through thickets of birch, sassafras, and witch-hazel; and sometimes tripped up or entangled by the wild grape vines that twisted their coils and tendrils from tree to tree, and spread a kind of network in his path.

At length he reached to where the ravine had opened through the cliffs to the amphitheatre; but no traces of such opening remained. The rocks presented a high impenetrable wall, over which the torrent came tumbling in a sheet of feathery foam, and fell into a broad, deep basin, black from the shadows of the surrounding forest. Here, then, poor Rip was brought to a stand. He again called and whistled after his dog; he was only answered by the cawing of a flock of idle crows, sporting high in air about a dry tree that overhung a sunny precipice; and who, secure in their elevation, seemed to look down and scoff at the poor man's perplexities. What was to be done? The morning was passing away, and Rip felt famished for want of his breakfast. He grieved to give up his dog and gun; he dreaded to meet his wife; but it would not do to starve among the mountains. He shook his head, shouldered the rusty firelock, and, with a heart full of trouble and anxiety, turned his steps homeward.

As he approached the village he met a number of people, but none whom he knew, which somewhat surprised him, for he had thought himself acquainted with every one in the country round. Their dress, too, was of a different fashion from that to which he was accustomed. They all stared at him with equal marks of surprise, and whenever they cast eyes upon him, invariably stroked their chins. The constant recurrence of this gesture induced Rip, involuntarily, to do the same, when, to his astonishment, he found his beard had grown a foot long!

He had now entered the skirts of the village. A troop of strange children ran at his heels, hooting after him, and pointing at his gray beard. The dogs, too, not one of which he recognized for an old acquaintance, barked at him as he passed. The very village was altered: it was larger and more populous. There were rows of houses which he had never seen before, and those which had been his familiar haunts had disappeared. Strange names were over the doors—strange faces at the windows— everything was strange. His mind now misgave him; he began to doubt whether both he and the world around him were not bewitched. Surely this was his native village, which he left but a day before. There stood the Kaatskill Mountains—there ran the silver Hudson at a distance—there was every hill and dale precisely as it had always been—Rip was sorely perplexed— "That flagon last night," thought he, "has addled my poor head sadly!"

It was with some difficulty that he found the way to his own house, which he approached with silent awe, expecting every moment to hear the shrill voice of Dame Van Winkle. He found the house gone to decay—the roof fallen in, the windows shattered, and the doors off the hinges. A half-starved dog, that looked like Wolf, was skulking about it. Rip called him by name, but the cur snarled, showed his teeth, and passed on. This was an unkind cut indeed. "My very dog," sighed poor Rip, "has forgotten me!"

He entered the house, which, to tell the truth, Dame Van Winkle had always kept in neat order. It was empty, forlorn, and apparently abandoned. This desolateness overcame all his connubial fears—he called loudly for his wife and children—the lonely chambers rang for a moment with his voice, and then all again was silence.

He now hurried forth, and hastened to his old resort, the village inn—but it too was gone. A large rickety wooden building stood in its place, with great gaping windows, some of them broken, and mended with old hats and petticoats, and over the door was painted, "The Union Hotel, by Jonathan Doolittle." Instead of the great tree that used to shelter the quiet little Dutch inn of yore, there now was reared a tall naked pole, with something on the top that looked like a red nightcap, and from it was fluttering a flag, on which was a singular assemblage of stars and stripes—all this was strange and incomprehensible. He recognized on the sign, however, the ruby face of King George, under which he had smoked so many a peaceful pipe, but even this was singularly metamorphosed. The red coat was changed for one of blue and buff, a sword was held in the hand instead of a sceptre, the head was decorated with a cocked hat, and underneath was painted in large characters GENERAL WASHINGTON.

There was, as usual, a crowd of folk about the door, but none that Rip recollected. The very character of the people seemed changed. There was a busy, bustling, disputatious tone about it, instead of the accustomed phlegm and drowsy tranquillity. He looked in vain for the sage Nicholas Vedder, with his broad face, double chin, and fair, long pipe, uttering clouds of tobacco smoke, instead of idle speeches; or Van Bummel, the schoolmaster, doling forth the contents of an ancient newspaper. In place of these, a lean bilious-looking fellow, with his pockets full of handbills, was haranguing vehemently about rights of citizens—election—members of Congress—liberty—Bunker Hill—heroes of seventy-six—and other words, that were a perfect Babylonish jargon to the bewildered Van Winkle.

The appearance of Rip, with his long, grizzled beard, his rusty fowling-piece, his uncouth dress, and the army of women and children that had gathered at his heels, soon attracted the attention of the tavern politicians. They crowded round him, eyeing him from head to foot, with great curiosity. The orator bustled up to him, and drawing him partly aside, inquired "on which side he voted?" Rip stared in vacant stupidity. Another short but busy little fellow pulled him by the arm, and rising on tiptoe, inquired in his ear, "whether he was Federal or Democrat." Rip was equally at a loss to comprehend the question; when a knowing, self-important old gentleman, in a sharp cocked hat, made his way through the crowd, putting them to the right and left with his elbows as he passed, and planting himself before Van Winkle, with one arm a-kimbo, the other resting on his cane, his keen eyes and sharp hat penetrating, as it were, into his very soul, demanded in an austere tone, "what brought him to the election with a gun on his shoulder, and a mob at his heels, and whether he meant to breed a riot in the village?"

"Alas! gentlemen," cried Rip, somewhat dismayed, "I am a poor, quiet man, a native of the place, and a loyal subject of the King, God bless him!"

Here a general shout burst forth from the bystanders:

"A tory! a tory! a spy! a refugee! hustle him! away with him!"

It was with great difficulty that the self-important man in the cocked hat restored order; and having assumed a tenfold austerity of brow, demanded again of the unknown culprit what he came there for, and whom he was seeking. The poor man humbly assured him that he meant no harm, but merely came there in search of some of his neighbors, who used to keep about the tavern.

"Well—who are they?—name them."

Rip bethought himself a moment and inquired, "Where's Nicholas Vedder?"

There was silence for a little while, when an old man replied, in a thin, piping voice, "Nicholas Vedder? why, he is dead and gone these eighteen years! There was a wooden tombstone in the churchyard that used to tell all about him, but that's rotten and gone too."

"Where's Brom Dutcher?"

Oh, he went off to the army in the beginning of the war; some say he was killed at the storming of Stony Point—others say he was drowned in the squall, at the foot of Anthony's Nose. I don't know—he never came back again."

"Where's Van Bummel, the schoolmaster?"

"He went off to the wars, too; was a great militia general,

and is now in Congress."

Rip's heart died away at hearing of these sad changes in his home and friends, and finding himself thus alone in the world. Every answer puzzled him, too, by treating of such enormous lapses of time, and of matters which he could not understand: war—Congress—Stony Point!—he had no courage to ask after any more friends, but cried out in despair, "Does nobody here know Rip Van Winkle?"

The bystanders began now to look at each other, nod, wink significantly, and tap their fingers against their foreheads. There was a whisper, also, about securing the gun, and keeping the old fellow from doing mischief; at the very suggesting of which the self-important man with the cocked hat retired with some precipitation. At this critical moment a fresh, comely woman passed through the throng to get a peep at the gray-bearded man. She had a chubby child in her arms, which, frightened at his looks, began to cry. "Hush, Rip," cried she, "hush, you little fool; the old man won't hurt you." The name of the child, the air of the mother, the tone of her voice, all awakened a train of recollections in his mind.

"What is your name, my good woman?" asked he.

"Judith Gardenier."

"And your father's name?"

"Ah, poor man, his name was Rip Van Winkle; it's twenty years since he went away from home with his gun, and never has been heard of since—his dog came home without him; but whether he shot himself, or was carried away by the Indians, nobody can tell. I was then but a little girl."

Rip had but one question more to ask; but he put it with a faltering voice:

"Where's your mother?"

Oh, she too had died but a short time since: she broke a blood-vessel in a fit of passion at a New England peddler.

There was a drop of comfort, at least, in this intelligence. The honest man could contain himself no longer. He caught his daughter and her child in his arms. "I am your father!" cried he—"Young Rip Van Winkle once—old Rip Van Winkle now!—Does nobody know poor Rip Van Winkle?"

All stood amazed until an old woman, tottering out from among the crowd, put her hand to her brow, and peering under it in his face for a moment, exclaimed, "Sure enough! it is Rip Van Winkle—it is himself. Welcome home again, old neighbor! Why, where have you been these twenty long years?"

Rip's story was soon told, for the whole twenty years had been to him but as one night. The neighbors stared when they heard it; some were seen to wink at each other, and put their tongues in their cheeks; and the self-important man in the cocked hat, who, when the alarm was over, had returned to the field, screwed down the corners of his mouth, and shook his head—upon which there was a general shaking of the head throughout the assemblage.

Rip now resumed his old walks and habits; he soon found many of his former cronies, though all rather the worse for the wear and tear of time; and preferred making friends among the rising generation, with whom he soon grew into great favor.

Having nothing to do at home, and being arrived at that happy age when a man can do nothing with impunity, he took his place once more on the bench, at the inn door, and was reverenced as one of the patriarchs of the village, and a chronicle of the old times "before the war." It was some time before he could get into the regular track of gossip, or could be made to comprehend the strange events that had taken place during his torpor. How that there [had] been a revolutionary war—that the country had thrown off the yoke of old England—and that, instead of being a subject of his majesty George the Third, he was now a free citizen of the United States.

He used to tell his story to every stranger that arrived at Mr. Doolittle's hotel. He was observed, at first, to vary on some points every time he told it, which was doubtless owing to his having so recently awaked. It at last settled down precisely to the tale I have related, and not a man, woman, or child in the neighborhood but knew it by heart. Some always pretended to doubt the reality of it, and insisted that Rip had been out of his head, and that this was one point on which he always remained flighty. The old Dutch inhabitants, however, almost universally gave it full credit. Even to this day, they never hear a thunderstorm of a summer afternoon about the Kaatskill but they say Hendrik Hudson and his crew are at their game of nine-pins; and it is a common wish of all henpecked husbands in the neighborhood, when life hangs heavy on their hands, that they might have a quieting draught out of Rip Van Winkle's flagon.

INDEX

INDEX

Photo Credits